Virginia in the War of 1812

Virginia in the War of 1812

Christopher M. Bonin

McFarland & Company, Inc., Publishers
Jefferson, North Carolina

LIBRARY OF CONGRESS CATALOGUING-IN-PUBLICATION DATA

Names: Bonin, Christopher M., 1976– author.
Title: Virginia in the war of 1812 / Christopher M. Bonin.
Description: Jefferson, North Carolina : McFarland & Company, Inc., Publishers, 2018 | Includes bibliographical references and index.
Identifiers: LCCN 2018026981 | ISBN 9781476671086 (softcover : acid free paper) ∞
Subjects: LCSH: United States—History—War of 1812—Campaigns. | Virginia—History—War of 1812.
Classification: LCC E355.1.V8 B66 2018 | DDC 973.5/23—dc23
LC record available at https://lccn.loc.gov/2018026981

BRITISH LIBRARY CATALOGUING DATA ARE AVAILABLE

ISBN (print) 978-1-4766-7108-6
ISBN (ebook) 978-1-4766-3330-5

© 2018 Christopher M. Bonin. All rights reserved

No part of this book may be reproduced or transmitted in any form or by any means, electronic or mechanical, including photocopying or recording, or by any information storage and retrieval system, without permission in writing from the publisher.

Front cover image: "Capture of the *Dolphin*, 3rd April 1813," John Irwin Bevan, watercolor drawing, 10¼" × 16¾" (Bailey Collection, Naval Battles, War of 1812, The Mariners' Museum, Newport News, Virginia)

Printed in the United States of America

McFarland & Company, Inc., Publishers
 Box 611, Jefferson, North Carolina 28640
 www.mcfarlandpub.com

To Clare Stone,
Long ago you asked me to
dedicate my first book to you.
I have not forgotten.

Acknowledgments

This book is an adaptation of my master's thesis, *War on the Doorstep: Virginia in the War of 1812* (2015). I dedicate it:

To the faculty of the History Department, University of Nebraska at Kearney, especially Doug Biggs, thesis adviser; Mark Ellis, Jinny Turman, and Vern Volpe, defense committee; and Amber Alexander and Stacey Stubbs, program coordinators: you are my friends and colleagues on the Great Plains.

To the kind and helpful staff at the Library of Virginia, especially Dale Neighbors and Meghan Townes, Special Collections, a hearty thanks for your help organizing illustrations.

Finally, to my wonderful family. Thanks for everything. I love you all

Table of Contents

Acknowledgments — vi
Author's Note — viii
Introduction — 1

1. "BRITISH OUTRAGE!" The *Chesapeake-Leopard* Affair — 9
2. The Road to War: 1808–1812 — 22
3. The War of Words: Support and Opposition for the War of 1812 in Virginia — 39
4. The Opposing Forces: The Americans — 54
5. The Opposing Forces: The British — 67
6. Virginians in the Northwestern Campaign — 80
7. "The guns are roaring at this moment!" The 1813 Campaign — 100
8. "VIRGINIANS TO ARMS!" The 1814 Campaign — 120
9. The Aftermath — 140

Conclusion — 151
Chapter Notes — 155
Bibliography — 168
Index — 173

Author's Note

In quotations from contemporary documents, spelling and grammar have been kept intact. To constantly add *sic* after each quotation would be needlessly intrusive. While the style and spelling might appear archaic to modern readers, it is an excellent way to portray the spirit of the times. The author is confident readers will wholeheartedly agree.

Introduction

It is often said that the War of 1812 is a neglected subject in American history. While there are in fact several secondary sources covering the conflict, many continue to spread myths and misconceptions, most commonly that this was America's second war of independence. Other, more reliable works cover a great deal of material, but the experiences of individual states—such as Virginia—are neglected. This is a shame, for many notable events occurred in the state. When writing about Virginia's role in the War of 1812, historians must scour secondary sources for bits and pieces. At present, there is not a single-volume work on the Old Dominion at war (Butler's 2013 book *Defending the Old Dominion* focuses exclusively on the state militia). This is certainly an oversight, especially when one considers that there are only three state-level studies covering this period. In 1970, Victor Sapio published *Pennsylvania and the War of 1812*.[1] In 1973, Sarah McCulloh Lemmon published *Frustrated Patriots: North Carolina and the War of 1812*.[2] This was an expanded version of an earlier study Lemmon produced for the North Carolina Division of Archives and History.[3] While Pennsylvania and North Carolina certainly contributed to the American war effort, they did not suffer British incursions to the same extent as Virginia. For that reason alone, Virginia deserves its own state-level study.

Benson J. Lossing, a popular 19th-century historian and engraver, published his lavishly illustrated *Pictorial Field Book of the War of 1812* in 1869.[4] Lossing conducted research throughout the 1850s and 60s. He visited many sites associated with the war and interviewed surviving participants. Though a secondary source, Lossing's *Field Book* has a sense of immediacy, which gives lasting value to the work. That being said, Lossing perpetuated the myth that the War of 1812 was the second war of American independence. This interpretation is at best an exaggeration, for the British were not attempting to re-conquer the United States. This myth still has life; in 2006, A.J. Langguth published *Union 1812: The Americans Who Fought the Second War of Independence*.[5] This popular history has certainly been more widely read than many scholarly monographs and articles on the subject.

Albert Marrin's *1812: The War Nobody Won* provides another possibility for why the war has not been more widely covered.[6] What lessons are to be learned from a war that did not end in a triumph? In addition, Marrin's book appeared in the 1980s, when the fear of nuclear war with the USSR was very much a reality. Perhaps "the war nobody won" seemed too close to the zero-sum game of World War III. It is far more reassuring to bask in the glory of Jackson's triumph at New Orleans than to accept the fact that the war was an exercise in futility.

Donald R. Hickey is America's preeminent scholar on the War of 1812. *Don't Give Up the Ship! Myths of the War of 1812* is an informative reference guide in a handy question-and-answer format.[7] It debunks common myths and misconceptions about the conflict and traces the origins of these inaccuracies. In the 1970s, Hickey examined the political dimensions of the war. His doctoral dissertation, "The Federalists and the War of 1812," examines Federalist opposition to the war and how the Republicans blamed them for American defeats.[8] Though Hickey examined Federalists throughout the United States in his dissertation, his best-known book, *The War of 1812: A Forgotten Conflict*, concentrates on the New England branch of the party, with a full chapter devoted to the Hartford Convention. In this justly acclaimed volume, Hickey argues the Federalists were actually in the right. Though they ceased to be a viable party, the Republicans actually adopted many of their policies postwar (a somewhat stronger military and national bank, for example). In this case, imitation is surely vindication.[9] At the same time, proving the Federalists were in the right challenges the American narrative of forward progress. If a doomed political party was actually in the right, what does that reveal about the party that emerged from the trouble and strife?

The War of 1812 was not in the best interests of the state of Virginia. It was a war ostensibly fought for sailors' rights and free trade. But most of the U.S. Army served on the Canadian border, leaving the American coastline wide open to British assault. For their loyalty to the Union, Virginians received little benefit. Postwar, they began turning away from nationwide patriotism. They abdicated their national leadership role and turned inward. The Commonwealth of Virginia—rather than the United States of America— became the focal point of their loyalty.

Chapter 1 examines the *Chesapeake-Leopard* affair of 1807. The British attack on an American frigate brought both nations to the brink of war. The action occurred off the Virginia Capes. For weeks, tensions were high in Hampton Roads. Most Virginians expressed outrage at the British action and supported measures condemning it. Had the United States declared war in 1807, the *Chesapeake-Leopard* affair offered a straightforward *casus belli*. But cooler heads prevailed and the crisis passed.

Introduction 3

Chapter 2 chronicles the road to war, from 1808 to 1812, linked to members of the so-called Virginia Dynasty, the Jefferson and Madison administrations. During the Napoleonic Wars, the United States attempted to follow a neutral course. This required a steady hand at the tiller. President Jefferson attempted to uphold American rights through "peaceful coercion"—by imposing an embargo. President Madison attempted a similar policy of non-intercourse. Unfortunately the embargo was unsuccessful. The Americans also blundered on the diplomatic front. Neutrality was finally abandoned in 1812. The United States declared war on Great Britain in June.

Chapter 3 examines support and opposition to the War of 1812 among Virginians. Many residents were diehard supporters of the war and the Madison administration. But a significant number of Virginians opposed the war. Some were Federalists, but Republicans also articulated their dissent. During the War of 1812, Virginia newspapers engaged in a lively war of words. Through the pages of 200-year-old newspapers, the past is vividly brought to life.

Chapter 4 covers the forces defending the Old Dominion. The U.S. Army and Navy contributed to Virginia's defense, but most of the regular forces served on the Canadian border. This meant that Virginia militiamen shouldered most of the burden. This chapter examines the organization of the Virginia militia and analyzes its performance on campaign.

Chapter 5 examines British forces in the Chesapeake. It also briefly covers forces in the Northwestern Campaign, as Virginia sent significant forces to this front. For the British, the War of 1812 was an unwanted conflict. Their primary objective was the defense of Canada. British strategy in the Chesapeake was meant as a diversion from Canada. Nevertheless, the British deployed significant forces to a secondary theater. Virginians were hard-pressed to meet this threat.

Chapter 6 covers the War of 1812 in the Northwest and Virginia's role in it. Ever since young Washington led an expedition to the Ohio Valley, Virginians had been intimately involved in the battle for the Old Northwest. The finale of this 60-year conflict came in the War of 1812. Virginia sent a militia brigade and a separate volunteer company to the Ohio wilderness, where they battled British and Indians.

Chapter 7 returns to Virginia and details the 1813 campaign. The Royal Navy arrived in Chesapeake Bay in early February. This was the start of a two-year blockade. British forces attempted to capture Norfolk in June. They sacked Hampton and threatened Richmond. It was an eventful year, and the citizens of the Old Dominion struggled to effectively defend their state.

Chapter 8 chronicles the 1814 campaign. American and British delegates began peace negotiations in Ghent, but many Britons wanted to punish the United States for declaring war. The first abdication of Napoleon meant thousands of British reinforcements were now available for service in America. Several regiments arrived in the Chesapeake. Once again, Virginia endured amphibious assaults. The climax came in late summer, with the embarrassing defeat at Bladensburg and the burning of Washington, D.C. Virginians looked for scapegoats for this national trauma. The city of Alexandria fit the bill. It surrendered to a British squadron without firing a shot. The partisan press reached a fever pitch in its denunciation for—and explanation of—the "Donation of Alexandria." Some honor was salvaged in the successful defense of Baltimore. Virginians played a role in the defense of the nation's third largest city. But as the year came to a close, many Virginians viewed the coming year with foreboding. They expected hard fighting in 1815.

Fortunately, news of the Treaty of Ghent arrived in February 1815. The Senate swiftly ratified the treaty, bringing the war to a close. Chapter 9 tallies the costs of the War of 1812 for the state of Virginia. It also details the fates of several characters introduced in the preceding chapters. The aftermath of the war is also examined. After the War of 1812, Virginia's status within the Union declined. Clearly, the war was not in the best interests of the Old Dominion.

There is much to be learned from an in-depth study of the Old Dominion during the War of 1812. This book will become a part of the hopefully expanding body of literature on this important period in Virginia history. It combines elements of military, political, and economic history, with a healthy dose of media criticism. If this book sparks interest and leads to further research, it will more than fulfill the author's ambitions.

In the early 19th century, Virginia was approximately 67,004 square miles, for West Virginia did not become a separate state until 1863. According to the U.S. Census of 1810, Virginia's population was 970,093, of which 390,634 were slaves. New York had just surpassed Virginia as the most populous state in the Union. Virginia's capital and largest city was Richmond, with 9735 people, of which 3748 (38.5 percent) were slaves. Norfolk followed closely behind, with 9193 residents, of which 3825 (41.6 percent) were slaves. Petersburg's population totaled 5668 people, of which 2173 (38.3 percent) were slaves. Hampton was not incorporated as a city until 1849. In 1810, Hampton was a part of the now-defunct Elizabeth City County. The county's total population was 3608, of which 1734 (48.1 percent) were slaves. Unfortunately, the numbers of free blacks in these cities were not given.

Alexandria was actually a part of the District of Columbia from 1791 to 1846, but it naturally retained many ties to Virginia. It is therefore appropriate to include Alexandria in a study of the Old Dominion in the War of 1812. In the Census of 1810, its population was 7227. A city-wide census conducted in 1817 gives a total population of 8159: 5513 whites, 1599 slaves, and 1047 free blacks.

In many ways, Virginia state government resembled its colonial predecessor. The courthouse was the center of county politics, a practice which continued until well into the 20th century. Many local magistrates also served in the House of Delegates, which meant power was not widely shared among the people.

Indeed, most of the populace did not have the right to vote. The franchise was limited to landowning white males. This rankled residents in the western part of the state. Many of them were in the process of establishing themselves and were confident that they would achieve prosperity. But it was galling that for the intervening years, they would be unable to cast their vote. Many argued that this was an attempt by the Tidewater elite to maintain control. By the 1820s, Virginia was one of the last states to limit voting to landowners. Ultimately, universal white male suffrage was granted, but not until the Constitution of 1830.

Virginia society was traditional, but it was also in a state of flux. Until 1786, there was no religious freedom. Methodists, Baptists, Presbyterians and others were unable to practice their faith openly. They could be fined or flogged for doing so. A law passed that year guaranteeing freedom of worship. The old Anglican Church was disestablished and replaced by the Episcopalian Church. Now that the premier church lost its exclusive status, many people joined other denominations. In the years before the War of 1812, the number of Episcopal parishes sharply declined. Postwar, there was an Episcopal revival in Virginia, but with a decidedly evangelical bent.

There was some industry in the Old Dominion, especially coal mining. Before it was displaced in the 1820s by anthracite coal, Virginia coal was in demand outside the state. That being said, Virginia remained very much an agrarian state. The primary crops were wheat and tobacco. These staple crops usually found their way to market by river. From riverine and Chesapeake ports, they found markets worldwide.

Agriculture was also in a state of flux. Tobacco is notoriously hard on the soil, draining it of nutrients. Planters worsened the damage by failing to rotate their crops. Much of the labor was performed by slaves. By 1800, Virginians found they had a surplus in human property. The solution was to sell excess slaves further south, especially to the cotton frontier of the Old Southwest.

The slave-master dynamic created tension. Most masters considered themselves benevolent toward their "people," but the reality was more complex. Masters who encouraged slaves to marry and raise families might threaten to sell family members as punishment (of course, many masters were actually related to their slaves, but this was an inconvenient fact not mentioned in polite society). When a master died, slaves might also be sold to pay off outstanding debts.

Many Virginians lived in fear of slave insurrection. Thomas Jefferson alluded to this fear in the Declaration of Independence, when he accused George III of exciting domestic insurrections. Several Virginia counties had substantial numbers of slaves; in 12 of them, slaves comprised more than 60 percent of the total population. One of the primary duties of the militia was to defend against such uprisings. Most of the time, such fears were kept under control. But when evidence of a slave conspiracy emerged, these anxieties leapt to the fore. In 1800, a slave named Gabriel Prosser attempted a revolt in the Richmond area. Bad weather and informers foiled the rebellion, but Gabriel and 25 others went to the gallows. With the coming of the War of 1812, fear of slave revolts loomed large among white Virginians.

Four of the first five U.S. presidents hailed from Virginia: Washington, Jefferson, Madison, and Monroe. They are known collectively as the Virginia Dynasty. This placed the Old Dominion in a national leadership role. But seeds of disunion had been sown by some of these very same leaders. Thomas Jefferson, while serving as vice president, co-authored the Virginia and Kentucky Resolutions, also known as the Principles of '98. The other author was James Madison, "Father of the Constitution" and one of the authors of *The Federalist Papers*. These resolutions were written in response to Adams' Alien

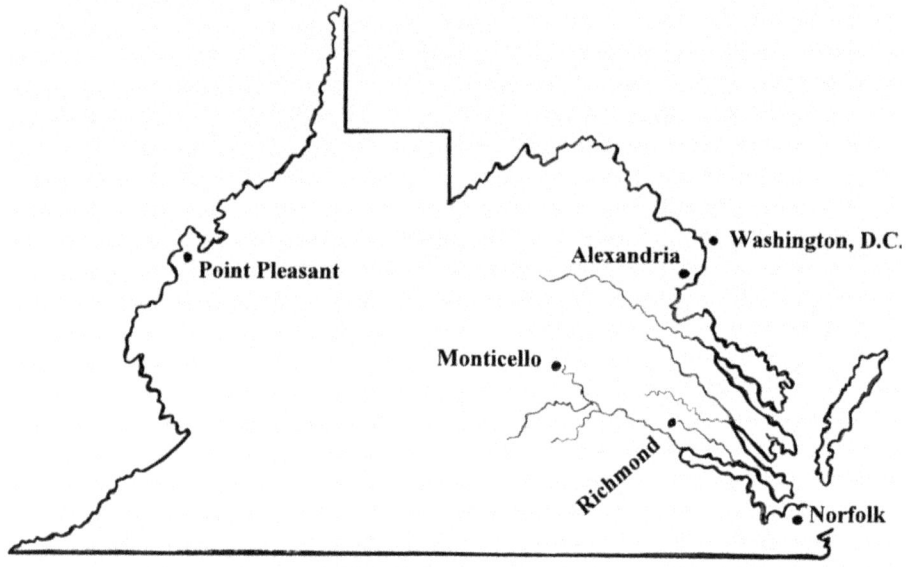

Virginia 1812-1815

Map of Virginia by Bonnie Bonin showing Virginia during the War of 1812, with principal cities and locations mentioned in the text (map by Bonnie Bonin).

and Sedition Acts. On the face of it, the Principles of '98 took a bold stand for free speech. But they also declared states had the right to disobey or negate federal laws. This was the argument followed later during the nullification controversy and, ultimately, by the Confederacy.

And now, without further ado, let us repair to the deck of an American frigate, off the Virginia Capes. It is 3 p.m., June 22, 1807.

1

"BRITISH OUTRAGE!"
The *Chesapeake-Leopard* Affair

In 1807, a violent encounter between two warships of the U.S. Navy and the British Royal Navy pushed both nations to the brink of war. American public opinion was almost unanimous in its support for war. President Thomas Jefferson ultimately decided not to go to war at this time. He opted for a policy of economic embargo, which caused more harm to the United States than it did to Great Britain. The *Chesapeake-Leopard* affair serves as a prologue, as well as a contrast, to the War of 1812. The attack on the *Chesapeake* provided a simple *casus belli*, easily understood by the American public, and Virginians in particular, for the events occurred on their very doorstep. When war was finally declared in 1812, Virginians were not so supportive.

On June 22, 1807, the American frigate *Chesapeake* (40 guns) departed Hampton Roads for the Mediterranean. At 3 p.m., approximately three leagues off the Virginia Capes, she was hailed by HMS *Leopard* (52 guns), a fourth-rate man-of-war. The *Leopard* sent over a lieutenant, who was received by Commodore James Barron. (*Chesapeake* was commanded by Captain Gordon, but Barron, appointed to command U.S. naval forces in the Mediterranean, was the senior officer aboard.) The lieutenant informed Barron he was searching for "runners"—Royal Navy deserters known to be aboard *Chesapeake*. The captain of the *Leopard*, Salusbury Pryce Humphreys, was under orders from Vice Admiral Berkeley (in command at Halifax) to apprehend these deserters.[1]

During the Napoleonic Wars, Great Britain had an insatiable need for sailors. When recruiting parties failed to produce enough men, ship's captains resorted to impressment. Press gangs were a familiar sight in British ports. But the Royal Navy also stopped ships on the high seas, and removed likely hands. They did not limit this practice to British merchantmen. Neutrals such as the United States were considered fair game. Service in the Royal Navy was despised by many. Sailors were desperate to escape life aboard a floating hell, and would take any chance to do so. When Royal Navy ships visited Hampton Roads, several hands seized their opportunity and ran.

Barron was not about to let the Royal Navy search his ship. He told the lieutenant no runners were aboard *Chesapeake*. The British knew this to be false—the men they were looking for were well known to them. In February 1807, three seamen deserted HMS *Melampus* in Hampton Roads, using the captain's gig to make good their escape. They promptly joined the U.S. Navy. These men were American citizens impressed into British service. William Ware, a Native American, came from Maryland. John Strachan (no relation to the Anglican clergyman and hero of the War of 1812) also hailed from the Old Line State. The third man, Daniel Martin, was an African American from Massachusetts.[2] The British alleged these men were actually volunteers, rather than pressed men. (In the Royal Navy, pressed men were sometimes allowed to "volunteer," to be eligible for a cash bounty.)[3] A fourth man, Jenkins Ratford, formerly of HMS *Halifax*, was a bona fide Briton. He made himself obnoxious to his erstwhile shipmates, openly taunting them while ashore.[4] Such provocations were too much to bear for the proud Royal Navy.

After the lieutenant returned to *Leopard*, Humphreys hailed Barron by trumpet, rather arrogantly stating that "Commodore Barron must be aware that the orders of the [British] vice-admiral must be obeyed."[5] Humphreys repeated this message several times, and then sent a shot across *Chesapeake's* bows. Then the shooting began in earnest. *Leopard* fired into *Chesapeake* for approximately 12 minutes. Twenty-one round shot pierced the American frigate's hull. Her sails and rigging were heavily damaged by grapeshot. *Chesapeake* managed to fire one gun before striking her colors. She suffered three killed and 18 wounded (one mortally). A boarding party from *Leopard* took the four wanted men into custody.[6] According to naval custom, Barron informed Humphreys that *Chesapeake* was now a British prize, but the Royal Navy captain refused to take possession: "My instructions have been obeyed, and I desire nothing more."[7] The British—rather belatedly—expressed sympathy and offered assistance. This was angrily rejected, and the *Chesapeake* limped back to Hampton Roads while *Leopard* rejoined the Royal Navy squadron in Lynnhaven Bay."

The *Chesapeake-Leopard* affair was greeted with outrage by Americans. Norfolk and Portsmouth citizens wore black crepe mourning bands for ten days, in honor of the dead Americans.[8] War between Great Britain and the United States seemed imminent. Americans were almost unanimous in their resolve, if not desire, for war. Political dissent was nonexistent. The *Virginia Argus* observed the crisis "seems to have buried in oblivion all party spirit. Federalists and Republicans are united in expressing their abhorrence of the conduct of the perfidious nation, and in the resolution of encountering them in War to avenge the unparalleled insults and injuries which they have inflicted on our country."[9]

1. "BRITISH OUTRAGE!"

The city of Alexandria was well known for its Federalist sympathies. But the local newspaper, the *Alexandria Daily Advertiser* (later renamed the *Daily Gazette*), supported the Jefferson administration during the crisis. It began its account of the attack on the *Chesapeake* with these words: "BRITISH OUTRAGE! We give the public the particulars of the following outrage on the American flag, under the influence of feelings which, we are certain, are in unison with those entertained universally by our fellow citizens."[10] This is in sharp contrast to 1812. When the United States eventually declared war on Great Britain, popular support was distinctly lacking. Samuel Snowden, owner and editor of the *Daily Advertiser*, proved a bitter opponent of "Mr. Madison's War."

President Thomas Jefferson was quick to condemn the attack on *Chesapeake*. He noted that Americans had tried to maintain strict neutrality, but escalating British outrages could not go unpunished. Jefferson applauded the national unity in the face of this outrage. At the same time, he reminded citizens that the ultimate handling of the crisis would be in his hands:

> There has been but one sentiment upon this occasion: the outrage is insulting to our national character beyond forbearance—Ample reparation must be made, but the *mode* of obtaining it ought to be left up to the Executive, who is confident of the support of the *whole* nation, if satisfaction is not given. It is not to be expected that the same unanimity will be found as to the means, tho' all agree in the end.[11]

William H. Cabell served as governor of Virginia from 1805 to 1808. He received news of the *Chesapeake-Leopard* affair before the president, and took immediate action. On June 24, he sent orders to the militia commanders in Hampton and Norfolk, Colonel John Wray and Brigadier General Thomas Mathews. These orders commanded the militia officers to defend their cities by any means necessary. Governor Cabell also sent 1,500 small arms from the Virginia Arms Manufactory to Hampton Roads.[12]

Jefferson sent his first letter to Cabell regarding the affair on June 29. He called for cooperation between the state and federal executive branches. Federal assistance was somewhat slow in materializing, so, in the words of historian Edwin M. Gaines, "for the first two and one-half weeks following the sea engagement Cabell actually exercised sole authority over military operations in Virginia."[13] But Jefferson trusted his friend not to do anything rash. Cabell confirmed this trust when he reminded the fiery General Mathews that he was to retain a defensive posture. No offensive moves were to be made by the Americans.[14]

Jefferson had great trust in Cabell, but he also wanted reliable firsthand information. He asked William Tatham, an old acquaintance in Hampton Roads, to observe the British movements. Tatham was to send daily reports by post to the president.[15] It was an inspired choice. The English-born Tatham was a man of many talents. He fought for the Americans during the Revolutionary

War. Postwar, he served in the North Carolina legislature. He was an accomplished civil engineer, and a passionate supporter of canals, which he believed would improve American commerce. He was also an experienced sailor. This skill served him well. Throughout the month of July, Tatham observed the British squadron on land and at sea, bringing his whaleboat well within range of the guns. It was a delicate—and potentially dangerous—assignment, but Tatham faithfully carried out Jefferson's instructions.

On July 2, Jefferson issued his *Chesapeake* proclamation. He condemned the British conduct in the strongest terms, and argued that "hospitality under such circumstances ceases to be a duty."[16] He ordered "all armed vessels bearing commissions under the government of Great Britain now within the harbors or waters of the U.S. immediately and without delay to depart."[17] If British ships did not leave American waters, all contact with them was prohibited, including food and supplies. American citizens violating this proclamation were liable to be prosecuted.[18]

The day after the incident, a Committee of Correspondence met at Norfolk's Eagle Tavern. General Mathews chaired the meeting. The minutes were widely published in newspapers across the state, including the *Virginia Argus*. The committee met almost one week before the president issued his proclamation, but its resolutions share much in common with the executive communication. Therefore, it can be concluded Jefferson approved of these resolutions. The committee members unanimously condemned the British attack as a violation of the laws of war. They resolved to sever all communication between British ships and the American shore. They also selflessly pledged "our lives and our properties to co-operate with the government in any measures which they may adopt, whether of vengeance or of retaliation."[19]

St. Memin portrait of President Thomas Jefferson. This likeness, circa 1804–05, shows Jefferson at the start of his second term (Library of Congress).

The resolutions adopted by the committee offer insight into this shadowy period between war and peace. Both sides felt war was a distinct possibility, but waited for word from higher authorities before taking drastic steps. For instance, the Committee of Correspondence felt that a British officer, carrying dispatches for Colonel Hamilton, the British consul, should have been detained, for he did not observe protocol by hoisting a flag of truce. In fact, this officer was lucky to escape a beating at the hands of an American mob. Fortunately, Hamilton was well liked in Norfolk. According to the consul's interpretation, hoisting a flag of truce was inappropriate, as war had not been declared. Only Hamilton's reputation for sincerity kept the mob in check.[20] Hamilton's rapport with the community also prevented would-be arsonists from burning his house.[21]

The Committee of Correspondence resolved not to permit commerce with the British squadron. The *Publick Ledger* noted on July 3 that "there has been no communication with the British squadron in Lynnhaven-bay for some days.—This squadron begins to feel some serious inconvenience from the want of water and fresh provision."[22] The British commander, Commodore Douglas, responded with a rather undiplomatic letter addressed to the mayor of Norfolk. The contents of this letter created a sensation:

> I beg leave to represent to you that having observed in the Newspapers a resolution made by a committee on the 29th ult. [June 29] Prohibiting and communication between His Britannick Majesty's Consul at Norfolk, and his ships lying at anchor in Lynnhaven Bay; and this being a measure extremely hostile, not only in depriving the British Consul from discharging the duties of his office, but at the same time preventing me from obtaining that information so absolutely necessary for his majesty's service. I am, therefore, determined, if this infringement is not *immediately annulled*, to prohibit every vessel bound either in or out of Norfolk, to proceed to their destination, until I know the pleasure of my government, or the commander in chief of this station. You must be perfectly aware that the British flag never has, nor will be insulted with impunity. You must also be aware that it has been, and is still in my power to obstruct the whole trade of the Chesapeake, since the late circumstance which I desisted from, trusting that general unanimity would be restored. Respecting the circumstance of the deserters, lately apprehended from the United States frigate Chesapeake, in my opinion, must be decided by the two governments *alone*. It therefore, rests with the inhabitants of Norfolk, either to engage in a war or remain on terms of peace.
>
> Agreeable to my intentions, I have proceeded to Hampton Roads with the squadron under my command, to await your answer, which I trust you will favor me with, without delay.[23]

Mayor Richard E. Lee refused to be intimidated. After conferring with the aldermen, he quickly drafted a reply to Commodore Douglas:

> I have received your menacing letter of yesterday. The day on which this answer is written [July 4], ought of itself prove to the subjects of your sovereign, that the

American people are not to be intimidated by menace, or induced to adopt any measures, except by a sense of their perfect propriety. Seduced by the false shew of security, they may sometimes be uperior and slaughtered, while unprepared to resist a supposed friend; that delusive security is now however passed for ever. The late occurrence has taught us to confide our safety no longer to any thing but our own force. We do not seek hostility, nor shall we avoid it. We are prepared for the worst you may attempt, and will do whatever shall be judged proper to repel force, whensoever your efforts shall render any act of ours necessary. Thus much for the threats of your letter, which can be considered in no other light than as addressed to the supposed fear of our citizens...

If you, sir, please to consider this act of individuals [Committee of Correspondence resolution to block British communications with shore] "extremely hostile," and shall commence hostility without waiting the decision of our two governments, although you yourself acknowledge that it properly belongs to them alone to decide, the inhabitants of Norfolk will conform to your example and protect themselves against any lawless aggression which may be made upon their persons or property; they therefore leave it with you "either to engage in a war," or "to remain on terms of peace" until the pleasure of our respective governments shall be known.[24]

Mayor Lee asked Littleton Waller Tazewell, a local politician and a future governor of Virginia, to deliver his reply. Tazewell delivered the letter as requested. The details of his meeting with Commodore Douglas were reported in the *Publick Ledger*. After reading Lee's reply, Douglas began rapidly backpedaling. According to Tazewell, Douglas denied his letter contained overt threats. If it seemed that way to the mayor, it was the fault of Douglas' clerk, who drafted the letter. Clearly, Douglas realized he had been intemperate in his choice of language (his flagship *Bellona* was named for the Roman goddess of war). While war might indeed be declared, it would be best to wait for instructions from home, or at least for orders from Halifax. Douglas said as much in his reply, in which he promised "that as far as I am individually concerned, every exertion shall be used that can, consistent with the honour and dignity of the British flag, tend to an amicable termination."[25]

As Mayor Lee mentioned in his reply to Commodore Douglas, the date of his reply—Independence Day—held special significance for Americans. In Norfolk, the Fourth of July was ordinarily a time for merriment and good cheer. July 4, 1807, was instead devoted to military drill and parades.[26] The commander of the 9th Brigade of militia invited those "not subject to the laws for regulating the militia (boys under 18 and men over 45) to volunteer for the duration of the crisis."[27] Considering the powerful British squadron menacingly anchored in the roadstead (*Bellona*, 74; *Triumph*, 74; *Leopard*, 52; and *Melampus*, 36) the militia needed every man it could get. Patriotic citizens volunteered their slaves to make repairs to Fort Norfolk.[28] The *Norfolk Herald* doubtless spoke for many with the following editorial, which was reprinted in the *Alexandria Daily Advertiser*:

1. "BRITISH OUTRAGE!" 15

Let us remember that we are MEN, and if we can do no better, let each man take his tree [like the Minutemen of '76] and kill one. In the name of all that is holy, powerful, manly or just, are we to FEED THEM for KILLING US? Are we to suffer them to send a BOATLOAD of MURDERED CITIZENS ashore and take a LOAD of PROVISIONS in return? Are we to pay them, to hire them with the luxuries of our land, to cut our throats? Away with such words as COOLNESS and MODERATION, they are the *cloak*, the *coverings* of *treachery*, and we have heard too much, seen too much, and *know* whence this moderation proceeds—from people who would tie our hands and bend our heads to the butcher! Let them beware, let us have no more of this—no MODERATION now—the storm is up, and at the least varying of the wind it will overwhelm *domestic* treason in due course.[29]

The last part about domestic treason was likely a reference to the Federalists. But as previously noted, the Federalists in this case either supported the actions of the Jefferson administration, or kept their dissenting views to themselves. Considering the tone of editorials such as these—and the fact that it was reprinted in a Federalist newspaper—this was a wise course to follow.

In such a tense atmosphere, rumors abounded. The Norfolk Committee of Correspondence heard the British were planning an amphibious assault on Hampton. Four gunboats were dispatched to Hampton, and 300 citizens volunteered to man them. It was acknowledged there might not be any truth behind the rumor, but considering the unprovoked attack on *Chesapeake*, it was best to err on the side of caution.[30] At the same time, a Hampton mob vented its anger by destroying 200 casks of water meant for the British squadron.[31]

The *Richmond Virginia Argus* joined in the rumor-mongering. On June 27, under the headline "Naval Despotism," editor Samuel Pleasants claimed to have a copy of secret instructions from 1793. These were issued by none other than George III himself, and commanded his naval ships and privateers "to seize neutral vessels and cargoes contrary to the law of nations." The Republican Pleasants included an attack on Federalists, claiming these orders "coerced" the United States into signing Jay's Treaty. He urged all American printers to circulate copies of these illegal orders.[32] It seems unlikely Pleasants had such orders in his profession; if he did, they were most likely forgeries. The printing of such sensational items gives a real indication of Virginians' mood during the crisis.

One incident that was not mere rumor occurred in early July, and was included in the July 8 edition of the Washington *National Intelligencer*. Vice President George Clinton and his daughter, aboard a cutter, were fired upon off the Virginia Capes. No casualties were suffered, but tempers flared. Those not already serving in the state militia requested Governor Cabell find room for them in the ranks.[33]

The *Argus* carried an account of further British aggression on July 6, from a report made to the Norfolk Collector's Office. The *Cynthia Ann*, a schooner out of Folly Landing, was fired on by a 14- to 16-gun British vessel. The British missed, and Captain Harrison, master of the *Cynthia Ann*, continued on his way. Suddenly, a British tender appeared immediately ahead. The tender dispatched a boarding party. The leader of the party called Harrison a "damned rascal," and demanded to know why he did not stop when fired upon by the first vessel. Harrison replied a foreign navy had no reason to stop him in his own waters. After further verbal abuse, including wishes that the gunfire had sunk the *Cynthia Ann*, the British boarders demanded a tow back to their craft. Harrison towed the British tars back to their vessel, and was then allowed to go on his way.[34]

The *Cynthia Ann* was not an isolated incident. The *Argus* carried further reports of British stoppages of shipping in Hampton Roads. The barque *Petersburg* was stopped and boarded, but Captain Davis was treated with great courtesy. On the other hand, Captain Chapman of the *Ruby* reported he was "treated rudely." Both ships were eventually allowed to pass. The item concluded rather obviously, "If the British commander is disposed for peace, he should cease to stop vessels in the waters of the United States."[35]

When the *Chesapeake-Leopard* affair occurred, the treason trial of Aaron Burr was the big story. The trial was held in Richmond, but the threat of war with Britain overshadowed the proceedings in court. When Commodore Douglas brought his squadron into Hampton Roads, Governor Cabell dispatched reinforcements to the threatened sector. He wrote the commanding officers of several brigades of militia: "I have the request that you will with all possible expedition march your troops to Norfolk for the purpose of repelling an invasion." From the Richmond area, four companies of infantry and two companies of cavalry were dispatched to Norfolk.[36]

The prospect of war with Great Britain inspired Richmond resident William Wirt with dreams of martial glory. Wirt was a 35-year-old lawyer, serving as prosecutor in the Burr case, and a future attorney general of the United States. He wrote his friend Dabney Carr, telling him of plans to raise a volunteer legion of brigade strength.[37] This legion was not meant for duty in the Tidewater; rather, it was to be part of a force mobilized for the invasion of Canada. Wirt planned to be a colonel of one of the regiments. He felt that Canada and Nova Scotia could be conquered in "a single campaign," and that the war would not last longer than one year.[38]

It might seem strange that the possibility of war—and the threat of maritime invasion—led to calls from Virginians to invade Canada. The *Alexandria Daily Advertiser* discussed the possibility at length, declaring "the conquest of Canada ought therefore in the first instance to be the object of this country." The conquest of Canada seemed a rather simple matter to this armchair strategist. An army of 15,000 to 20,000 should suffice, as British military strength in Canada was estimated at 4,000 men. Conquering Canada would also eliminate the Indian menace once and for all, for it was well known that these tribes were in the pay of the British. The *Daily Advertiser* also envisioned an expedition to the West Indies. Ten thousand militiamen would depart Charleston, South Carolina, for the Bahamas, which would quickly fall to such a large force. American possession of the Bahamas would deny them to the Royal Navy, thus diminishing the threat to American merchantmen.[39]

In this editorial from the *Daily Advertiser*, we see the roots of the divided strategy of the War of 1812. The War of 1812 was ostensibly a war to protect sailors' rights and to guarantee free trade. But in 1807, we see plans for the conquest of Canada openly discussed in American newspapers. One might argue that the best defense is a bold offense, but where were the troops to be found for this war of conquest? The author places a dangerous overreliance on untrained militia. In the event of war, these men would be hard-pressed to defend their homes, let alone conquer British territory. All of these points were confirmed during the War of 1812.

After Mayor Lee called his bluff, Commodore Douglas withdrew his squadron to Lynnhaven Bay.[40] In light of these developments, Governor Cabell cancelled the order sending 500 militia of White's Brigade to Hampton. General Mathews was confident that his own 9th Brigade, in addition to the earlier reinforcements from Richmond and Petersburg, were "amply sufficient to repel any attack that can be made by any force which can be spared from the British squadron."[41] The British withdrawal from Hampton Roads indicated a less aggressive posture on their part.

Still, tensions remained high. The *Alexandria Daily Advertiser* carried news of a skirmish near Cape Henry on July 17. A British watering party of five men—two midshipmen and three ratings—landed on the east side of the cape. A detachment of Kempsville militia guarded this sector. They opened fire on the party, forcing them to retreat to nearby woods. The militiamen surrounded the woods at dawn. The British, seeing no hope of escape, surrendered.[42] At first, they were placed in custody of a picket of Petersburg cavalry, led by a young corporal named Winfield Scott. After sharing a sumptuous repast—including wine and porter—with their prisoners, they were taken to the home of local resident Lemuel Cornick, while local authorities awaited further orders on what to do with them.[43]

The British sailors were ordered held by Governor Cabell pending further instructions from Washington.[44] Tatham suggested to Jefferson that the British prisoners be held as hostages in exchange for the four seamen removed from *Chesapeake*.[45] Not surprisingly, Commodore Douglas was "greatly incensed" by the capture of his men. In retaliation, five Americans were seized from a coastal craft. Douglas vowed "he would capture every American vessel going in or out, until the British prisoners were restored."[46]

On July 24, Jefferson advised—but did not order—Cabell to return the British prisoners. In his letter to the governor, the president recommended this course of action as "we should avoid every act which may precipitate immediate and general war," for the nation needed time to prepare. At the same time, Jefferson praised "the vigilance and activity" of the militia cavalrymen. Also, the return of the captives was not to be interpreted as a retreat from the presidential proclamation. If force became necessary, the Virginians were "unequivocally to understand that force is to be employed without reservation or hesitation."[47]

Governor Cabell concurred with President Jefferson's recommendation. The prisoners were duly returned to their ship. Though no casualties were suffered in the skirmish, war between Great Britain and the United States remained a distinct possibility. Both sides had to tread lightly. One false move by either side could result in open conflict.

By late July, the militiamen from Richmond and Petersburg had to be relieved by fresh troops. Samuel Pleasants of the *Argus* hoped the relief would be prompt, for many of the capitol's citizen soldiers were seriously ill. "It is with no small degree of pain we learn that a considerable number are already on the sick list, and everybody knows how destructive to the health of strangers a residence in the vicinity of Norfolk even for a short time is at this season of the year."[48]

Public support remained high throughout the summer. Town meetings were held all across Virginia, which passed resolutions expressing support for the administration and solidarity with the citizens of Hampton Roads. A typical example is from the meeting at Charles City Courthouse, July 13, 1807. It was chaired by John Tyler, father of the future president, and governor of Virginia from 1808 to 1811. The committee unanimously praised Jefferson's handling of the crisis. It approved of the "dignified answer" of Mayor Lee to Commodore Douglas' "insulting and menacing letter." The citizens of Charles City also praised "the manly and spirited conduct of our fellow citizens of Norfolk, Portsmouth, and Hampton." The committee waxed eloquent at the outrage it felt over the attack on the *Chesapeake*:

> What sort of feelings must Englishmen have? One hour to be in habits of peace and friendly intercourse, not only with Commodore Barron, but with the citizens of Norfolk (that hospitable port from which no stranger returns unsatisfied) and in another within view of our harbors, to commit so deliberate and wicked a murder on an unsuspecting, unoffending crew! Slaves and tools of a fool and tyrant, we uperior your country's destiny; what has it to boast of now but treachery, bribery, hypocrisy, and murder? We will plant a dagger in the heart of it. The vengeance of your own people shall be upon it!

The committee also expressed confidence that the United States could survive without British trade, declaring that "your commerce has not corrupted the great mass of our people, we can exist without it, and will return to habits of economy, industry, and our own internal resources."[49]

The *Alexandria Daily Advertiser* echoed the sentiments of the Charles City convention, declaring, "The effects of war are not to be dreaded so much as the peace we have experienced for some time past. We want no supplies and will require none. We can at all times subsist upon the means which the country affords. With these advantages, we have no occasion to ask or pray for peace."[50] Jefferson eventually pursued a policy of embargo, putting to the test the assertions of the Charles City committee that the United States could survive without trade with Britain and France. Unfortunately, the embargo was a failure.

In the meantime, the federal government made preparations for war. Heavy artillery, including two ten-inch mortars, was dispatched to Norfolk. Captain Stephen Decatur, hero of Tripoli, was given command of all naval forces in Hampton Roads (Barron was relieved from duty following the *Chesapeake-Leopard* affair, pending an inquiry into the incident). One hundred thousand militiamen were to be raised from all the states.[51] Virginia had the largest population in the Union. Its quota was placed at 11,563 men, comprising 8,673 infantrymen, 1,156 riflemen, 1,156 cavalrymen, and 578 artillerymen. The state governors were directed "to organize, arm and equip according to law, and hold in readiness to march at a moment's warning, their respective proportions of one hundred thousand militia."[52]

Commodore Decatur mostly had gunboats under his command, but by the end of July, *Chesapeake* was once again ready for action. On July 2, Naval Constructor Josiah Fox arrived with 20 shipwrights to repair the badly damaged frigate.[53] Fox kept his men hard at work. By July 27, the *Chesapeake*, which had been "little better than a hulk, without a mast of shroud standing," was "compleatly ready for sea." The *Publick Ledger* could not resist adding "that this circumstance ought to prove to the navy department the superior advantages of this place over Washington for naval equipments. Had the Chesapeake been sent to Washington for refit, we do not believe she would have been ready for sea under six weeks or two months from this date."[54]

Ultimately, Great Britain and the United States did not go to war in 1807. As the summer waned, tensions relaxed. By August 5, Governor Cabell ordered all militia on 24-hour alert to stand down. The garrison of Norfolk was reduced to one company of infantry. A single troop of horsemen patrolled the shore. No doubt, this was welcome news to the sick militiamen, who could return home to their families. By the end of October, the British squadron was withdrawn from its position near the Virginia Capes.[55]

On August 31, 1807, Jenkins Ratford, the native-born Englishman seized from the *Chesapeake*, was executed at Halifax, following a court martial for desertion. He was hanged from the yardarm of his old ship, HMS *Halifax*.[56] The three Americans were sentenced to 500 lashes each, but this was suspended. Ware died in captivity before he could be repatriated, but Martin and Strachan were returned to Boston on July 11, 1812, after the outbreak of war.[57] The return of the Americans was part of a deal made on November 12, 1811, in which the British disavowed the action taken by the *Leopard*. They also agreed to pay reparations, though they do not seem to have fulfilled this part of the agreement.[58] Captain Humphreys never commanded a ship again, though he was eventually promoted to rear admiral in the 1830s.[59]

Commodore Barron also paid a heavy price for the *Chesapeake-Leopard* affair. A court martial charged him with neglect of duty. As Benson Lossing described it, "she [*Chesapeake*] had gone to sea without preparations for hostile service, either in the drilling of her men or in perfecting her equipments. She was littered and lumbered by various objects, and her crew had been mustered only three times."[60] After the affair, all American men-of-war left port ready for action. Barron was suspended from the service for five years, but he did not return to active duty until 1824. In the meantime, the fallout continued. A quarrel with Decatur over the affair led to a duel (1820) in which Barron killed Decatur. For his part in the affair, Captain Gordon received a reprimand. Gordon fought a duel in January 1810 with the editor of the Baltimore *Federal Republican* over comments related to the affair. Gordon received a severe wound in the abdomen. Though he eventually returned to service, his health never fully recovered. Gordon died on September 6, 1816.[61] Lieutenant Hall of the Marines also received a reprimand. The gunner was dismissed from the service.[62]

As for the ships involved in the incident, during the War of 1812 *Chesapeake* had a moderately successful cruise in West Indian and African waters (December 13, 1812, to April 9, 1813), capturing five British merchantmen.[63] She returned to Boston, which she departed once again on June 1, 1813. On that date, *Chesapeake* fought one of the most famous frigate duels in history, against HMS *Shannon*. After 15 bloody minutes, *Chesapeake* once again struck her colors. *Leopard* also continued in service, though she was downgraded to a troop transport. It was in this capacity that she was wrecked in the St. Lawrence River near Anticosti Island, on June 18, 1814. No lives were lost.[64]

The *Chesapeake-Leopard* affair brought the United States and Great Britain to the brink of war. Had war broken out in 1807, Virginia would likely have been on the front lines. Most residents of the Old Dominion would have supported war at this time. An unprovoked attack on a U.S. Navy frigate, just a few miles off the Virginia Capes, provided a simple, straightforward *casus belli*. Cooler heads prevailed, and the crisis was averted. But tensions between the two nations remained. During the years of uneasy peace that followed, the U.S. government pursued a policy of economic embargo. The embargo did not achieve the desired results. What is more, the American diplomacy during this period was decidedly amateurish. The failures and blundering policies of 1808–12 left Americans—including Virginians—confused and reluctant to go to war, as the next chapter reveals.

2

The Road to War
1808–1812

The *Chesapeake-Leopard* affair did not occur in a vacuum. During the French Revolutionary and Napoleonic Wars, Great Britain and France battled for supremacy. The United States tried to maintain neutrality; at the same time, the rising republic flexed its mercantile muscles. In a period of global war, with so much of the nation's prosperity riding on the waves, maintaining profitable trade involved a delicate balancing act. Like Odysseus, the United States would have to sail carefully between Scylla and Charybdis, or Britain and France.

As early as 1793 (March 24, 1793), Thomas Jefferson wrote—to James Madison of all people—of the possibility that the United States might need to resort to embargo in the near future. According to Jefferson, "I think it will furnish us a happy opportunity of setting another example to the world, by shewing that nations may be brought to do justice by appeals to their interests as well as by appeals to arms."[1] This letter, written at the beginning of the French Revolutionary Wars, shows a remarkable grasp of the challenges the young republic would soon face. While Jefferson identified the problem, his solution—embargo—proved ineffective.

In 1794, Great Britain and the United States signed the Jay Treaty. This resolved several lingering issues from the Revolutionary War, and led to unprecedented prosperity for the young republic. In 1794, American exports totaled $33 million. In 1801, they stood at $94 million. A new era of Anglo-American amity seemed assured.[2]

But the Jay Treaty also drew criticism. The fallout from the treaty led to the formation of the first political parties, the Federalists (who favored the treaty) and the Democratic-Republicans (who opposed it). Washington himself favored the treaty, which assured its passage through the Senate. But opponents believed it was a return to British dominion. They also argued that the Franco-American treaty of 1778 was still in effect. Revolutionary

France agreed with this argument, and responded by attacking American merchantmen. From 1795 to 1799, France seized more than $20 million in American property.[3] This led to the Quasi-War (1798–1800), a Franco-American conflict on the high seas. The United States successfully asserted its maritime rights, thanks to the excellent performance of the navy. But conflict with France smacked of allegiance to Britain. Also, most Americans chafed under the higher taxes.

Jay's Treaty had a ten year life. When it expired in 1805, U.S. minister to the United Kingdom James Monroe negotiated a replacement. The Monroe-Pinkney Treaty (1806) improved on the foundations of the Jay Treaty, offering American merchantmen profits at low risk. The price for the United States, according to historian Donald Hickey, was "little more than a promise of benevolent neutrality."[4] This seemed a small price to pay, but Jefferson rejected the treaty without passing it to the Senate. He argued that the British made no concessions over impressment. Jefferson also believed France would triumph in the Napoleonic Wars, forcing greater concessions from Britain. Also, Jefferson placed great faith in the power of economic sanctions.[5] In retrospect, Jefferson's rejection of the Monroe-Pinkney Treaty was a grave error, which helped pave the way to war with Great Britain.

After victory at Austerlitz, Napoleonic France was the major power in Europe. But Nelson's crushing victory at Trafalgar meant Britannia ruled the waves. In retaliation, Napoleon devised the Continental System, which tried to exclude Britain from European trade. The Continental System came in two parts. Under the Berlin Decree (1806), the British Isles were off limits. French controlled ports would not permit ships that had called in British occupied ports. Furthermore, all British goods could be confiscated, even when carried by neutral ships. The Milan Decree (1807) went even further, allowing French authorities to seize neutral ships who followed British trade policies. Even ships which had allowed British boarding parties to search their vessels were subject to French seizure.[6] In the aftermath of the *Chesapeake-Leopard* affair, what chance did an unarmed American merchantman stand against the Royal Navy? A Yankee skipper who prudently submitted faced the loss of his cargo to the French.

In retaliation, the British government issued the Orders in Council (1807). These decrees forbid trade with ports which left out Britain, unless ships paid transit duties en route. The British hoped that by these measures, Napoleonic Europe would open its ports once again to British merchantmen. In the meantime, the British government sold licenses to neutrals heading to these ports.[7]

Between 1803 and 1812, Britain and France seized approximately 1,700 American merchantmen. Losing 200 ships per year in this manner was galling, but not particularly crippling to American trade. Donald Hickey states this amounted to roughly 4.4 percent of the U.S. merchant fleet. Before the outbreak of war, insurance averaged 7 percent, meaning these losses were covered. Hickey further argues that the total number of American ships during this period peaked in 1810.[8] If one went beyond pure statistics and examined individual cases, surely some ship owners and merchants went into debt and suffered bankruptcy due to Anglo-French seizures. But Hickey's larger point is well taken. For the majority of Americans involved in European commerce, these losses were sustainable.

Federalists argued that France was the worst offender. In July 1808, the Norfolk-based Marine Insurance Company published losses of $250,000 on cargoes it had insured. All of these losses were at the hands of the French. In contrast, the British seized $50,000 worth of property insured by the Marine Insurance Company. The British also helpfully returned $50,000 worth of property previously captured by the French. These statistics were published in the Federalist *Norfolk Gazette and Publick Ledger*, in an attempt to reveal the true enemy to the American people.[9]

Federalist hostility to France was firmly rooted in the violence of the French Revolution. In 1808, on the anniversary of the storming of the Tuileries, the editor of the *Staunton Political Censor*, lamented, "It is Sixteen Years this night, since the principles of murder and massacre were established in France—and from that period to the present, Good God! what bloodshed—what butchering and inhuman massacres, have marked the tracks of the French nation!!"[10] The perceived French bias on the part of Jefferson proved he was a Jacobin. In the early 19th century, this was the equivalent of calling a man a communist.

According to the Federalists, the only sane course was strict neutrality, though if there must be bias; it should be toward Great Britain. The Federalists saw in Britain the only nation with similar respect for liberty, tempered by a natural conservatism. To the Federalists, Napoleon was a conqueror who would not be content with Europe. Eventually, Napoleon would set his sights on the Americas. The wooden walls of the Royal Navy were the only barrier that stood between Napoleonic aggression and the United States. If a few seamen were impressed, so be it. It was a small price to pay to keep the tyrant from American shores.

The Republicans, for their part, were sensitive to slights from Great Britain. Every highhanded act was an attempt at re-colonization by the mother country. In early 1810, a high-ranking Republican wrote an extraordinary letter to Madison. Attorney General Caesar A. Rodney (nephew of the signer of the Declaration of Independence) declared Great Britain to be "our old & inveterate enemy." He acknowledged wrongdoing on the part of France, but British impressment "is worse than all we have sustained from France."[11] Rodney believed England was vulnerable on land and at sea and boldly declared that the United States could conquer Canada, while American privateers would cut a swath through British shipping.[12] Rodney did not propose a formal alliance with France, but felt American policy should favor Bonaparte. Rodney believed the British would not prevail against the mighty French Empire, for they were hobbled by debts and cursed with a mad king and a regent of "broken constitution." France, on the other hand, was not merely "Colossus of Europe," but master of the entire world, with unrivalled power in the history of mankind. Even the mighty Russians were mere satellites of Bonaparte.[13]

Rodney's letter is remarkable. The anti–British bias is clearly apparent, and not surprising. But Rodney certainly misjudged British resolve. His infatuation with French power blinds him to the power of the Royal Navy, which triumphed at Trafalgar in 1805. The British were engaged in a struggle for national survival. "Perfidious Albion" would not quit until Napoleon was utterly defeated. But Rodney sees vulnerabilities that can be exploited. Officially, the war was about sailor's rights and free trade, but Rodney seems intent on territorial acquisition. Such ulterior motives muddied the waters,

A cartoon from 1808 criticizing the Embargo Act. A giant snapping turtle named "Ograbme" (Embargo spelled backwards) bites a would-be smuggler carrying superfine tobacco to the British (Wikipedia).

allowing the opposition to claim—with merit—that the Republicans lacked a clear-cut *casus belli*.

Instead of war, Jefferson pursued a policy of embargo. The Embargo Act (1807) was supposed to protect American ships and sailors by keeping them in port. The complete withdrawal of American exports and shipping was in turn designed to place pressure on belligerent nations, who would be forced to respect American neutrality. Unfortunately, the embargo ended up hurting the United States the most. American exports in 1807 totaled $49 million. The next year, they declined drastically, to $9 million.[14] The U.S. government now found itself enforcing a decidedly unpopular law, preventing merchantmen from leaving port. A popular cartoon depicts the United States as a large turtle, for the nation had retreated into its shell. But this turtle is also a snapping turtle, biting a would-be smuggler attempting to bring superfine tobacco to the British. The captured smuggler curses "Ograbme" (embargo spelled backwards), while the turtle's handler marvels at his abilities. The British mocked the American policy, describing it as "a Rod which produced no other sensation on the rough hide of John Bull, than the pleasurable one which arises from titillation."[15] Perhaps this was a case of classic British understatement; nevertheless, the embargo hurt the United States more than Great Britain.

Virginia merchants and seamen had a premonition the embargo would be bad for business. Before the law took effect, ships scrambled to clear Norfolk. Elijah Cobb, master of a Cape Cod vessel docked in Norfolk, raced against time to leave port with three thousand barrels of flour. Cobb made the deadline, and managed to outrun the port collector, who had launched a boat in pursuit. For Cobb and those whose cargo he carried, the gamble paid off. In Cadiz, the flour sold for an incredible $20 per barrel.[16]

The embargo took a terrible toll on Norfolk. Thomas J. Wertenbaker paints an evocative portrait of the once-bustling port city:

> Her warehouses were locked, her wharves empty, the ships in port moved away to fresh water to avoid the worms, property values declined, many merchants faced ruin, her shipyards were idle, her artisans out of work, hundreds of sailors walked the streets or packed their bags to leave for foreign countries, the gangs of Negro stevedores loafed in the back alleys, the taverns and boarding houses were without guests.[17]

The election of 1808 is seen by many historians as a referendum on the embargo. If so, it would seem that the majority of Americans supported the policy, for the Democratic-Republican James Madison won a decisive victory over the Federalist Charles Pinckney of South Carolina (122 to 47 in the Electoral College, and 124,732 to 62,431 for the popular vote). But appearances can be deceptive. The early 19th-century South had a large number of subsistence farmers. Such people had little connection to overseas trade.[18] As long as they could put food on their table, they were satisfied. Also, even if they were not satisfied with the current leadership, subsistence farmers in Virginia often lacked the property requirements for voting. This effectively neutralized opposition from the underclass.

Despite the election of his former secretary of state, Jefferson repealed the embargo just before he left office. The embargo was replaced with a non-intercourse act. This act reopened American trade, with the exceptions of Britain and France. However, since American ships were now free to leave port, it was impossible to keep them from trading with the belligerents in neutral ports, or even going directly to the British Isles. As Donald R. Hickey concludes, "It was designed primarily to save face, to keep up the appearance of commercial warfare while giving up the rigors of the embargo."[19] Non-intercourse also brought some economic recovery, with annual export revenues between $31 and $45 million.[20] The increase in revenues gained public support for the Republicans, while Federalists could no longer use hard times for political gain.

The new president took office in March 1809. In his first inaugural address, Madison declared he wanted "To cherish peace and friendly intercourse with all nations having correspondent dispositions; to maintain sincere neutrality towards belligerent nations ... to exclude foreign intrigues and foreign partialities."[21] Many Federalists took heart in Madison's words. They hoped it meant an end of the pro–French bias of the Jefferson administration. The Richmond *Virginia Gazette* (soon renamed the *Virginia Patriot*) expressed a desire to give the new president "a *fair trial* ... if he administers the government according to the Constitution; if he acts fairly and impartially toward *foreign nations;* far from being opposed to him, he will find us in company with his warmest friends, admiring and approving."[22]

The honeymoon did not last. Just one month into the new administration, a golden opportunity beckoned. David M. Erskine, newly-appointed British minister to the United States, indicated Great Britain's willingness to repeal the Orders in Council. Not surprisingly, Madison jumped at the chance to reach a rapport with Great Britain, for it appeared that the Republican policies were vindicated. In mid–April 1808, President Madison issued a proclamation restoring trade with Great Britain, to take effect on June 10, 1809.[23]

Federalists initially applauded Madison's measures. It seemed that the new administration was genuinely interested in pursuing sensible policies. Federalist ship owners rejoiced, sending their ships to sea once again. But hopes were soon dashed, as the British government declared Erskine exceeded his instructions. The Orders in Council remained in effect. In response, Madison once again suspended trade with Britain.

At first, Federalists shared in the general outrage. Some accused the British of luring American ships out to sea, so that they could be captured en masse. But cooler heads—and party bias—prevailed. The Federalist *Norfolk Gazette and Publick Ledger* initially criticized the British government for its duplicity. By early August, the editor requested its readers wait until all facts were known. On August 14, the *Norfolk Gazette* concluded that the British government was blameless. Erskine was also not at fault, having acted in good faith.[24]

As Federalists gradually exonerated Erskine and his government, they once again took a negative view of Madison. Francis James Jackson, Erskine's replacement, received a frosty reception in Washington. Before he met with Jackson, Madison wrote, "My general impression is that he has been represented by King as arrogant in his temper & manners, and that he has been the instrument for certain offensive transactions."[25] Relations did not improve, and by November, the administration refused to meet with him again. At the same time, the American minister in Great Britain also returned home.[26] Tensions increased, and a diplomatic solution seemed out of reach.

In November 1809, Senator William Branch Giles, a prominent Virginia Republican, presented a resolution vowing "to stand by and support the executive government in its refusal to receive any further communications from.... Francis J. Jackson, and to call into action the whole force of the nation ... to assert and maintain the rights, the honour, and the interests of the United States." The Senate easily passed the resolution. It received more opposition in the House of Representatives, but finally passed by a vote of 72–41. On January 12, 1810, Madison signaled his approval by signing the resolution.[27] Giles' resolution sparked a vigorous Federalist counterattack. Congressman Jacob Swoope, also from Virginia, accused Republicans of orchestrating the diplomatic crisis. Swoope accused Republicans of "rooted animosity to England" and "wicked" allegiance to

Engraving of James Madison. The "Father of the Constitution" proved a mediocre president (courtesy Library of Virginia).

France.[28] According to Federalists, it was a diabolical plot to force Britain into declaring war.

American diplomacy during this period was amateurish at best. In May 1810, Congress repealed the Non Intercourse Act and replaced it with Macon's Bill No. 2. The new law permitted trade with both Britain and France, but in the words of Donald R. Hickey, would "reimpose non-importation against either belligerent if the other rescinded its restrictions on neutral trade."[29] Napoleon saw an opportunity to hurt Britain, and to drive a wedge in Anglo-American relations. In August 1810, John Armstrong, U.S. minister to France, received a letter from the duc de Cadore, French foreign minister. Cadore quoted the emperor, declaring the Berlin and Milan Decrees "are revoked, and from the 1. Nover., they shall cease to be in force, it being understood that in consequence of this declaration the English shall revoke their Orders in Council, and renounce the new principles of Blockades which they have att(empted) to establish; or that the United States, conformably to [the terms of Macon's Bill No. 2], shall Cause their rights to be respected by the English."[30] In his cover letter to Madison, Armstrong referred to French ambitions as "gigantic and terrible," but believed that European affairs would keep them occupied for the next 20 years. In other words, Armstrong believed Cadore's offer was sincere.[31]

Federalists believed Cadore's letter to be a ruse. Federalist newspapers, including the *Norfolk Gazette and Publick Ledger*, pointed out that Cadore's offer depended on British cooperation.[32] Since Great Britain was engaged in a fight for national survival, it would be highly unlikely they would relax their Orders in Council based on a tenuous promise from a French diplomat. They knew enough not to take the words of Napoleon—"The Ogre"—at face value. But Madison accepted Napoleon's offer in good faith. On November 2, 1810, Madison proclaimed the Berlin and Milan Decrees had been revoked, and declared all American restrictions against France lifted.[33] Under the terms of Macon's Bill No. 2, Britain had 90 days to respond in kind.

At the end of 90 days, with no revocation of the Orders in Council, Madison declared non-intercourse against Great Britain. Congressional Republicans responded with a bill approving the ban. Federalists responded with heat, asking for proof of the repeal of the Continental Decrees. The Federalist press reported continued seizures of American vessels by the French. They attacked the Madison administration for its gullibility and pro–French bias.[34]

During his first term, James Madison faced challenges from within his own party. In 1808, Madison was hardly the universal choice for president among Republicans. Madison owed his election to prominent Republicans such as Wilson Cary Nicholas and William Branch Giles of Virginia, and two brothers from Maryland, Robert and Samuel Smith. But the loyalty of these powerful men could never be taken for granted.[35]

"To the victor goes the spoils" is a venerable aphorism, but the victor must distribute these spoils carefully. When Madison attempted to appoint Secretary of the Treasury Albert Gallatin to secretary of state, he generated animosity among the Smith brothers. The Smiths personally despised Gallatin; also, they felt that by their efforts for Madison, such an important job was rightfully theirs.[36] Robert Smith was eventually appointed secretary of state, while Gallatin remained at the Treasury Department.

In his tenure as secretary of state, Robert Smith proved difficult and disloyal. He repeatedly questioned the president's foreign policy decisions, particularly over the Cadore Letter and non-intercourse against Britain. The animosity between the Smiths and Gallatin intensified, which was exacerbated by Samuel's efforts in the Senate to block the re-charter of the Bank of the United States. Gallatin threatened to resign. While Madison would be sorry to see Gallatin go, firing the secretary of state would make reelection in 1812 that much more difficult, as the Smiths would mobilize their supporters against the incumbent.[37] Madison eventually made the difficult decision to fire Robert Smith. At the same time, he made efforts to unify the disparate factions of the Republican Party.

In March 1811, Madison offered James Monroe the position of secretary of state. Monroe was a leader of the Old Republicans, and it was hoped he would gain their support for the administration. Monroe replied that he would like to accept the office, but with important qualifications. He reminded Madison that "I was sincerely of the opinion … that it was for the interest of our country, to make an accommodation with England … even on moderate terms, rather than hazard war."[38] He hoped the president would allow him to express his opinions freely, even when they were contrary. Monroe also asked for a public invitation from Madison, so that he could resign the governorship on terms acceptable to Virginians.[39]

Madison acknowledged past differences of opinion with Monroe, but minimized their differences, claiming to see "no serious obstacle on either side, to an association of our labors in promoting them." Madison also reasoned that the failed Monroe-Pinkney Treaty was part of "the general policy of avoiding war," and that "there is & has been an entire concurrence among the most enlightened [Republicans] who have shared in the public Councils since the year 1800."[40] Madison accepted that differences of opinion were to be expected "within the compass of free consultation and mutual concession," but they were to be "subordinate to the necessary Unity belonging to the Executive Dept."[41] Monroe's conscience was sufficiently mollified by Madison's reply. He accepted the office of secretary of state.

Robert Smith was furious at his dismissal from the cabinet. In late June 1811, he published a pamphlet addressed directly to American citizens. In this *Address*, Smith put the administration's dirty laundry on public display. He denounced the president as weak on foreign policy. He questioned once again the repeal of the Berlin and Milan Decrees, and whether Madison sincerely believed this to be true. The publication of the pamphlet came just as Monroe was negotiating with the new British minister, Augustus Foster. Smith's bombshell allowed Foster to ask why the United States should receive preferred treatment as a neutral. If Madison cynically made deals with the insincere emperor of the French, why should Britain be expected to make extraordinary concessions to the United States?[42]

Robert Smith's *Address* revealed serious infighting in the cabinet. Madison appeared indecisive at home and abroad. This emboldened a group of Republicans historian J.C.A. Stagg terms the "malcontents," who attacked the president for his weak foreign policy. They advocated a more bellicose stance in response to foreign policy challenges, for the honor of the United States was at stake.

Faced with the dismal prospect of being a one-term president, Madison changed gears. He adopted the aggressive policies of the malcontents. He called the 12th Congress to assemble one month early, in November 1811. Madison and his cabinet informed key members of Congress to make preparations for war. It is often said that a particularly militant faction in Congress—the War Hawks—were the driving force behind the push for war. According to Stagg, the driving force actually came from the Executive Branch; specifically, from the president. While the War Hawks pushed the program through Congress, they received their marching orders from Madison.[43]

The president also attempted to neutralize political opposition from outside his party, particularly from New England Federalists. On March 9, 1812, Madison delivered an explosive message to Congress. The president announced that the State Department had in its possession letters from a British intelligence agent formerly active in the Massachusetts state government. His mission was to foment "disaffection to the constituted authorities of the nation; and in intrigues with the disaffected, for the purpose of bringing about resistance to the laws, and eventually, in concert with a British force, of destroying the Union and forming the Eastern part [New England] thereof, into a political connection with Great Britain."[44] It certainly sounded like a diabolical plot. Jefferson wrote to Madison that here was proof to ordinary Britons that the upcoming war was caused by the nefarious activities of their own government.[45]

The truth of the matter was decidedly underwhelming, and yet another example of the administration's gullibility. The author of the letters was John Henry, an Irishman and former U.S. Army officer. Frustrated by lack of opportunity in the United States, Henry moved to Montreal. Eventually he found employment as a low-level secret agent for the governor-general of Canada. He traveled to New England in 1809, to gather information on public opinion.

If possible, Henry was to make contacts among discontented American citizens. When Henry returned to Montreal, he received £200 for his efforts. He felt this was not nearly enough, and petitioned for a larger payment or political office. The British authorities denied his requests, and Henry looked for compensation elsewhere. At this point, the Irishman met Paul Emile Soubiran, a confidence man masquerading as a French aristocrat. The two grifters ingratiated themselves with Elbridge Gerry, Republican governor of Massachusetts, who provided the proper introduction to the Madison administration.[46]

Seizing an opportunity to damage the Federalists, Secretary of State Monroe spent $50,000—the entire annual secret service budget—on the Henry letters. After Madison dropped the expected bombshell, the awful truth was revealed. Henry spent his time in New England among denizens of taverns and coffeehouses. No one of importance was implicated in treason, and Monroe was forced to admit as much. The entire affair showed a profound lack of judgment on the part of the administration, and revealed the lengths to which Madison would go to discredit the opposition.[47]

Meanwhile, many American citizens were distressed at the warlike noises emanating from Washington. They appealed to party luminaries in an attempt to halt the march to war. In mid–April 1812, Jefferson received a letter from Philadelphia, signed "U.M." The identity of this correspondent is unknown, but he was not a member of the former President's inner circle. Rather, it seems to be a plea for peace from an ordinary American citizen, who reckoned Jefferson had Madison's ear. U.M. noted that Jefferson's administration "was conspicuous for preserving the blessings of peace to your Country." He also observed that Great Britain was not the only nation which had committed outrages against the United States. U.M. cited France, but also stated that Denmark seized American vessels. U.M. concluded that the nation was ill-prepared for what he predicted would be a disastrous war. Jefferson filed the letter with a notation that it was "against war."[48]

The reference to Denmark by U.M. is interesting. During the Napoleonic Wars, the tiny nation attempted to maintain strict neutrality, while championing the rights of free trade. The British rather heavy-handedly searched Danish merchantmen, which led to violence. In 1801, the Royal Navy defeated the Danish fleet. Both sides quickly concluded an armistice, but not a binding treaty.[49] In 1807, the French occupied Holstein, and seemed poised to invade Denmark. Britain feared the Danish fleet would fall into French hands. To prevent this, a powerful expeditionary force, including 30,000 soldiers and 27 ships of the line, sailed in mid–August for Copenhagen. After a brief siege, the Danes capitulated, delivering their fleet into British hands.[50]

That October, the Danish crown prince concluded an alliance with France, and declared war on Great Britain in early November. Over the next seven years, Danish gunboats proved a major nuisance to British shipping in

2. The Road to War

the Baltic. As major British trading partners, American merchantmen also suffered from Danish depredations. A letter from Gothenburg, dated April 19, 1811, painted a gloomy picture: "The markets in the Baltic are becoming more gloomy, and the Danes are capturing every vessel they meet with; two out of three American vessels which have attempted to pass the Sound this year, have been captured.... There are fifty new privateers fitted out from Denmark this year."[51] The losses to American shipping at the hands of the Danes reveals there were more threats than Britain and France on the high seas. But Madison never considered war with Denmark. By the time U.M. wrote to Jefferson, Madison already concluded war with Britain was a *fait accompli*. Madison expressed this sentiment in a letter to the elder statesman on April 3, informing him of the recommendation of the 60-day embargo to Congress.[52]

For his part, Jefferson supported Madison's decision. U.M.'s letter—if it ever stood a chance—arrived too late to sway the elder statesman. Why did Jefferson support war with Great Britain? Jefferson actually put his reasoning in writing. Soon after the outbreak of war (June 28, 1812), Jefferson explained the reasons for war with Britain to the Polish revolutionary Tadeusz Kosciuszko. It is worth quoting at length:

> It is now 10 years since Great Britain began a series of insults & injuries which would have been met with war in the threshold by any European power. this course has been unremittingly followed up by increasing wrongs, with glimmerings indeed of peaceable redress, just sufficient to keep us quiet, till she has had the impudence at length to extinguish even these glimmerings by open avowal. this would not have been borne so long, but that France has kept pace with England in iniquity of principle, altho' not in the power of inflicting wrongs on us. the difficulty of selecting a foe between them has spared us many years of war, & enabled us to enter into it with less debt, more strength & preparation.[53]

This letter is extraordinary for several reasons. On the one hand, Jefferson accuses the British of ten years of outrage, which European nations would not bear peacefully. Jefferson then claims that France has committed similar abuses. The only reason the United States has remained at peace was because it was difficult to choose which nation to fight. As for Jefferson's statement that the intervening years allowed the United States to enter the fray stronger and better prepared, a cursory glance at the lack of military preparedness would suggest otherwise.

Jefferson also claims that while France behaved outrageously, it did not possess the same means to inflict wrongs. This seemingly contrary statement is clarified later in the letter, when he informs Kosciuszko that "the partisans of England here [Federalists] have endeavored much to goad us into the folly of chusing the ocean, instead of the land, for the theatre of war. that would be to meet their strength with our weakness, instead of their weakness with our strength."[54]

What was Jefferson hinting at? The answer seems to indicate what Federalists and dissident Republicans claimed—war with Britain was a means to acquire more territory. In 1801, Jefferson wrote that American success furnished "a new proof of the falsehood of Montesquieu's doctrine, that a republic can be preserved only in a small territory. The reverse is the truth."[55] Montesquieu, the very embodiment of the Enlightenment, clearly had the example of Rome in mind. As Rome expanded her borders, the old Republic became too unwieldy to govern. Chaos and civil war was the result. From the ashes emerged the Roman Empire, behind the façade of the old Republic. But American republicans ignored the lessons of the past in favor of territorial expansion. At this point, American territory, while extensive, did not span the North American continent. The Louisiana Purchase more than doubled the size of the United States. It also eliminated the French presence from the continent.

Great Britain still controlled Canada. When choosing which of the two powers to strike, it seems that British North America, sparsely populated and thinly garrisoned, was a prize too rich to ignore. For his part, James Madison agreed with the former President. As early as 1787, he wrote, "The question is, whether small or extensive republics are more favorable to the election of proper guardians of the public weal; and it is clearly decided in favor of the latter."[56]

The Southern Federalists made several attempts to argue against war. John Marshall, the most prominent Federalist in Virginia, was astonished Madison so quickly accepted Napoleon had revoked the Berlin and Milan Decrees. Party members in Hampshire County, Virginia, declared war with Britain would be "the extreme of folly, little short of madness."[57] Indeed, the statistics confirm this argument. Great Britain was the nation's biggest trading partner. This trade amounted to $39 million annually, while France accounted for just $4 million. As for the question of sailors' rights, while Great Britain (according to a report issued by the secretary of state) impressed approximately 6,257 native-born Americans, most had been released from their service. Just 400 to 600 remained in the Royal Navy. Surely, the issue was resolving itself.

The Federalists even voted several times against military preparations. In this way, they hoped to prevent the Republicans from mobilizing for war. Southern Federalists even voted against naval bills. This is particularly telling, for a strong navy was something Federalists held dear. Virginia Federalists were reluctant to vote against naval funding. They voted five times in favor of naval funding. But they also voted seven times against it.[58]

On April 1, 1812, Madison called on Congress to issue a 60-day embargo. The Senate extended this to 90 days. A non-exportation act passed at the same time. All of this was designed to keep American ships from leaving port, so that they would not be at sea when war was declared. To War Hawks such as Henry Clay, this was "a direct precursor to war."[59] But the administration continued to send mixed signals to the British. Augustus Foster, British minister in Washington, asked the president if the embargo signaled imminent war. Madison replied: "Oh! No, Embargo is not war." At the same time, Madison added that the United States would be justified in declaring war, for Britain had been waging war against the United States for some time. Foster concluded that war was not imminent, and passed on his impressions to his government.[60]

Meanwhile, word of the embargo reached the general public while the bill was still in committee. It is probable John Randolph of Roanoke was the culprit. Whoever was responsible, American ships rushed to get to sea, to avoid a new round of trade restrictions. As late as May, many Americans believed war was not in the offing.[61]

Why did Madison push for war? If the previous narrative seems confusing, imagine how it seemed to legislators and the general public at the time. The *Chesapeake-Leopard* affair offered a simple reason for war that most Americans understood and supported. The intervening years of failed embargo and non-intercourse—not to mention the diplomatic blunders—confused many Americans. It seems that Madison believed war with Britain would solve several problems. On the surface, war would prove the nation intended to defend its honor and to fight for its maritime rights. War would unify American citizens. The majority, except for the most ardent Federalists, would patriotically support the war. Westerners in particular would support war with Britain as a way to end the Indian threat. They might also acquire more territory in the process. Madison also had personal reasons for wanting war. War with Britain would unify the Republican Party, bringing dissidents back into the fold. This would almost certainly guarantee the Madison's re-election. While Madison never completely unified the Republican Party, he managed to win nomination for reelection in May 1812.

On June 1, 1812, Madison delivered a message to Congress. The president accused Great Britain of "a series of acts, hostile to the United States, as an Independent and neutral nation."[62] In lawyerly fashion, Madison made his case, cataloging outrages by Britain and the failure of the United States to gain redress by peaceful means. The president declared, "We behold, in fine, on the side of Great Britain a state of war against the United States; and on the United States, a state of peace towards Great Britain."[63] Would the nation be allowed to passively endure further insults? The decision was now in the hands of Congress. Madison was confident they would make the right decision.

As Congress deliberated on the question of war, what was the state of affairs in Virginia? From January 1811 to January 1812, no less than five men served as governor of Virginia. John Tyler, father of the president, resigned on January 15, 1811. George William Smith served four days until James Monroe was elected on January 15. Monroe lasted until early April, when he accepted Madison's appointment as secretary of state. George William Smith returned as acting governor, and was formally elected on December 6. Tragically, Smith perished on December 26 in a Richmond theater fire. Peyton Randolph briefly assumed the governorship, ending a year of turmoil at the highest level of state government.[64] Such lack of continuity of leadership would have been bad enough in tranquil times, but with war looming, the absence of leadership was deeply felt. Fortunately for Virginia, the next man to serve as governor provided both continuity and solid leadership.

In early January 1812, James Barbour (1775–1842) became governor of Virginia. He had previously served as speaker of the House of Delegates. Virginia governors served a one year term, but could not serve more than three consecutively. Barbour proved a popular choice, for he served three terms, from January 3, 1812, to December 1, 1814. For his effective leadership, Barbour became known as "the war governor."

On March 30, Barbour wrote a letter to the president. The new governor felt that war was imminent, and he wanted further information on the issue, as far as the president was willing to take him into his confidence. Barbour revealed to Madison the nature of his dilemma:

> In endeavouring to form a correct opinion as to the probable course of events by which to be governed in the discharge of my official duties I have experienced great difficulty from my limited information. Under this embarrassment I have been apprehensive that on the one hand I might create by some act of mine false or unnecessary alarms of an approaching war when one was not likely to ensue or on the other hand by supineness to leave the state defenceless and unprotected against sudden invasion should hostilities commence.[65]

Portrait of James Barbour, Virginia's "war governor," 1812–14 (courtesy Library of Virginia).

Most of all, Barbour wanted to know "what share of the national defence in the event of war will be extended to Virginia." Barbour assured the president of his complete cooperation and steadfast loyalty. Though Madison received Barbour's letter, it does not appear that he replied. A simple note in Volume 4 of *The Papers of James Madison: Presidential Series* reads "Docketed by JM."[66]

With no reply from Washington, Barbour made a statewide inspection tour in April and May. When the governor visited Norfolk in early May, he met with Lieutenant Colonel Robert B. Taylor. They discussed the problems of the defense of Norfolk at length. Both men agreed that Craney Island, at the mouth of the Elizabeth River, needed to be fortified.[67] Taylor impressed Barbour with his intelligence and dedication to duty, and marked him for further promotion. The governor also met with William Tatham,

Brigadier General Robert Barraud Taylor, commander at Norfolk during the Battle of Craney Island (Benson Lossing's *Pictorial Field Book of the War of 1812*).

Jefferson's lookout during the *Chesapeake-Leopard* affair. Tatham made a favorable impression; Barbour requested a report on the state of the defenses of Hampton Roads. The indefatigable Tatham produced a report, which contained several excellent suggestions.

Tatham suggested a telegraph from Cape Henry to Norfolk. From there, it would continue to Williamsburg, then Richmond, and hopefully, to Washington. Tatham guaranteed that with his telegraph, signalers could "put a question from Lynnhaven, & get your Excellency's answer from Richmond in twenty-five minutes."[68] Tatham suggested a similar plan to Jefferson in 1807.[69] He also proposed to Madison (March 1811) a plan for a telegraph from Cape Henry to Washington, with an estimated total cost of $15,000.[70] The idea was not without precedent. During the French Revolutionary Wars, Claude Chappe persuaded his government to adopt a semaphore telegraph line. The speedy transmission of information — 150 miles in five minutes — allowed French armies to concentrate at the point of greatest danger.[71] This was a tremendous tactical advantage. Tatham believed such a plan was feasible, though he worried about finding a reliable group of men to man the relay stations, as most young men were "so fond of talk, pleasure, indolence, & dissipations, that the energy of 1776 is lost."[72]

Tatham also called for the establishment of an observation post at the Pleasure House. This was an establishment that catered to "gamblers, tipplers, & those gentry of pleasure who love idleness."[73] Tatham conducted observations of the British squadron from the Pleasure House in 1807, for it had an excellent view of Lynnhaven Bay. Tatham wanted to strongly fortify the vicinity of Lynnhaven Bay, with a strong fort on Crump's Hill. He emphasized the importance of the bay as the first line of defense: "Make Lynnhaven bay too hot to hold a maritime enemy. Take the Bull by the horns and fight an enemy at his entering point."[74] Tatham also recommended fortifying Craney Island, but according to his plan, it would be part of the second or third line of defense.

Unfortunately, the outbreak of war came much too quickly for Tatham's plans to be put in place. Craney Island was eventually fortified, but not until 1813. Frustrated at the lack of progress, Tatham warned of the impending danger. He also predicted the federal government would not provide adequate assistance. It was up to Virginians to prepare their defenses. "John Bull's fleet will be in Lynnhaven Bay in the Spring." They would certainly attempt to capture Norfolk, "as they easily will, if they have any brains."[75]

As Congress debated matters of national importance, citizens of the president's home state viewed these developments with anxiety. As war with Britain approached, many patriotic Virginians, loyal and true to Madison, had an impending sense of doom. They attempted to address their concerns through official channels, but to no avail. In the meantime, those less loyal to the president and his party expressed their displeasure in the sharpest possible terms. Even after the declaration of war, they continued to give voice to their dissent. Let us now turn to the war of words which rocked the Old Dominion from 1812 to 1815.

3

The War of Words
Support and Opposition for the War of 1812 in Virginia

In 1807, when the United States and Great Britain stood on the brink of war, most Americans supported military action. By 1812, support for war was distinctly lacking. Conventional wisdom holds that political dissent in wartime is disloyal, even treasonous. In Virginia during the War of 1812, opponents of the war felt no qualms over expressing their dissent, loudly and often. When political opposition to the War of 1812 is considered, New England is usually identified as the seat of discontent, mostly due to the Hartford Convention (1814–15), where secession from the Union was proposed. While Virginia Federalists and dissident Republicans did not contemplate secession, they were a significant force. The opposition made effective use of newspapers to articulate their views. At the same time, editors loyal to Madison fired back. Throughout the War of 1812, editors of rival Virginia newspapers engaged in a lively war of words.

On June 18, 1812, the United States declared war on Great Britain. One week after the declaration of war, Virginia governor James Barbour called for unity for the duration: "In a moment like this let all party distinctions be forgotten, and whilst we offer them up as the most acceptable sacrifice upon the altars of our country and embrace each other as brothers, let us present an undivided front to the enemy." Initially, Virginians heeded Barbour's call for unity. Independence Day 1812 saw several sincere toasts to "Annihilation to Party spirit and Unison in sentiment, with a firm determination to support American independence."[1] But such unity proved short-lived.

This is not surprising, considering the distinct lack of popular support. The Congressional vote for a formal declaration of war was the closest in U.S. history—79–49 in the House, and 19–13 in the Senate. The conventional interpretation identifies the greatest support in the South and West, with opposition concentrated in New England. According to this view, one might assume that Virginia—a Southern state, and home of President Madison—solidly supported the war. The reality was more complex. Though Madison enjoyed support from a majority of Virginia Republicans, a minority faction—the Quids—loudly opposed the war. The Federalists were never a majority, but they enjoyed significant support in some parts of the state. In fact, Richmond was home to John Marshall, perhaps the most famous Federalist in the nation. But Marshall's position as Chief Justice largely removed him from the rough-and-tumble of party politics.

In the 12th Congress, a group of Republicans—dubbed the War Hawks—vociferously called for war. Historians have differed on the size of this faction, from a low estimate of five, to a high of 82.[2] According to preeminent scholar Donald R. Hickey, the group was led by Speaker of the House Henry Clay (Kentucky), and also included Richard M. Johnson (Kentucky), Felix Grundy (Tennessee), Langdon Cheeves (South Carolina), William Lowndes (South Carolina), John C. Calhoun (South Carolina), David R. Williams (South Carolina), George M. Troup (Georgia), John A. Harper (New Hampshire), Ezekiel Bacon (Massachusetts), and Peter B. Porter (New York).[3] Hickey's list of War Hawks tends to support the conventional interpretation with Southerners and Westerners predominating (the two New Englanders are rather surprising). But it is significant that no Virginians are on the list.

Virginia sent two senators and 22 representatives to the 12th Congress. Senators William B. Giles and Richard Brent were Republicans. As for the House, 15 were Republicans, five were Federalists, and two were Quids.[4] The term Quid came from the Latin *tertium quid*, or "a third thing." They were not mainstream Republicans, but they were certainly not Federalists. The Quids broke from the Republican mainstream in 1806, during Jefferson's Presidency. They originated in New York, and also emerged in Pennsylvania and Virginia, but no attempt was made to form a separate party, or to unify the disparate state factions.

The leader of the Virginia Quids was John Randolph of Roanoke, a slightly built, boyish man (he did not experience puberty, due to juvenile tuberculosis), who combined personal antagonism for Madison with eloquent opposition of the mainstream Republican platform. Randolph broke with the mainstream Republicans following the Louisiana Purchase. According to the French philosopher Montesquieu, a republic must remain small in size. If it acquires too much territory, it becomes ungovernable under republican principles. The increase in population also guarantees violent disagreements. Montesquieu based his assumptions on the example of the Roman Republic, which eventually became an autocratic empire. Randolph worried this would be the fate of the United States, if it continued to acquire territory. But mainstream republicans like Jefferson and Madison believed the United States was an exception to the rule.

Randolph summed up his principles as "love of peace, hatred of offensive war, jealousy of the state governments toward the general government; a dread of standing armies, a loathing of public debts, taxes, and excises; tenderness for the liberty of the citizen; jealousy, Argus-eyed jealousy of the patronage of the President."[5] Randolph's oratory attracted a great deal of attention. Virginia newspapers frequently printed his speeches verbatim.

Some of Randolph's sharpest rhetoric came during the months leading up to war. On December 16, 1811, he denounced calls for war to defend sailor's rights as a blatant falsehood. "Agrarian cupidity, not maritime right, urges the war. Ever since the report of the Committee on Foreign Relations [urging war preparations] came into the House, we have heard but one word—like the whip-poor-will, but one eternal monotonous tone—Canada! Canada! Canada!"[6] Unfortunately for Randolph, his constituents were not as vehemently antiwar. A Congressman since 1799, he was defeated in 1813, but returned to office in 1815.

It was not certain how even the loyal Virginia Republicans would vote. Gaining a majority for war remained in doubt until the closed-door sessions in June 1812. In the end, party loyalty won out. Fourteen House Republicans (one was absent) voted for war, while four Federalists and one Quid (the Federalists and Quid each had one man missing) voted against. The two Republican senators also voted for war.[7] It was by no means a ringing endorsement.

Though he was not in government at this time, John Taylor of Caroline, planter and political theorist, was a Republican (not a Quid), who opposed going to war. A personal friend of James Monroe, Taylor regularly corresponded with the secretary of state. In a letter dated January 2, 1812, Taylor sincerely hoped that the Madison administration was merely playing a game of brinkmanship with Great Britain, to force the repeal of the Orders in Council.[8] An astute judge of character, Taylor felt that "the people do not seem to possess the slightest tincture of a disposition for war."[9] He warned Monroe that the president was playing a dangerous game. Madison's aggressive posturing might "prime Congress so high, that it will not be in his power to prevent an explosion."[10]

In the same letter (a gold mine of antiwar rhetoric), Taylor was quick to reassure Monroe that he wished the administration well. But he hoped that Madison's brinkmanship would not result in a shooting war, which would be "a remedy worse than the disease."[11] Taylor firmly believed war with Great Britain would bring ruin to the United States. Six months before the declaration of war, John Taylor of Caroline saw the grim future with an astounding clarity of vision.

For his part, James Monroe expressed optimism. The secretary of state joined the Madison administration as an outsider. He seems to have quickly adjusted his views to correspond with those of the president. Monroe felt this might be seen by his Old Republican friends as a betrayal of his principles. In a letter dated June 13, 1812, he expressed reluctance to write to Taylor, for he knew his friend expected the secretary of state to affect a compromise between Great Britain and the United States.[12] But Monroe felt war with Britain would be short and successful: "My candid opinion is that we shall succeed in obtaining what it is important to obtain, and that we shall experience little annoyance or embarrassment in the effort."[13] Monroe believed that war would result in a change of government in London, who would quickly sue for peace. If the war did happen to drag on, "I do not apprehend either invasion, the desolation of our coast, the battering of our towns, or even any greater injury to our commerce than has existed since 1807, the period of the first embargo."[14] Compared to Taylor's prescient pessimism, the secretary of state's optimism appears recklessly short-sighted.

On June 18, 1812—the day war was declared—Taylor wrote once again to Monroe. The tone of the letter was conciliatory. "You will see that the object of this letter is to obviate the too usual consequence of a difference in opinion. War being determined on, it is useless to reason farther about it."[15] Taylor once again expressed his best wishes for success. He reckoned that "my chance therefore of reaping from the war a crop [of] odium for defending integrity is, I really think, better than the government's for reaping a crop of applause."[16] One suspects that Taylor still felt a great deal of anxiety about the prospect of war with Britain. It is likely he was simply trying to bridge the gap that had developed between old friends.

In November 1812, Madison was reelected to a second term (Madison 128 electoral votes, Clinton 89 electoral votes). He won 75 percent of the votes cast in Virginia.[17] On the face of it, this is a respectable margin of victory. But Taylor wrote Monroe about the apathy among voters. In Caroline County (Taylor's home), over 700 freeholders were eligible to vote. No more than 130 cast their votes.[18] Taylor himself did not vote, out of principle. Having spoken against the administration's policies, Taylor felt that it would be hypocritical to vote for Madison's reelection, as it would be a tacit endorsement of the war. At the same time, he stated that he preferred Madison to the Federalist King.[19]

In the same letter, Taylor noted that approximately 20 of the 130 freeholders voted for dissident Republican DeWitt Clinton, or Federalist Rufus King.[20] This must have been shocking to a longstanding Republican like Taylor. In 1808, when Monroe considered running for president, Taylor warned him about forming an alliance with the Federalists: "You cannot count upon any permanent friendship from them, both because they mean only to use you for their special objects, and because your principals can never unite with theirs."[21] Considering his strong antifederalist prejudices, it is no wonder Taylor decided to abstain from voting. He simply could not bring himself to cross party lines into the enemy's camp. This partisan mistrust went both ways. In the election of 1812, Madison's principal opponent was the dissident Republican DeWitt Clinton. Nationwide, many Federalists voted for Clinton, but Virginians nominated a "straight" Federalist, Rufus King of New York. While voting for Clinton might prove the best strategy to defeat Madison, Virginia Federalists turned against him after a pro-war speech which also praised Jefferson.[22] There was simply not enough of a difference between the mainstream Madison and the dissident Clinton to justify crossing party lines.

The election of 1812 in Virginia was characterized by low voter turnout. Less than half the eligible voters participated—20,700 out of 50,000.[23] King won 5,600 votes in Virginia, 27 percent of the total. Most of these were cast in traditional strongholds of Federalist support, such as the Eastern Shore.[24] It is quite possible more Virginia Federalists would have voted for King, if not for the General Ticket Law. This piece of legislation, passed by the Virginia General Assembly in 1800 (just in time for Jefferson's election), gave an extra advantage to Republicans. Before the passage of this law, electors came from individual districts. This meant that Federalist candidates might win a few Virginia electors. Thanks to the General Ticket Law, according to James H. Broussard, "by providing a statewide popular vote for all twenty-one [in 1800] electors, any local Federalist majorities would be submerged in the general Republican tide."[25] This had the effect of keeping many Federalist voters from turning out, as the saw the cause as hopeless, and wished to avoid harassment from their Republican neighbors.[26]

While some parts of Virginia were undoubtedly Federalist, in other parts, the extent of support is more difficult to determine. According to Myron F. Wehtje, Federalists were concentrated in "the Tidewater, the Northern Neck, the Shenandoah Valley, and the transmontane West."[27] The Tidewater also contained a fair amount of Quids. In *The Southern Federalists*, Broussard divides Federalist support into quartiles, and presents the data on a county map of the state. His findings partially confirm Wehtje, though he also includes the Eastern Shore (Northampton and Accomack counties) as solidly Federalist. The counties clustered around Richmond, such as Henrico, Chesterfield, Prince George, and Powhatan, are in the lowest two quartiles. In other parts of the Old Dominion, Broussard presents a more complicated picture. While Wehtje identifies widespread Federalist support in the Tidewater, Broussard's map is a checkerboard. For instance, York County is placed in the second quartile, while neighboring James City and the now-defunct Warwick and Elizabeth City counties are in the lowest two quartiles. In the Northern Neck, John Taylor's Caroline County is—not surprisingly—in the lowest quartile, but nearby Westmoreland and King George counties is highly Federalist. Even the western part of the state shows the same county divisions along party lines.[28] After examining Broussard's map, one realizes why Republicans felt the need for the General Ticket Law. Without a law to tilt the scales in the Republicans' favor, the checkerboard distribution of Federalists and Republicans left too much to chance.

How many Virginians opposed the War of 1812? Wehtje estimates perhaps one-quarter of the state population. While this was a minority, Wehtje argues "the opposition in Virginia rivaled that of New England in intensity."[29] Stymied at the polls, opponents of the war expressed their views in print. Virginia during this period boasted a large number of newspapers. The dispersed nature of settlement in the South made newspapers critical for the spread of information. This was particularly true for the Federalists, who were often surrounded by Republican neighbors.[30] Naturally, there were those who expressed support for the war and the administration with chest-thumping bellicosity. The *Richmond Enquirer, Virginia Argus,* and *Alexandria Herald* represented the pro-war Republican press. On the Federalist side, the *Alexandria Daily Gazette, Norfolk Gazette and Publick Ledger, Virginia Patriot,* and—despite its name—the *Staunton Republican Farmer*—proved tenacious adversaries. The editors of these rival sheets waged a lively, acrimonious, and frequently entertaining war of words.

Perhaps the most aggressively Republican newspaper in the Old Dominion was the *Richmond Enquirer*. It was founded in 1804 by Thomas Ritchie, a bookseller and former schoolteacher. From the start, Ritchie was a steadfast champion of the mainstream Republican agenda. He was also politically well connected. His cousin was Spencer Roane, the leading judge on the Virginia Court of Appeals. Another ally was Dr. John Brockenbrough, director of the Virginia State Bank. All three men came from Essex County, and were collectively known as the "Essex" or "Richmond Junto." (Undoubtedly Ritchie and his comrades preferred the name Richmond Junto, for the Essex Junto was also the name of a faction of ardent Massachusetts Federalists.) Ritchie's unstinting support for the Republican cause made the *Enquirer* Jefferson's favorite newspaper. It also made the *Enquirer* a newspaper of note nationwide.[31]

Also in Richmond, the editor of the *Virginia Argus*, Samuel Pleasants, was very much a pro-war Republican. He frequently reprinted items from the *National Intelligencer*, the Washington, D.C.-based paper, considered the house organ of the Madison administration. On April 23, 1812, the *Argus* ran an editorial from the *Intelligencer*, expressing confidence that the British would be unable to wage war in America:

> Do we apprehend danger to ourselves? From what quarter will it assail us? From England and by invasion? The idea is too absurd to merit a moment's consideration. Where are her troops? [Most were fighting the French or scattered across the globe in colonial garrisons].... Can any one believe, that, under such circumstances, the British government could be so infatuated, or rather mad, as to send troops here for the purpose of invasion?[32]

In May, Pleasants contributed his own editorial voice to the discussion. He projected the same breezy optimism as his compatriots at the *National Intelligencer*, and added a slap at the opposition:

> It makes one smile to hear the tory [Federalist] boast that the Americans would be swept from the ocean in a war with Great Britain.... Surely the British cannot be so omnipotent at sea as is pretended; or, if they are, the tory tales of [the French] burning [American] vessels must be false. The British are strong at sea, to be sure; but they are not quite so strong as they pretend to be.... The U. States, on the contrary, have never been over-rated as to strength; they have, in fact, been under-rated. And come the tug of war when it will, the world will be ccouterm into admiration of the real energy of the nation.[33]

In the pages of the *Argus*, before war was even declared, the battle was already won by the United States. But a small amount of doubt seems evident from an advertisement printed May 21. The owner of a paper mill, John J. Johnson, "earnestly recommended" Richmond residents save linen, rags, and old ropes. The proceeds from cash for these recycled items could be used to feed and clothe the needy.[34] While a paper mill would certainly welcome rags as a source of pulp, it seems Johnson thought the war would last longer than the optimists believed it would. His advertisement is a modest bit of foresight in an aggressively pro-war newspaper.

The *Norfolk and Portsmouth Herald*, though a Republican newspaper, viewed the approach of war with anxiety. "If we are on the verge of war with England, the only nation upon the globe that possesses the immediate means of annoying us, how can our rulers answer to their country and to their consciences for the consequences which must inevitably follow our unprepared situation?"[35] After the events of 1807, when British men-of-war sat menacingly in Hampton Roads, it is not surprising that Norfolk Republicans would display more reluctance than their Richmond brethren. This is an indication that support for the war in Madison's home state, and from his own party, could not be taken for granted.

A month before the declaration of war, the Federalist *Norfolk Gazette and Publick Ledger* called for a change in leadership. The editor castigated leading Republicans, and exhorted responsible citizens of all political persuasions to vote Madison out of office, before a great calamity befell the nation. The editor appealed to "thinking men of all parties" to "unite in their efforts to snatch the nation from the brink of ruin." The editor argued that the Republicans bore sole responsibility for the economic downturn, a cornerstone of Federalist rhetoric. Now the Republicans were on the verge of precipitating an even greater folly, a fact which even "the most hardened ccouter" could not deny.[36] Such dire warnings were not unique to Norfolk. Samuel Snowden (1776–1831), editor and owner of the *Alexandria Daily Gazette*, also argued against war with Great Britain.

The details of Snowden's early life are vague, but it is known that he was born in Piscataway, New Jersey.[37] At some point before 1800, Snowden moved to Alexandria. On December 8, 1800, he purchased the *Alexandria Advertiser* (founded 1784), which he later renamed the *Daily Gazette*.[38] Carrol H. Quenzel, who wrote a brief biography of Snowden in 1952, believes he may have been attracted to the city because most of the mechanics (artisans) hailed from eastern Pennsylvania, a region sharing much in common with New Jersey.[39] Whether or not Snowden was a Federalist before he settled in Alexandria is unknown, but he was in good company; as Quenzel notes, "A safer Federalist haven in the South than Alexandria would have been difficult to find, since even as late as March, 1814, nine of the sixteen members of its Common Council were Federalists."[40] In September 1812, Snowden hired John Douglass Simms as an editorialist.[41] This was significant, for John Douglass Simms was the son of Mayor Charles Simms. Hiring such a man indicates official sanction—or at least tacit consent—by the local government of the opinions expressed by the *Gazette*. Snowden certainly did not shy away from expressing Federalist views.

Snowden vehemently opposed going to war. In January 1812, pro-war arguments were sarcastically dismissed as "such as disgrace an animal pretending to rationality."[42] In an editorial from mid–May, Snowden warned his readers of the folly of war with Britain. It is worth quoting at length, for many of the Federalists' core beliefs are encapsulated in this editorial:

> We are decidedly of the opinion that the people of this once free, prosperous and happy country are to experience in a short time the calamities of war.... Without a fleet, an army, and with a treasury exhausted through the blind folly of our rulers, we are to be plunged into a war with one of the most formidable powers in Europe, in aid of a system laid down by one of the greatest tyrants the world ever saw [Napoleon], for the ruin of the only nation on earth capable of setting bounds to his insatiable ambition.[43]

Federalists frequently noted the unpreparedness of the United States for war, though it is important to add that they also had a fear of standing armies, though they did advocate a stronger navy (much like Great Britain). At the 1812 Federalist state convention, held in Staunton, delegates ridiculed the Madison administration as "the first that ever went to war, in order to raise an army, and to borrow money to obtain it."[44] The Federalists were also quick to criticize war with Britain on the grounds that France was the true enemy. By fighting the British, Americans would be aiding a tyrant, to the detriment of the only other nation on Earth dedicated to liberty. George Hay, son-in-law to James Monroe, expressed similar sentiments in a letter to the secretary of state.[45]

In the same editorial, Snowden speculated that war offered a chance to eliminate political opposition: "The war offers Whigs and the current admin-

3. The War of Words

istration an opportunity to purge the counties of 'tories.'"[46] In the overheated rhetoric of the times, Federalists were branded with the epithet "Tory," and accused of traitorous allegiance to Great Britain. In turn, Republicans were often called "Whigs" by their Federalist enemies. The continued use of British political identities is certainly remarkable.

On June 4, 1812, the *Gazette* published the first of a four-part series of editorials, written by "Senex" (quite possibly Snowden using an alias, a common conceit in early 19th-century journalism). The Senex editorials are rather verbose, but the central arguments are expressed in the first part:

> TO THE PEOPLE OF AMERICA.
>
> The men who are precipitating this country into a war with England, pretend that the *spirit of the Nation, the voice of the People*, call upon them to avenge their wrongs and assert their rights in this way. These pretenses have never been wanting in the mouths of demagogues, for the support of their own wicked views. This pretended "voice of the people" has ever been the Syren song to lure them to their ruin.[47]

Senex also predicts war with Great Britain will be calamitous for the United States.

The contrast between 1807 and 1812 is striking. During the crisis caused by the *Chesapeake-Leopard* affair, Snowden was quick to condemn British aggression. Though a dedicated Federalist, Snowden did not accuse the Republican Jefferson administration of ulterior motives. In 1812, Madison and his cohorts are denounced as demagogues of the worst kind. These blackguards wrap themselves in the flag, and silver-tongued, employ the rhetoric of patriotism to whip up popular support.

Two days after the declaration of war, the *Gazette* imparted the news in a decidedly unenthusiastic tone:

> It is now WAR between the United States and Great Britain. Congress have at length opened a "Pandora's Box," and from it has issued one of the deadliest evils which ever ccout a nation, particularly one situated as these U. States are—they [the Madison administration] have done us all the harm they can; but although they have exercised their power as far as in them lies of *taking away our living* thank Heaven they have *left us with life!*[48]

The sense of foreboding is palpable. Anxiety over ships and cargoes on the high seas is also expressed. Alexandria was a thriving port, which had not suffered greatly under the embargo. Much of the credit for this lies in the profitable grain trade with Spain and Portugal, which supplied Wellington's Peninsular army. This was a major reason for Alexandrians' reluctance to go to war, and will be examined later in greater detail.

The *Daily Gazette* was not the only paper in Alexandria. In 1811, the *Alexandria Herald* published its first edition. Co-editors J. Corse and N. Rounsavell adopted a much more mainstream Republican stance. In a July 1, 1812, editorial, the editors of the *Herald* responded directly to a piece in the *Gazette*, authored by "Cato." The *Herald* expressed displeasure at Cato's inflammatory language, at a time when passions were running high: "This last desperate plunge of a domineering faction and of an ambitious and prejudiced chief magistrate, it is hoped, has opened your eyes and dissipated your fears as to the intentions of their political opposers."[49] The *Herald* ridiculed the idea that the motion for war, debated at length in Congress, and approved by the required two-thirds majority, was evidence of legislative tyranny. The notion that Madison's personal ambitions played a role in the declaration of war is dismissed as preposterous.[50]

While Corse and Rounsavell thoroughly dissected and sharply criticized Cato's arguments, they also held out an olive branch to the opposition. They felt that "Cato's language suits but a small proportion of the federal party," though out of stubbornness, the majority might prove reluctant to disavow the more radical elements.[51] The members of this minority faction were denigrated as Tories, or Federalists of the "Boston Stamp."

"True-Blue" told the readers of the *Herald* all about these dastardly characters, denouncing them as "a base and unprincipled Faction whose object is to rise into power by *any* means." These scoundrels baselessly attacked President Madison, portraying him as a cartoonish tyrant oppressing the people. In their deluded worldview, the war itself was "unjust and unnecessary ... in order to please 'the ruler of France' and to protect British seamen against their lawful sovereign." Tories minimized America's grievances against Britain, and declared peace within reach, if voters put Federalists in office. Federalists of the Boston Stamp minimized American successes on the battlefield (few and far between for much of the war). "Everything is represented in the darkest colours, nothing but imbecility, venality, profligacy, profusion, waste, and speculation on the part of our rulers, on the part of the people distress, misery, hunger, taxes, and oppression." If the people refused to be taken in by these lies, the worst of the Tories would attempt "the last act," presumably a *coup d'etat*. Thankfully, most would be unwilling to take such drastic measures, for "it is the villain who has little to lose, who sets fire to the house for the purpose of plundering."[52]

True-Blue certainly delivers a devastating indictment of the Federalist opposition, in a fine example of the purple prose of the period. But one has the distinct feeling that he uses a rather broad brush, and that *any* discontent can be condemned as seditious. The *Herald* implies this in a later edition: "Government is of too sacred and serious a nature, of too great importance to the welfare of society, to be a subject for the carping of a discontented few; and in time of war, it is doubly atrocious to endeavor, by diffusing their venom, to counter the strong arm of national power."[53] War certainly has a way of sharpening divisions in society. What might be tolerated in peacetime is intolerable in wartime.

For his part, Samuel Snowden did not soften his criticism as the war dragged on. When word of the repeal of the Orders in Council reached the United States, he called for an immediate armistice, so that lingering differences between the warring nations could be worked out.[54] He frequently reprinted editorials from New England Federalist newspapers. In early 1814, Snowden seemed to confirm True-Blue's accusation that Boston Federalists spread preposterous lies, with an item taken from the *Salem Gazette*:

> THE FACT CONFESSED
> We have often considered that our own Vice-roy Madison was in fact a naturalized Citizen of France; and the following extract from a French Biography of Mr. Barlow, proves that he also had become a French Citizen.... This fact is a key to many mysteries.[55]

It is shocking—and rather amusing—that such allegations were ever taken seriously. Then again, considering some of the more outlandish conspiracy theories circulated in recent years (President Obama's forged birth certificate), perhaps we should not judge our ancestors too harshly.

The *Alexandria Daily Gazette* was not the only antiwar newspaper in the Old Dominion. Federalist editors in Richmond and Norfolk also expressed opposition to the war. The *Richmond Virginia Patriot* accused the administration of allegiance to France, and the worst kind of hypocrisy. In the not-so-distant past, Republicans declared their undying support for the principles of "liberty, equality, and the rights of man," and proclaimed themselves the enemies of "unlimited despotism." But such lofty sentiments fell by the wayside; such was their infatuation with Napoleon, "tho' almost every vestige of freedom has forsaken France." Discarding cherished principles requires "a change in the mental constitution" of Republicans. Since they now fight for the cause of "pure, absolute despotism," freedom of speech must be suppressed. "Now those who dare mistrust the purity of motive or the wisdom of the proceedings of government, are branded as traitors, tories, and advocates of England."[56]

The *Patriot* also resorted to ridicule. On April 30, 1814, a mock letter "from a little Man to a tall Man" lampooned both Jefferson and Madison. "Madison" addressed his "Illustrious Predecessor," telling him that "to the world my language is always equivocal when necessary: to you I always am plain." The gist of the letter was Madison's lament over Napoleon's downfall. The defeat of "this favorite brat" meant that Britain could devote its entire war effort to the United States, exposing both Jefferson and Madison "as two short sighted block heads." The Federalist press would have a field day. After several more lines of lamentation, Madison took solace in the fact that the Republicans had spin doctors of their own. "There are newspapers enough to make us both patriots, statesmen, and philosophers."[57]

Naturally, such open ridicule angered Madison's supporters. It is apparent that they would have liked to stifle dissent. This is ironic, for in 1804, Samuel Pleasants of the *Argus* published a pamphlet by "Marcellus." This pamphlet, entitled "Essays on the Liberty of the Press," defended the necessity of a free and unfettered press. It was far preferable to allow editors to published inflammatory and libelous words, than for newspapers to be muzzled by overzealous magistrates. Marcellus criticized at length the Sedition Act passed during the Quasi War with France (1798–1800). This act was a direct assault on the 1st Amendment.[58] Then again, the Sedition Act was passed by the Adams administration, a political rival. One wonders if Marcellus would have been so quick to criticize similar legislation passed by good Republicans, such as Jefferson or Madison. When reading Marcellus, the reader gets the distinct impression that principles are dependent on political affiliation.

Pleasants was quick to return fire at opponents of the war. In September 1812, the *Argus* denounced the opposition as a pack of ingrates, who did not appreciate how blessed they were to be U.S. citizens:

> It is a truth, that there never yet has been a government which has received the united support of a *people*—if there ever was one, however, that merited it, we are confident *our's* is that one: but ingratitude is so congenial to the feelings of some of mankind, that it is not unfrequently the case, that the quarter from which they receive *protection*, is the very one against which they level their *spleen*—Like the surly Mastiff, they are willing to *bite* the hand that feeds them—willing and anxious to frustrate the designs of government, unexceptionally the most equitable in the known world—It is a fact, that such now appears to be the disposition of many who *call* themselves *federalists!*[59]

Pleasants' attitude leaves little room for dissent of any kind. By July 1813, the war was not going well for the United States. The conduct of the war was now openly criticized on the floor of the House of Representatives. Pleasants took exception to this, and penned an editorial remarkable for its willingness to excuse military incompetence:

> That there have been failures of our military enterprises in one or two instances, is too true. The war commenced with one, not only more disgraceful than any which has since happened [Hull's surrender of Detroit], but more so than could have been imagined before it occurred.... If there have been failures on the one hand, there have been victories more brilliant than the failures have been lamentable. And considering the unmilitary character of the nation at the time this war was declared; considering that, in the lapse of time, the skill and science acquired in the Revolution had mouldered away, or descended with its possessors to the tomb ... we are not surprised that we have sometimes been unsuccessful. But in every battle which has been fought, in every rencontre with the enemy, if our brave soldiers have not commanded success, they have at least deserved it. When was a war waged with unvaried success?[60]

The editorial goes on to invoke the example of the American Revolutionary War. American armies were defeated time and again by the redcoats, but they persevered to achieve final victory. Pleasants rather conveniently ignores the fact that British victories during the Revolution tended to be tactical rather than strategic in nature. By July 1813, American defeats tended to be both tactical *and* strategic. Also, many of the American generals were in fact veterans of the Revolutionary War. In the case of Hull and Dearborn, they were honest men well past their prime. As for Wilkinson, he was one of the greatest scoundrels in American history, and a thoroughly incompetent military commander. Far from being descended to the tomb, these commanders were leading American armies to defeat. One wonders what it would take before a single iota of criticism would find its way into the pages of the *Argus*.

The *Stanton Republican Farmer*—despite its name—was a staunchly pro–Federalist newspaper. Staunton was the site of the 1812 Virginia Federalist convention. The *Republican Farmer* served as a voice of Federalism in the western part of the state, frequently reprinting items from New England Federalist papers. The *Republican Farmer* also reprinted items from other Virginia Federalist publications. In November 1812, Virginia Federalists took Madison to task for remaining at peace with France, the true enemy. The *Republican Farmer* reprinted a piece of righteous indignation from the *Norfolk Gazette and Publick Ledger*: "The Berlin and Milan decrees are not revoked, yet we are at war with France! The British Orders in Council are rescinded, yet we are at war with Great Britain!"[61]

"An Old Federalist" expanded upon this theme in December, alleging that the president maintained that France had indeed repealed the Berlin and Milan Decrees. The aged Federalist declared this "really astonishing," and accused Madison of gross prevarication. The president kept the full truth from Congress, which violated the Constitution.[62] It would seem logical that impeachment should follow, but this did not happen. The Federalists had nowhere near the support for this, even if they enlisted dissident Republicans in their cause. The expression of such sentiments in the *Republican Farmer* were merely manifestations of impotent rage.

Throughout the war of words, tempers flared. In June 1812, Jefferson suggested to Madison a simple, brutal expedient to stifle dissent: "A barrel of tar to each state South of the Potomac will keep all in order, & that will be freely contributed without troubling government."[63] It is shocking to hear Jefferson, who famously who famously proposed using the blood of tyrants to water the tree of liberty, express such reactionary sentiments to a fellow Founding Father. It is also significant that Jefferson specifies states south of the Potomac, suggesting a great deal of antiwar feeling in a region commonly considered pro war. The prescient sage John Taylor of Caroline warned James Monroe that due to the unpopularity of the war, the government might become increasingly authoritarian:

> To me it appears that an usurpation of tyrannical persons or a peace, will very soon become the alternative, and that the longer the latter is deferred, the more unavoidable will be the former. For the war cannot be carried on without such powers, and Congress shall determine to carry it on, they will compel their instruments to do every thing necessary for its success, altho' they will at last become the victims of their own measures.[64]

Due to their opposition to the war, Federalist newspaper editors were threatened. Augustine Davis, editor of the *Virginia Patriot*, was informed of a plot to destroy his offices on July 4, 1812. He personally appealed to Governor Barbour for protection. Fortunately for Davis, and perhaps thanks to the governor's protection, the plot failed to materialize.[65] Shortly after the outbreak of war, Samuel Snowden also received word of a credible threat. He pugnaciously vowed to protect his life and property:

> *A warning.*—The editor of this Gazette having been informed by some of his friends, that threats of violence against his person and property have been uttered, if he persevers in the course, guaranteed to every citizen of the United States by the constitution thereof, in the full and free expression of his sentiments in relation to the course the government has determined to pursue;—takes this method and opportunity of warning all such as have been so indiscreet as to make use of them, that he *is*, and at all times *will be*, prepared to defend both at the hazard of his life, and that the lives of those attempting to commit such violence will most certainly pay the forfeit of such unlawful procedure.[66]

Perhaps Snowden's warning worked. At any rate, he was not attacked in 1812. But on the night of January 27, 1814, an unknown arsonist set fire to the offices of the *Gazette*. The fire was discovered and extinguished without serious damage.[67]

The *Norfolk Gazette and Publick Ledger* made much of ill-disciplined militiamen tarring and feathering a townsman. The rival *Norfolk and Portsmouth Herald* argued that the not-so-innocent citizen brought the harsh treatment on himself, by taunting the local militiamen. He even threatened to give away their positions to the British.[68] Fortunately, such incidents were rare in Virginia. For the most part, the war of words remained just that.

The worst case of mob violence during the War of 1812 actually occurred in Baltimore. But it involved a notable Virginian, none other than Major General Henry "Light Horse Harry" Lee, a Revolutionary War hero and former governor of Virginia. In June 1812, a Baltimore mob destroyed the offices of the *Baltimore Federal Republican*, perhaps the most prominent Federalist newspaper in the nation. Undaunted, the editor, Alexander Contee Hanson, vowed to resume printing from a new location.[69]

Light Horse Harry was a good friend of Hanson's. He gathered armed supporters to protect the plucky editor. On July 26, 1812, a mob surrounded the fortified house where the *Federal Republican* had resumed publication.

3. The War of Words

Shots were fired, and the mob suffered one killed and several wounded. Eventually, Hanson, Lee, and company realized they were surrounded, and the situation was hopeless. They surrendered to authorities, and were placed in the city jail for their own protection.[70]

The jail did not prove a sanctuary. The mob dragged the prisoners from the jail, screaming, "Kill the Tories!" The jailers did nothing to protect their prisoners. Lee was beaten and stabbed severely, one eye brutally gouged out. He never fully recovered from the trauma he suffered in Baltimore.[71] This was a terrible injustice for a man who had distinguished himself during the Revolution. Ironically, Lee was a friend of Madison. The president arranged for the wounded hero to travel to the British colony of Barbados to convalesce.[72] In Barbados, Lee corresponded with the colonial governor, Lieutenant General Sir George Beckwith. Lee attempted to act as a peace agent, to bring the war to a close.

Beckwith did not feel he had the authority to negotiate with Lee. "But having neither sought it nor shunned it [Lee's peace proposal]," he passed on the correspondence to Lord Bathurst, Secretary of State for War and the Colonies.[73] A peace conference began in St. Petersburg in 1813, independent of Lee's attempted mediation. Ultimately, Lee's proposal came to naught. But it reveals the depth of antiwar feeling among Federalists.

To its credit, the *Virginia Argus* repudiated vigilantism. "Cadwallader" declared "public exposure to ridicule is, indeed, the *just* punishment of those who advocate a surrender of their country's rights at the foot stool of British Insolence; but no *violence*, even against such persons, will be committed by any true republican."[74] Suspected traitors were to be arrested by the proper authorities. Fortunately, the terrible scenes in Maryland were not repeated in Virginia.

Republicans were quick to brand their Federalist opponents as Tories and British agents. This was, of course, a gross mischaracterization. In fact, many Federalists served when called for militia duty. Chief Justice John Marshall, one of the leading Federalists in the state, served on the Richmond vigilance committee when the capitol was threatened by British invasion. But the rancorous partisanship of the time was not known for nuanced distinctions. Fortunately for the Old Dominion, most of the slings and barbs traded by political opponents remained confined to the pages of newspapers.

Virginia's war of words offers a great deal of insight into the political controversies of the day. The contrast between 1807 and 1812–15 is immediately apparent. Poring over microfilm copies of 200-year-old newspapers, the passions of the times come vividly to life.

4

The Opposing Forces
The Americans

During the War of 1812, most of the U.S. Army served on the Canadian border. That meant states such as Virginia were forced to rely on militia for their defense. Militiamen were not regulars—their conduct during the war was mediocre at best. In contrast, their British opponents tended to be long service professionals. Fortunately for Virginians, British objectives in the Chesapeake were limited. This, more than anything else, preserved much of Virginia from the ravages of war.

"Every one knows how difficult it is to establish that discipline among the militia, which is necessary to render it efficient."[1] This statement appeared in the *Norfolk Gazette and Publick Ledger* in June 1813. It was actually part of a story on how General Taylor was doing an excellent job preparing the defenses of Norfolk. Yet it addresses a fundamental truth—militiamen were not regulars, and could not be expected to perform like regulars. In spring 1814, in preparation for the Niagara campaign, Brigadier General Winfield Scott put his troops through an intensive training regimen, drilling the men ten hours per day for three months.[2] The regulars' improved performance on the Niagara reflected the benefits of this training. Unfortunately, this well-drilled little army was confined to the northern frontier. This meant the militia became the primary defense force for the Old Dominion. In a letter to President Madison, a resident of the Northern Neck summed up the militia as "undisciplined, indifferently armed, worse clad and still worse commanded."[3] The shortcomings of the militia contributed to the difficulties of defending the state against British regulars.

The Founding Fathers feared standing armies as a threat to liberty. Throughout this period, the U.S. Army was kept as small as possible, with periodic expansions during periods of crisis. Once the crisis passed, the additional men were swiftly discharged. American society valued individual liberty. Why would any self-respecting man join an undemocratic institution such as the army? This tended to attract recruits from the margins of society. Some were even deserters from the British forces in Canada. As for the officers, the fluctuating size of the military establishment dissuaded good men from seeking commissions. Winfield Scott, commissioned captain in 1808, characterized the officer corps as a group "of swaggerers, dependants, decayed gentlemen, and others—'fit for nothing else.'"[4] The war eventually brought competent leaders to the fore, but it was a long, painful process.

The small size of the U.S. Army led to a dependence on militia. In the wake of the *Chesapeake-Leopard* affair, Congress increased the size of the 3,000-man army (April 12, 1808) by 6,000 men. But full strength was never achieved. Between April 1808 and the outbreak of war, the army numbered between 5,500 and 7,000 men. Regiments varied in strength from 362 to 680 men.[5] Low pay did nothing to encourage enlistment. A private earned $5 a month, less than an unskilled laborer. The outbreak of war brought a massive expansion, and added incentives to recruits. Upon enlistment, recruits received a $16 bounty. After five years of honorable service, veterans were entitled to 160 acres of land and three months' pay. Congress even offered a shorter, 18-month enlistment, despite the conventional wisdom that it took at least two years to make a man into a soldier.[6] By 1814, pay was raised to $8 a month, with a $124 enlistment bounty.[7] Even these incentives did not cause men to flock to the colors. No more than 57,000 regulars served during the war, and peak strength rarely rose above 20,000 men.[8]

U.S. regulars were often poorly clothed. The official uniform consisted of a blue coatee and felt shako. The massive wartime expansion led to shortages. Many regiments had to make do with coats of many colors. The 20th Regiment of Infantry served in the vicinity of Norfolk for much of the war. Instead of the regulation blue, they were issued drab and brown coatees. The regiment did manage to receive the new leather shakos in 1813.[9] But replacement for worn-out clothing remained a problem. As Gregory J.W. Urwin noted, "In the meantime, the men went about in rags and worn-out shoes, not a very inspiring sight to other lads who contemplated answering their country's call."[10]

Dismal recruiting results led some to call for conscription. In the June 1, 1814, edition of the *Virginia Argus*, "An Old Federalist" offered a solution:

> Such is the love of liberty and the independence of the yeomanry of this county that great numbers will not enlist for five years or during the war, but they would draw lots and serve their country for two years.... Let Congress call forth now the energies of the nation, and raise by draft Seventy Thousand additional troops for two years, who have the same pay as other soldiers, bounty, &c.... Thence we shall have a force sufficient to restrain our oppressors. Not once in 20 times will a draft take place—You make every man in each division, but one, a recruiting officer— Each one will give more or less to induce a hearty, brave soldier to serve his country in place.... Raise soldiers; let your Militia stay at home & cultivate their farms.[11]

The August 31, 1814, edition of the *Richmond Enquirer* proposed raising 30,000 troops, "so many men either to furnish a soldier among themselves, or contribute money to furnish a substitute—to act during the war. Thus, such as do not wish to risk their *persons*, may open their purses."[12] In the event, the federal government did not resort to conscription until the Civil War. The U.S. Army of the War of 1812 was an all-volunteer force, and thinly spread. This placed much of the burden on state militias.

During the war, 458,463 men served in militia or state volunteer units.[13] Militia service was much shorter than a regular enlistment, usually no more than six months, though some men served multiple tours of duty. It is difficult to determine how many served in individual state militias. For Virginia, Stuart L. Butler estimates 65,000 men served in the state militia. No more than 10 percent were on duty at any time.[14] The defense of the Old Dominion rested in the hands of these untried, undertrained citizen soldiers.

The governor of Virginia was commander-in-chief of the state militia. He was assisted by a military advisor known as the Adjutant General, appointed by the Assembly. All generals were also approved by the Assembly. County officers—ensign to lieutenant colonel—were chosen by the county courts, with the approval of the governor and the Council of State.[15] In 1812, every county had at least one regiment. The cities of Richmond, Williamsburg, Norfolk, and Petersburg also had one regiment apiece. Regiments were commanded by lieutenant colonels, and divided into two battalions, commanded by majors. There does not appear to have been a set number of companies; according to Butler, "Each county had as many companies that would sustain company level units with no less than forty or no more than eighty men. New companies would be created by local courts when sufficient population of young men would make it possible to divide the regiments into additional companies."[16] Captains commanded companies. Each company also had one lieutenant, one ensign, four sergeants and corporals, one fifer, and one drummer.

In early 1812, Governor Barbour announced new uniform regulations for Virginia militiamen. Generals strongly resembled their regular counterparts, with blue and buff coats, yellow buttons, and gold epaulettes, topped with a black cocked hat. Artillerymen wore blue coats lined and faced in red, buff vests, blue overalls with red stripes, and a black cocked hat with red cockade. Cavalrymen wore short blue coats faced red. On their head they wore a Tarleton helmet. Sturdy jackboots protected their legs. While some regiments had companies of grenadiers and light infantry, most militiamen were ordinary infantrymen. These men wore blue hunting shirts with red fringe, blue overalls with red fringe, and black round hats. Riflemen wore perhaps the boldest uniforms of all, purple hunting shirts and overalls fringed red, topped with a black round hat.[17]

4. The Opposing Forces: The Americans

At the beginning of the war, Virginia's militia comprised approximately 83,000 men, organized into regiments, brigades, and divisions.[18] (Not all of these men were called out at the same time. In April 1812, the federal government called for 100,000 militiamen. Virginia's quota was 12,000.) Brigades consisted of four to five regiments. Several brigades made up a division. In 1815, the Virginia militia had four divisions, 21 brigades, and 124 regiments.[19] The force contained cavalry, artillery, and rifle units, but most were ordinary infantry.

In theory, all able-bodied white men between the ages of 18 and 45 were liable for militia service. There were exemptions, of course, including those holding federal office.[20] Virginia also exempted pacifist sects such as Quakers and Mennonites, but they were required to find substitutes to serve in their place.[21] Men over the age of 45, known as "silver grays" volunteered and saw active service. Many of these men were Revolutionary War veterans. Junior volunteers—boys under the age of 18—also volunteered to serve.[22]

States required militiamen to have a musket, with sufficient powder and shot. Virginia was unique in having its own state arms manufactory in Richmond, which opened in 1802. By 1815, it produced 35,616 .69 caliber muskets, and 721 .45 caliber rifles. A further 2,000 rifles were made by independent contractors across the state. Virginia also bought 13,000 muskets before the Virginia Arms Manufactory began production.[23] These numbers suggest that Virginia militiamen were adequately armed. But state-manufactured muskets were not always well made. Lieutenant Colonel William Sharp (54th Regiment, Norfolk) noted in April 1812 that his men questioned the quality of their weapons. They would not use them, even "with common bird shot.... Many persons have said they would not march with these guns, knowing from experience that no dependence could be placed in them." The 54th also lacked sufficient cartridges and flints.[24]

Lieutenant Colonel Jonathan Cropper, Jr., commanding the militia on the Eastern Shore, wrote to Governor Barbour (March 20, 1813) about the poor quality of his soldiers' arms and equipment. In June 1812, Cropper received 18,000 cartridges from Richmond. One half of these cartridges were "good for nothing except the bullets." The powder and paper, of Revolutionary War vintage, were "mouldered to the finest dust." Cropper also noted shortages of foodstuffs, and requested 200 barrels of pork, and 100 each of beef and flour. According to Cropper, the geographic isolation of the Eastern Shore from the rest of the state made periodic resupply imperative.[25]

Cropper's letter to the governor was not unique. Militia commanders across the state alerted Barbour to the sorry state of the militia's arms. York County's commanding officer wrote that "not one man out of five or six has a musket."[26] Many muskets were in a state of disrepair. Some militiamen even sold their state-issued muskets, confident they would be issued another one if and when they were mustered. It must also be noted that the state government did not want local arsenals to be well stocked. They were afraid rebellious slaves would seize these arms.²⁷

War has been called 90 percent routine, and 10 percent sheer terror. Depending on the nature of service, soldiers throughout the ages might experience greater or lesser proportions of routine to terror. As for Virginia militiamen, their service was largely characterized by monotonous, mind-numbing routine. In September 1814, William Wirt, who had once dreamed of leading a legion to martial glory in Canada, found himself in command of a company of militia artillery. They camped near Worrenigh Church on the York River (New Kent County), to repel any British attempts on Richmond. The militiamen expected action was imminent. But as the days passed, and the possibility of battle decreased, Wirt found himself less a commanding officer than the headmaster of a class of unruly students.

On September 26—less than three weeks after mustering—he vented his frustrations in a letter to his wife. While the company was well fed and adequately supplied with tents, still the men "murmured incessantly." They grew tired of the endless drill. The men craved action, and found the mundane aspects of soldiering tedious. According to Wirt, "Being kept on the ground after the expectation of a battle has vanished, and not knowing how long they are to remain—looking every day for their discharge—they are enduring the hope of pain deferred, and manifest their disquiet in every form. Of such men, in such a state of mind, in such a service, I am heartily sick."²⁸

Fortunately for Captain Wirt, his men were discharged a few days later. The *Virginia Patriot* of October 5 welcomed home the Richmond militiamen. The paper praised the men's conduct, noting, "their gentlemanly and soldier-like deportment has obtained them the esteem and perfect confidence of their commander."²⁹ One wonders at Wirt's reaction to this glowing report of his men's service.

For some militiamen, their tours of duty were more like an extended holiday. Pleasants Murphy, a cavalry private in Captain Otey's troop (Bedford), saw service in an unfamiliar part of Virginia. On December 19, 1814, Otey's troop arrived in Williamsburg. The next day, Murphy went to see the sights:

> 8 or 10 of us went To the Lunatic hospital [the oldest in the U.S.] where there is between 20 and 30 poor unhappy Creatures Confined with madness. I walkd. over the greater part of the city which in its Greatest Length is nearly a mile. Several good houses, but generally the place has an antient appearance. [two days later] I walked about town most of the day merely for amusement, went into all the Stores which I find To be badly Supply'd with goods but what few they do contain Very high priced.³⁰

On Christmas, Murphy and his comrades fired their guns in celebration. They spent most of the day making merry in their barracks, drinking great quantities of eggnog and whiskey. The festive occasion concluded with an excellent supper.[31] Throughout his sojourn in Williamsburg, Murphy spent sent evenings at a tavern run by Mrs. Hansford. On January 7, 1815, he received a one-day furlough to attend a wedding approximately six miles from Williamsburg.[32] On January 9, Otey's troop moved to Yorktown. Murphy spent the next day sightseeing, also noting the houses had an "antient appearance" (He did not mention much of the town burned in 1814). Later that day, the troopers moved to Hampton, which Murphy described as "Low unhealthy, the town old irregular and the people inhospitable."[33] Murphy spent the rest of his tour in Hampton. News of peace arrived the next month, and he returned home to Bedford.

Those attempting to explain the lack of military activity during Murphy's service might note that it was late in the war, and in December and January (and the holiday season), when armies traditionally went into winter quarters. But Tappahannock, Virginia, and other points on the Rappahannock were raided in early December 1814. Murphy's unit actually went to Tappahannock before Williamsburg (Murphy missed this because he was convalescing at home from a broken arm), but were too late to hinder the raiders. The British continued raiding throughout the winter, so one might expect more martial exercises on the part of the militia. But apart from a few hours parade and drill (and not a daily occurrence), Murphy and his comrades seem to have been left very much to their own devices.

Discipline varied widely among militia units. Early in the war, on the march to Detroit, Private Peter Vassar, a militiaman in General Hull's army, while drunk on guard duty, shot and seriously wounded Private Joseph England. A court-martial found Vassar guilty. He had his ears cropped and was branded on both cheeks.[34] On February 21, 1815 (the day before news of peace arrived), six Tennessee militiamen were shot for disobedience at Mobile.[35] These punishments represent the extremes of military discipline. Most militiamen were not punished so severely.

We are fortunate to have the details of courts-martial of Virginia militia. The following cases come from early 1814, and the 3rd Brigade (4th, 5th, and 6th regiments) stationed in Norfolk. On February 23, 1814, Corporal Isaac Hughs was charged with sedition and riot, for fighting with Private Garland Lewis, and causing uproar throughout the barracks. Hughs was acquitted of sedition, but convicted of riot. As punishment, he was demoted to private.[36]

Private Lewis, Hughs' opponent, was brought up on a variety of charges for crimes committed over a three day period (February 8–10). Lewis was charged with disobedience, for quitting "the garrison without permission and not returning the next day." He was charged with drunkenness on guard duty, and was so incapacitated "that the officer of the day had him relieved." The next day brought a charge of sedition and riotous conduct, for the fight with Hughs. The court found Lewis guilty of all charges except sedition. As punishment, he was sentenced to straddle a gun for two hours a day for ten days, with a tin cup and a bottle tied around his neck. This was designed to be uncomfortable (straddling a cannon for prolonged periods is painful) and humiliating, with the bottle and cup revealing his shameful drunkenness to the entire garrison. The court also ordered Lewis confined to quarters at night, and reduced his rations for ten days to bread and water. His pay was also cut by half for three months (of a six month tour of duty).[37]

On March 4, 1814, the court met again. They heard the case of Private Reuben Frayly, who was found asleep on guard. The court found Frayly guilty, and sentenced him to "ride a cannon for two hours, with his hands tied behind him, and his feet tied together." He was also sentenced to hard labor for the rest of his period of service.[38] In contrast, the court dismissed the same charges against Private George Leonard,

> it not being proved to their Satisfaction that the prisoner was a Sleep, they are of the opinion that he was guilty of a breach of duty Sitting on his post, his gun being at a Little distance from him, they deem it proper to bring to View of the Commanding officer the practice that too frequently exists and is permitted by guard officers for want of proper Instruction, of Sitting on posts, which practice alone prevents them from offering some punishment for the prisoner's offence.[39]

The court displayed genuine sympathy for Private Thomas McGehee, charged with leaving his post and returning to the guardhouse. While the court found McGehee guilty, it was noted that he was an elderly Revolutionary War veteran, who suffered from painful rheumatism. The judges recommended the old soldier be discharged without punishment.[40]

Sleeping on guard and leaving a post were serious offenses in the regular army. Those found guilty were likely to receive corporal, or even capital, punishment. In the 3rd Brigade, the officers presiding over the courts-martial obviously felt they could not apply the same standard of discipline to militiamen. They also issued a reminder in General Orders (March 4) to officers and NCOs to prevent men from sitting on guard duty. Officers and NCOs were also expected to visit their men frequently, and to closely guard passwords and countersigns.[41] Such things would be second nature to regular officers and NCOs. It is quite revealing of the state of discipline in militia units that they needed to be reiterated in general orders.

Officers often had difficulty exerting authority. The *Publick Ledger* revealed the reason.

> The men, accustomed at home, to live on terms of intimacy with their officers—in many instances the private occupying a higher ground in talent and fortune, in their respective counties, than his officer, and last, though not least, the officers often being candidates for popular favor, all presented formidable difficulties to the establishment of discipline.[42]

In the regular army, officers had to work to gain obedience and respect from their men. But they were greatly assisted by the more rigid application of discipline.

Desertion and absent without leave were serious crimes, but the authorities proved reluctant to apply severe penalties. Occasionally, even the regular army offered amnesty. In 1812, President Madison promised to pardon all deserters who turned themselves in.[43] This was after Hull's surrender of Detroit; leniency was likely considered a wise policy. Not surprisingly, desertion among militiamen was usually punished less severely. In Virginia, deserters were fined $20 for each month they were absent from the ranks, or a total of $120 for a six-month tour. Imprisonment—usually for a period of three months, was also common. Captured deserters might be compelled to serve another six months in the militia.[44] Individuals encouraging desertion faced fines of up to $300 and one year in jail.[45] While the fines were relatively steep for the period, apprehended deserters at least escaped with their lives.

Despite the relatively lenient sentences, militia officers proved reluctant to charge their men—often friends and neighbors—with desertion. In August 1813, Captain John Miller of the 1st Cavalry Regiment took out an advertisement in the *Virginia Argus*. The apologetic tone is remarkable:

> Attention! The absentees in my Company (except those on furlough) are hereby required to repair, with all convenient dispatch, to HAMPTON, and join the troop; otherwise, I shall be compelled, though with much reluctance, to advertise them as deserters unless satisfactory proof be given of sufficient cause for their absence.[46]

Apparently, Miller's advertisement did not gain the desired results, for it ran twice that month. Another example comes from the September 3, 1814, issue of the *Argus*. The commander of the Manchester Cavalry published a "Notice to Delinquent Troopers." This advertisement actually *ordered* cavalrymen absent without leave to report to Camp Holly. But it seems to imply that the delinquent troopers who reported would not be punished.[47] These advertisements are far from the only examples to be found in wartime Virginia newspapers.

In *Defending the Old Dominion*, Butler describes a large-scale mutiny among men of the 4th Regiment at Norfolk in October 1814. The men were angry that their three-month tour had been extended to six months. Their pay was also in arrears. The mutineers stacked arms, and refused to fall in until they received three months' back pay. A court martial found the men guilty, with the exception of seven men, due to their youth. The rest were sentenced to hard labor at Craney Island for the rest of their tour. As added humiliation, the men had their left eyebrows shaved and one side of their faces blackened with lamp oil. They were also gagged with bayonets, and paraded before the loyal troops in this condition.[48] One imagines the mutineers harbored lasting resentment for this treatment, but at least they escaped with their lives. In the regular army, mutineers faced execution. Here is another case where citizen soldiers were treated more like citizens than soldiers.

Enlisted men were not the only ones to commit disciplinary infractions. Officers frequently broke the rules. Many of these incidents involved alcohol. Ensign Powell (2nd Brigade, Norfolk) "was charged twice with repeated drunkenness so severe that he could not perform his duties. The court found him guilty and he was dismissed from the service."[49] In another case—this one not involving alcohol—Lieutenant Nathan Perrell cheated his men out of much of their pay. The court found Perrell guilty and dismissed him from the service.[50] Yet Perrell was not required to repay the stolen money. Also, convicted officers were spared the indignity of corporal punishment. In the Virginia militia, rank had its privileges.

Officers also felt free to tender their resignations. Even the threat of invasion did not keep disgruntled officers at their post. Just nine days after warning Governor Barbour of the unpreparedness of the Eastern Shore militia, Colonel Cropper resigned his commission. Cropper was angry that Colonel Robert B. Taylor—a Federalist, no less—was promoted to brigadier general, and command of the 9th Brigade. Cropper expected the job would go to him, due to seniority and combat experience in the Revolutionary War. Taylor, on the other hand, had rather limited military experience. While he wished his old command well, Cropper informed Barbour, "Your excellency will no longer consider me bearing a military commission."[51] In the event, Taylor proved to be a good commander. After his resignation, Cropper spent most of the war at home.[52] In January 1815, he was finally promoted to brigadier general, commanding the newly-organized 21st Brigade.[53] But Cropper never led his troops in action against the British.

The Mathews County militia was plagued by a feuding officer corps. According to subordinates, Colonel Gayle "was a genial mediocrity," while his second in command, Major Billups, was "an elderly drunk who never showed up for duty."[54] Governor Barbour and the Council of State could tolerate Gayle, but they wanted a more competent major. Billups was persuaded to resign in March 1813. He was replaced by Captain Christopher Tompkins.

Tompkins' promotion revealed deep political and class tensions in Mathews County. Tompkins was a well-educated, well-to-do merchant and farmer. A letter, signed by "Seventy-Six," told the governor that the new major was one "of the most gainsaying, hard-hearted, stiff-necked, rebellious Federalists that ever disgraced the unsullied soil of the U.S. of America."[55] The real problem was that Tompkins was promoted instead of Captain Langley B. Eddins. Eddins was the local favorite, with deep roots in the community. He also enjoyed the patronage of Houlder Hudgins, county magistrate. Hudgins and his supporters were suspicious of outside authority, and felt that Richmond was trying to elevate its man—Tompkins—to gain greater control in Mathews County.[56] Major Tompkins found it difficult to carry out his duties, as militiamen refused to obey his orders, and Colonel Gayle turned a blind eye to their insubordination.[57] Partisan bickering and petty feuds did nothing to help Virginia's war effort.

Most Virginia militiamen spent their tours of duty in Norfolk. Butler estimates perhaps 40,000 (60 percent) served there. Others served in Richmond.[58] This meant the militia was spread rather thinly throughout the rest of the state. Before he tendered his resignation, Colonel Cropper illuminated the problems of defense in a letter (March 20, 1813) to the governor:

> At this time we are exposed in the extent of 180 miles to the incursions of the enemy. Accomack and Northampton are indented by navigable creeks at every five miles on the seaside and at every five miles on the bay, so that a large barge may land at almost everyman's door, if not opposed by the militia.... Two companies have been on duty in Northampton for three or four weeks, and one in Accomack for one week, to which one it will be necessary to add another in a short time. The whole of the militia are harrassed, and liable every day to be called to repel the enemy, especially the 27th regiment, which has already every member called out.[59]

The isolation of the Eastern Shore compounded the problem of organizing an effective defense. But Cropper's description of the geography of Northampton and Accomack counties is equally applicable to all of Tidewater Virginia. The region abounds with rivers, streams, and inlets. It was physically impossible to guard all of it. This gave the British an immense tactical advantage. They could—and did—conduct amphibious raids at numerous points throughout the war. The militia was hard-pressed to respond in a timely manner. As Northern Neck resident Walter Jones put it, "If all the petty resources of the State are collected at Norfolk, the Enemy knows that there are four equally productive peninsulas, within a few hours Sail, which they may ravage with little or no hazard."[60]

Also, militia service was not the only occupation for these citizen soldiers. Keeping large numbers of militiamen on duty kept them away from their civilian occupations. This could have negative consequences, both social and economic. In 1813, Virginia devoted 52 percent of its state budget ($433,363) to military expenses. This meant higher taxes, and Virginians were hard-pressed to carry the burden, with so many breadwinners away on militia service. The state proved unable to pay militiamen in a timely manner, causing further grumbling in the ranks. Virginians from the interior did not relish service in the Tidewater, where malaria and other ailments were common.[61] Finally, the fear of slave revolt made militiamen reluctant to serve extended periods far from home.

Richmond was not insensitive to the concerns of the populace. In February 1813, the General Assembly authorized the creation of a 1,000-man force of state regulars. These soldiers were to serve for the duration of the war, and to be drilled and disciplined as U.S. regulars. All expenses were to be paid by the state government. Most important of all, these troops were only liable for service within the borders of the Old Dominion.[62]

The Defense Force Act, as the legislation was called, was not without precedent. During the American Revolutionary War, several states, including Virginia, raised regular forces. This force, separate from the Continental Line, eventually comprised seven infantry regiments, one artillery regiment, one light dragoon regiment, three combined-arms legions, and numerous independent companies. The states offered recruits a $750 bounty.[63] State-raised "private armies" created competition for Washington's army. Patriotic Virginians could avoid arduous service—and be handsomely compensated for it—by serving in state units. While it is true that Virginia troops formed the bulk of George Rogers Clark's army in the Old Northwest, these men *volunteered* for this service. They could not be compelled to serve beyond the boundaries of the Old Dominion.

In 1813, the federal government, hard-pressed to find recruits for the U.S. Army, did not want competition at the state level. There were also serious constitutional implications. During the American Revolution, states possessed greater sovereignty. The ratification of the Constitution changed this state of affairs. Certain responsibilities, like providing for the common defenses, were now in the hands of the federal government. While the Madison administration did not want federal powers to devolve to the states, what particularly worried the president was the precedent set by Virginia's General Assembly. If Virginia raised a state army, would other states, not as loyal to the administration, follow suit?

The Madison administration was particularly concerned about the Federalist stronghold of New England. While some Virginians opposed the war, New England was a hotbed of dissent. At the start of the war, when Major General Henry Dearborn dispatched regulars stationed in New England to the Canadian border, he ordered New England's militia to take up garrison duties. The governors of Massachusetts, Connecticut, and Rhode Island refused to comply. These ardent Federalists argued that since their states were not facing the threat of invasion, their militias could not be called out. Taking a states' rights position, they reasoned that individual states had exclusive control of their militias.[64] But if the threat of invasion seemed imminent, as the British squadron in the Chesapeake indicated, how would New England respond? Would they clamor for state regulars of their own? Could these hypothetical soldiers be considered loyal to the administration and the United States?

Madison and Secretary of State James Monroe hailed from the Old Dominion. They felt Virginia's Defense Force Act set a dangerous precedent.

Monroe wrote to Barbour on the president's behalf, requesting repeal of the Act. As a compromise, the administration raised a regular unit, the U.S. 35th Infantry Regiment, which would serve exclusively in Virginia (the 20th Infantry also served in Virginia, though a sizeable detachment went to the northern frontier).[65] In a conspicuous display of political acumen, Barbour persuaded the legislature to repeal the Act. Nathaniel H. Claiborne and Peter V. Daniel of the Council of State maintained that the constitutional ban on state regulars did not apply in wartime (a disingenuous argument, for why would the state want them in peacetime?), but the majority voted for repeal.[66] In a special session of the General Assembly, the House of Delegates voted 182 to 2 for repeal of May 24, 1813, just three months after the law was passed.[67] By doing the president's bidding, Barbour proved his loyalty to the Madison administration. But Virginians paid a heavy price for this loyalty. The handful of U.S. regulars and thinly spread militiamen could not prevent British raiding and depredations.

While Barbour outwardly expressed support for the federal government, he privately condemned the Madison administration for leaving his state to the mercy of the invader. Council of State member John Campbell expressed this resentment in folksy terms: "The *General Government* has left us to *paddle our own Canoe*."[68] This resentment reached a boiling point in 1814. Napoleon's first abdication brought thousands of British reinforcements to North America. In the Chesapeake, this led to American defeat at Bladensburg, and the burning of Washington, D.C. The *Virginia Argus* related the news in tones of despair, crying, "Fatal, fatal apathy! monstrous, suicidal neglect! Why would not the American government cover their Capital with sufficient defence?"[69]

Governor Barbour attempted to calm his constituents with a proclamation, assuring them that measures were being taken to provide adequate defenses for the state.[70] As the federal government proved unable to meet this responsibility, politicians once again raised the issue of state regulars. Virginia was not the only state considering such measures. By the beginning of 1815, ten out of 18 states passed laws raising state regulars.[71]

Virginia's second Defense Force Act passed into law on January 18, 1815. The law condemned the current militia system as "wasteful, expensive, and improvident." Instead of the modest force of 1,000 men authorized in 1813, the new law called for a force of 10,000 state regulars. These men were to serve for the duration of the war, and to be clothed, equipped, and disciplined like U.S. regulars. As in 1813, the force was only liable for service in Virginia, but the federal government would cover all expenses.[72]

Remarkably, the federal government passed a law on January 27, 1815, agreeing to fund and equip these state armies.[73] Considering the nation's sorry financial state, it is difficult to see where Congress would find the money.

It does reveal the critical nature of the situation. In September 1814, James Monroe, now also serving as secretary of war, wrote to Governor Caleb Strong of Massachusetts that individual states must pay the cost of their defense. If the federal government was forced to carry this burden, Monroe argued, it would have a corrosive effect on its authority, creating a precedent "the tendency of which I forbear to comment."[74] Within the space of a few months, the Madison administration bowed to the inevitable and reversed its policy.

The federal government's agreement to pay for state regulars is particularly telling when it is remembered that this legislation came after the Hartford Convention, where radical New England Federalists proposed secession from the Union. Fortunately, the majority of the convention delegates were far more moderate.[75] But many loyal Republicans denounced the Hartford Convention as a seditious assembly. The New England States were among those who passed laws authorizing state regulars, with Massachusetts calling for 10,000 troops. When it is remembered that these states stubbornly refused to call out their militias at the beginning of the war, surly the raising of state armies in New England caused alarm in Washington. Once again, the specter of legal precedent returned to haunt the Madison administration. When the federal government proved unable to provide for the common defense, the floodgates opened. Now all the states were free to raise private armies of their own. Such a precedent threatened to dissolve the Union itself, with federal authority devolving to the states. How would this play out in 1815?

The end of the war effectively mooted further debate on the issue of state regulars. With the threat of invasion removed, Virginia and the other states cancelled their plans to raise regular troops. While many breathed a collective sigh of relief, the question remained effectively unanswered. Senator William Branch Giles of Virginia, a member of the Senate Committee on Military Affairs, issued a prescient warning for the future. According to Giles, this issue warranted resolution, for it threatened to "change the fundamental character of the Constitution itself, and thus eventually ... produce its destruction."[76] Giles' warning went unheeded, the cracks in the Union's foundation ignored. The nation would face the issue again in 1861. This time, the solution proved more violent and tragic.

5

The Opposing Forces
The British

For the U.S. Army, the War of 1812 was a painful learning curve. Poor leadership and inexperienced troops led to a series of embarrassing failures. As for the British army, they had experienced their nadir at the beginning of the Napoleonic Wars. The British expeditionary force in the 1793–94 campaign in the Low Countries turned in a dismal performance. Most officers did not display proper leadership or regard for their men's welfare. Many were drunk on duty. The men in the ranks were poorly disciplined and badly clothed.[1] One of the few who distinguished himself was Arthur Wellesley, lieutenant colonel of the 33rd Regiment of Foot. The future Duke of Wellington covered the army's retreat to the Waal River.[2]

The vast wealth of the West Indies made them tempting targets. This forced the British to send troops to garrison these islands. The West Indies were notoriously unhealthy. Disease would decimate entire regiments overnight. Some units mutinied rather than serve in the West Indies. It also made recruitment difficult. (The British army during this period was an all-volunteer force. Great Britain did not resort to conscription until 1916.) Under normal circumstances, soldiering was not the most highly regarded profession. It was a hard life, with privates receiving only one shilling per day, from which deductions for food and "necessaries" were taken.[3] Still, recruiting sergeants managed to find men suffering from hardship, escaping from trouble, or with a taste for adventure. A potential posting to the "fever islands" made young Britons think twice about taking the king's shilling.

But positive changes were in the offing. The appointment in 1798 of the Duke of York as commander in chief was a step in the right direction. The duke had a gift for administration, and he quickly introduced several reforms. These reforms improved discipline in the ranks, held officers and noncommissioned officers responsible for misbehavior, and improved commissary and medical services. The duke also sponsored standardized drill and maneuvers.[4]

Amazingly, the British army did not have a standardized drill manual. Forces mustered for a particular campaign might train together—the Duke of Cumberland famously drilled his troops before defeating the Jacobite rebels at Culloden. But Cumberland's formations were not adopted by the army as a whole. Training largely remained at the discretion of individual battalion commanders. When a new officer assumed command, he might completely undo the work of his predecessor. This happened often enough that it was satirized in a comedic work titled *Advice to the Officers of the British Army*:

> When promoted to the command of a regiment from some other corps, shew them that they were all in the dark before, and overturning their whole routine of discipline, introduce another as different as possible; I will not suppose of your own—you may not have genius enough for that: but if you can only contrive to vamp up some old exploded system, it will have all the appearance of novelty to those, who have never practised it before: the few who have, will give you credit for having seen a great deal of service.[5]

This state of affairs changed with the adoption of *Principles of Military Movements*. This manual was published in 1788 by General Sir David Dundas. Dundas observed several Continental armies on military maneuvers, and was considered an authority on the subject. The centerpiece of Sir David's manual was what became known as "The Eighteen Manoeuvres." These exercises represented practically every maneuver a competent infantry battalion should require in battle, from deploying from line into column, and concluding with volley fire. Until the appointment of the Duke of York as commander in chief, Dundas' *Principles* were not mandatory. In May 1798, the duke ordered "every Officer of Infantry shall be provided with a copy of these regulations."[6]

Thanks to these reforms, the British army's performance dramatically improved. The Egyptian Campaign of 1800–01, which ended the French presence in that country, revealed that the British had revitalized their forces. Confidence soared in the ranks. The Peninsular War, with Wellington in command, revealed the redcoats were in the ascendant. These were tough, veteran troops, bold in the attack and tenacious in the defense. They would prove to be dangerous opponents for their American counterparts.

The British arrived in force in the Chesapeake on February 5, 1813. In addition to powerful naval forces, they deployed a significant number of ground forces to the campaign. In 1813, this included two battalions of Royal Marines, of approximately 800 men each.[7] The Royal Marines were disciplined, reliable troops, accustomed to fighting both ashore and afloat.

In 1813, the Royal Navy in the Chesapeake was commanded by Admiral Sir John Borlase Warren (1753–1822). He was a veteran of the American Revolutionary War, but somewhat past his prime. In April 1814, he was relieved by Vice-Admiral Sir Alexander Forrester Inglis Cochrane (1758–1832), who

5. The Opposing Forces: The British

Portrait of Rear Admiral Sir George Cockburn. "Houseburn" proudly stands in front of a burning Washington, D.C. (Library of Congress).

commanded Royal Naval forces in theater until the end of the war. Though he was bolder than Warren, Cochrane usually left operational planning in the hands of his energetic subordinate, Rear-Admiral Sir George Cockburn (1772–1853).[8]

Under Cockburn, British forces carried out a series of raids in the Chesapeake, and caused a great deal of destruction of property. Cockburn was said to relish this duty, and became known as "Houseburn."[9] To the Americans, Cockburn became a hated figure. *Niles' Weekly Register* declared "that there breathes not in any quarter a more savage monster." A Virginia Irishman actually offered a $1,000 bounty for the hated admiral's head. His ears would fetch $500 apiece.[10]

Apparently, Cockburn felt some pride in the reputation he earned in the Chesapeake. A full-length portrait shows him standing in front of a burning Washington, D.C. But he was not insensitive to American threats and insults. When Washington was captured, Cockburn made sure his men burned the offices of the *National Intelligencer*. This paper, house organ of the Madison administration, was particularly vitriolic in its denunciation of the British admiral. The building was burned, but Cockburn went further. The typeset was scattered, and the Cs destroyed, "so they can't abuse my name."[11]

In 1813, British army units in the Chesapeake were commanded by Colonel Sir Thomas Sydney Beckwith (1772–1831). Beckwith joined the Royal Artillery in 1791, and served in India, Copenhagen, and the Peninsula before being appointed assistant quartermaster general in Canada in 1812. While he was undoubtedly an able and experienced soldier, Beckwith was not a strict disciplinarian, for the conduct of the troops under his command at Hampton was inexcusable.[12]

Beckwith departed for Halifax in September 1813. In 1814, the size of the British army in the Chesapeake dramatically increased. These reinforcements were commanded by Major-General Robert Ross (1766–1814). Ross was an aggressive Irishman, and a veteran of the Peninsular War. Under his command, the British triumphed at Bladensburg, and burned Washington, D.C. He was killed by Maryland riflemen while conducting his own reconnaissance at the Battle of North Point.[13]

As for the British army, the units first deployed to the Chesapeake did not have a particularly good reputation. The 102nd Regiment of Foot, formerly known as the New South Wales Corps, spent several years garrisoning the Australian penal colony. It was known somewhat derisively as the Botany Bay Rangers. Other nicknames included the Rum Corps, for the officers were heavily implicated in the liquor trade. The unit's officers also led the way when it came to indiscipline, mutinying in 1808 against Governor Bligh of *Bounty* fame.[14]

5. The Opposing Forces: The British

In 1810, after 20 years in Australia, the 102nd returned to England. Most of the rank and file were discharged, and replaced with young recruits. In January 1812, they received a new commanding officer, Lieutenant Colonel Charles Napier, a veteran of the Peninsular War. It fell to Napier to whip his men into shape, and he felt up to the challenge. "To get a regiment that is in bad order is agreeable; where no character could be gained and some might be lost. Caution is however necessary with these heroes; for, not making the regiment I unmake myself."[15] The 102nd performed well under Napier's command.

The same cannot be said for the two Independent Companies of Foreigners, 250 men sometimes known as the Canadian Chasseurs. These men wore the green of the famous 95th Rifles, but there the similarities ended. Unlike that illustrious regiment, The Independent Companies of Foreigners were destined for infamy. These companies were recruited among French prisoners taken in the Peninsular War. Many were brutalized by their experiences in Spain and Portugal. Some of the men were also "professional deserters who continually leapfrogged between armies in search of personal gain."[16] Their officers proved unworthy of their commissions; instead of providing a good example, they embezzled the men's pay. When unleashed on Hampton, Virginia, on June 25, 1813, the Independent Companies of Foreigners committed numerous atrocities. If better led, it is possible the Independent Companies would not have committed such outrages. In 1814, the 7/60th Regiment served as part of the British occupation force in the vicinity of Castine, Maine. The 7/60th was recruited from similar sources as the Independent Companies. But they had officers who practiced firm, but fair discipline. They also cared for their men's welfare. During their time in Maine, no atrocities were visited upon the populace by the 7/60th.[17]

The British received significant reinforcements in 1814. The 4th, 21st, 44th, and 85th regiments of Foot arrived in the Chesapeake, fresh from Wellington's triumph in the Peninsular War. These were reliable, veteran troops, though they served mostly in Maryland and the District of Columbia, and later, in the New Orleans campaign.

From the moment of the British arrival in the Chesapeake, slaves sought their freedom by escaping to Royal Navy ships. Many performed valuable service as scouts and pilots. Colonel Napier saw great potential and proposed an incredible, ambitious plan for raising an enormous army of runaway slaves. He recalled the plan in his memoirs. With 200,000 muskets and a cadre of white officers and NCOs from three regiments of black enlisted men, Napier would drill the escaped slaves, who would rally to his standard in droves. They would turn the Delmarva Peninsula into a vast armed camp. Napier optimistically predicted his recruits would learn the art of soldiering within a month. Then the juggernaut would sally forth and capture Washington, while British forces in Canada would counterattack the American army on the Northern frontier.[18] According to Napier, "Had this plan been accepted, two things must have happened: we should have dictated peace, and abolished slavery in America!"[19]

Napier's grandiose ambitions to form an army of liberated slaves were ignored by his superiors. Such a plan was beyond the scope of British plans in the Chesapeake. British West Indies planters would not have approved of the plan, for it might give their own slaves dangerous ideas. It was also felt that the liberated slaves would go on an uncontrollable rampage.[20] As an old man, and a distinguished general, Sir Charles Napier still thought his plan an excellent idea, though the logistical aspects alone seem impractical, to say nothing of the other ramifications.

The British did eventually enlist 300 runaway slaves in a unit known as the Corps of Colonial Marines. They were assembled and trained on Tangier Island, Virginia, which was occupied by the British for much of the war. Their baptism of fire occurred on the Eastern Shore at Pungoteague Creek, Virginia, on May 29, 1814. The British were initially uncertain how well the Colonial Marines would perform in combat. But in the action at Pungoteague Creek, Captain Ross of the Royal Navy noted, "Their conduct was marked by great Spirit and Vivacity and perfect obedience."[21] Admiral Cockburn happily observed "the most general and undisguised alarm" the Colonial Marines created among their erstwhile masters. "They expect Blacky will have no mercy on them and they know that he understands bush fighting and the *locality of the Woods* as well as themselves, and can perhaps play hide & seek in them even better."[22]

After the war, the Colonial Marines, and approximately 4,000 other escaped slaves, started a new life in Maritime Canada. Though they suffered from poverty, disease, and discrimination, their descendants can still be found there.[23] The Americans spread the lie that the runaways were sold into slavery by the treacherous British. This myth continued to be repeated as fact for years afterward. In his popular *Pictorial Field Book of the War of 1812*, Benson Lossing stated, "Among other 'property,' according to the laws of Virginia, taken away by the British, were negroes. Under a promise of freedom, a large number of them flocked to the British standard. Most of them whom Cockburn enticed on board his vessels by these promises were afterward sold into a worse slavery in the British West Indies."[24]

Major-General Isaac Brock (1769–1812) initially commanded British forces in the Northwest. His bold leadership inspired Indian warriors and Canadian militiamen. After his death at the Battle of Queenston Heights, the Northwest command passed to colonel, later Major-General Henry Procter (1763–1822). Procter was an experienced soldier, with 31 years of service in the army. A *Canadien* in Amherstburg recalled that "he was a very stout built

5. The Opposing Forces: The British

man, so stout that he did not like to ride on horseback. I guess his horse not like it pretty well neither. His face was very full and very red like the moon when she come up in the fog. He had a big bush of brown whiskers."[25] This homely description humanizes Procter, who has a reputation as a bungling incompetent. For the British, Procter is often rated the worst commander of the entire war, for his failure to conquer in Ohio, and his utter defeat at the Battle of the Thames. For Canadians, Procter is an uninspiring coward. For the Americans, Procter is an inhuman fiend, who allowed the Indians to massacre captured Kentuckians at the Raisin.

Indian warriors did not have the same command structure as European-style armies. But certain chiefs rose to prominence by skill and force of character. Tecumseh was one of these men. The Shawnee hoped to forge an Indian confederacy to preserve their lands from American expansion. An alliance with the British seemed to offer the best chance. Tecumseh explained his reasons:

> I have more confidence of a British than a Big Knife [American frontiersman]. Here is a chance presented to us; yes such as will never occur again for us Indians of North America to form ourselves into one great combination and cast our lot with the British in this war. Should they conquer and again get mastery of the whole of North America, our rights, at least a portion of the land of our fathers would be respected by the King.[26]

Procter, who failed to cultivate an effective relationship with Tecumseh, nevertheless recognized his "natural superiority of genius which, sometimes in civilized communities and almost always in a rude society challenge deference from common minds."[27] Americans knew Tecumseh as a dangerous opponent. In time, they also recognized him as an honorable man.

In the Northwest, Virginians battled British regulars, Canadian militiamen, and Native American warriors. The redcoats were primarily represented by the 41st Regiment of Foot. This unit had served in Canada since 1799. It was scheduled to return to England in 1812, but the threat of hostilities led to their retention in Canada.[28] The soldiers of the 41st were the epitome of long-service regulars. During the War of 1812, the 41st fought in more battles than any other British regiment.

Canadian militiamen shared much in common with their American counterparts. In fact, many were recent arrivals from the United States. In Uppermost Canada, the region between Buffalo and Detroit, perhaps 60 percent of the population was so-called "late Loyalists," who came from the United States primarily for cheap land and low taxes. When war broke out, the government held them in suspicion. But the capture of Detroit and victory at Queenston Heights kept potential dissenters quiet. During the war, Canadian militiamen served as useful auxiliaries to the redcoats, but British commanders knew that they were not equal to regulars. Eventually, the British raised a unit called the Incorporated Militia Battalion. These were militiamen who received training as regulars, and proved good troops on active service. But they were not encountered by Virginians in the Northwest, or in the Chesapeake.

Several thousand Native Americans fought for the British. In the Northwest, they actually outnumbered the redcoats and militiamen. They came from several tribes of the Great Lakes region, including Delaware, Shawnee, Potawatomi, Menominee, Winnebago, Ojibwa, and Sauk. Indians played an important role in British strategy, but they could be a source of frustration. The British frequently tried to treat them as auxiliaries, rather than allies. Also, warriors fought for personal prestige. They might choose to follow a charismatic leader, but they were under no obligation to remain. In battle, Indian warriors painted their bodies in a variety of colors and patterns. They evoked fear and loathing in their enemies. The sound of the war whoop unnerved American troops on more than one occasion.

For British troops, traveling to America meant many weeks at sea. Ocean crossings were usually unpleasant, and frequently terrifying. Though he was writing of the American Revolutionary War, Richard Ketchum's description is equally applicable to redcoats of the War of 1812:

> These transatlantic crossings were the stuff of nightmares. For the army officers, they were bad enough ... but to the common soldiers they were an unmitigated horror. Crowded belowdecks for six weeks and more, they had to endure the stench of vomit and unwashed bodies and the crudest sanitary facilities, with three men stacked in bunks in a space five feet high and seven feet wide, fed on the meanest rations— including water that was green with viscous algae and rock-solid hardtack, crawling with weevils.... Many passengers had never seen an oceangoing vessel before, let alone sailed aboard one, so along with acclimating themselves to shipboard life and the continuous, often violent motion, they had to face terrors to which even seasoned sailors never fully adjusted.[29]

These terrors included storms, though even relatively placid seas could be difficult for landlubbers. Monotonous shipboard diet and lack of exercise meant the men were in poor condition on arrival. In 1814, Lieutenant George Gleig of the 85th Foot noted several men died from heatstroke in the Chesapeake.[30] These were experienced campaigners, accustomed to marching long distances in Spanish heat, but several weeks at sea wore them down.

Throughout military history, there is an ongoing struggle to produce smart, soldierly uniforms and kit, which are also hard-wearing and practical. During the Napoleonic Wars, British infantrymen were certainly not helped by their uniforms and equipment. Enlisted redcoats wore a brick red coatee, which frequently faded to dull brown or pink. On their head they wore an awkward peaked cap known as a shako. In 1812, the lighter, felt version was replaced by a heavier one of leather, though many regiments did not immediately receive the new shakos.

British officers wore better-quality uniforms, though they were not particularly practical. On campaign, non-regulation clothing abounded. The satirical *Advice to the Officers of the British Army* told young officers to "never wear your uniform ... when you can avoid it. A green or a brown coat shews you have other clothes beside your regimentals, and likewise that you have courage to disobey a standing order. If you have not an entire suit, at least mount a pair of black breeches, a round hat, or something unregimental and unmilitary."[31] Senior officers also tended to turn out in non-regulation clothing. The Duke of Wellington famously wore a plain blue coat. He also stated that he did not care how his men dressed, as long as their weapons were in order and they were ready to fight.

British soldiers carried a flintlock musket, nicknamed "Brown Bess." It was a .75 caliber weapon, though the lead musket ball—which weighed slightly more an ounce—was actually .71 caliber. The musket weighed nine pounds, 11 ounces, and was just shy of five feet in length. The socket bayonet, when fixed, made the weapon nearly six feet. Brown Bess, like most muskets of the day, was a smoothbore. Theoretically, maximum range was 250 yards, but lack of rifling meant the preferred range was less than 100 yards. Well trained soldiers could fire three rounds per minute, but misfire rates could be as high as 40 percent. All of these factors made mass volley fire the preferred tactic. At 30 yards, Brown Bess could fire a soft lead musket ball through ⅜ inches of iron, or five inches of seasoned oak.[32] The effect on human flesh and bone is best left to the imagination.

On the march, soldiers carried 60-pound loads. Those who attempted to lighten their burden by "losing" equipment risked a flogging. Perhaps the cruelest item of equipment was the Trotter knapsack, introduced in 1805. Prior to this date, infantrymen had an envelope-shaped canvas pack. This was a fairly comfortable and practical item of equipment, but spit-and-polish types decided it looked sloppy on parade. Enter Mr. Trotter, army equipment contractor, who designed a rigid pack, with a neat wooden framework. The pack was carried by shoulder straps, which were connected by two straps across the chest. The Trotter knapsack caused a great deal of pain and suffering. The wooden framework bashed soldiers' backs. The shoulder straps cut off circulation to the arms, and the chest straps constricted breathing. Some men were actually invalided out of the service from a malady known as "pack palsy." But Trotter's pack continued in service—with minimal modifications—until 1871.[33]

Infantry officers also carried a great deal of personal kit. Junior officers—unless they served on staff or as battalion adjutant—did not have the luxury of a horse. They were themselves the beasts of burden. Gleig listed the things he carried:

> In the first place, then, I carried, as is usual on such occasions, a perfect equipment of military accouterments; that is to say, sabre, sash, belt, pistols, and telescope.

Strapped across my shoulders was a good cloak, which on many previous occasions had done the duty of a bed, and which I confidently anticipated would be called upon to discharge a similar duty in times that were yet before me. On my right flank, that is to say, slung over my left shoulder, lay a black leathern haversack, containing a spare shirt, a pair of stockings, dressing utensils, a foraging cap, three pounds of boiled pork, and two pounds and a half of sea-biscuit. On my left breast, again, rested a horn, filled with rum, such as pursers usually serve out, whilst a wooden keg, for the conveyance of water, hung over my neck, on the very middle of my back.

Gleig added that all of these things were necessities, to provide a minimal amount of comfort in the field. While subalterns carrying so much kit did not cut a particularly elegant figure, since all men were similarly burdened, they did not ridicule their fellow officers' equipment.[34]

The Royal Artillery did not carry as much personal gear as their infantry comrades, but the weight of their guns more than made up for it. Artillerymen had a hard, dirty job. For this reason, the British preferred larger men as gunners. They were clothed in a blue coat, which hid dirt and grime better than red. On active service, artillerymen usually deployed lighter guns, such as three- and six-pounders. This was the field artillery. Siege artillery was not nearly as mobile, and tended to be used when attacking fortified places. At Fort Meigs, the British employed 24-pounders, plus 12-pounders and 5½-inch mortars. The mortars were particularly useful for lofting projectiles over walls, rather like a major league pop-fly. But the British siege train at Fort Meigs was not particularly large, or well supplied with ammunition. This is not surprising in a wilderness campaign.

In the Chesapeake, the British army and the Royal Navy employed rockets. Rockets originated in the Far East, and were used in warfare for hundreds of years. The British faced rockets in 18th-century India, and sent captured samples to the Royal Arsenal at Woolwich. William Congreve, an employee of the arsenal, designed the rocket that bears his name. Congreve rockets came in several sizes, but the 12-pounder was most often used by ground forces. Congreve rockets were mounted on wooden frames. The 12-pounder had a range of 1.5 miles, which was twice the range of conventional light artillery. Unfortunately, they were not particularly accurate. Only a handful of men were killed in the Chesapeake by Congreve rockets.[35] But their eerie screech could be unnerving, especially for green troops.

The Royal Marines also wore a red coat, but in hotter climates, they frequently donned white cotton jackets. The Corps of Colonial Marines probably received this uniform, which was practical attire for campaigning in the Chesapeake. Royal Artillerymen originally manned bomb vessels. In 1804, they refused to perform other shipboard duties. This led to the formation of the Royal Marine Artillery. The new corps also served ashore, crewing rockets and howitzers. They wore a blue uniform, similar to the Royal Artillery.[36]

5. The Opposing Forces: The British

Royal Navy officers wore blue and white uniforms adorned with gold braid, though they tended to wear "undress" coats for everyday use. Enlisted seamen of the Royal Navy did not have an official uniform until 1857. But sailors' clothing followed a general pattern, typically consisting of waist-length jackets and loose-fitting trousers. Hats were coated with tar to make them waterproof. This clothing was both comfortable and practical. In the heat of action, sailors often stripped to the waist.

The Royal Navy blockaded the Chesapeake Bay for two years. This was intended to be a diversionary operation, to relieve pressure on Canada. But the scale of this secondary operation reveals the power of the Royal Navy. Approximately 183 rated vessels participated in the blockade. Rated vessels meant those commanded by a post captain, and did not include various brigs, sloops, and other vessels, commanded by junior officers. The rated vessels on the Chesapeake station included ships-of-the-line, or those warships which stood in line of battle during fleet actions. During the assault on Craney Island, the Royal Navy had six 74-gun ships-of-the-line.[37] Frigates tended to carry 32–44 guns. These were nimble warships, and carried out a variety of missions, including commerce raiding and intelligence gathering. Frigate captains often called out their opposite numbers. The War of 1812 featured several Anglo-American frigate duels, but none of them occurred in the Chesapeake.

The Royal Navy also employed bomb ketches and rocket ships. The bomb ketches carried massive ten- and 13-inch mortars, firing projectiles weighing nearly 200 pounds. They tended to have names that reflected their purpose, such as *Terror*, *Devastation*, and *Meteor*. Several bore the names of volcanoes. Rocket ships fired 32-pounder Congreve rockets. HMS *Erebus* was the only rocket ship in the Chesapeake, but her projectiles were immortalized by Francis Scott Key as "the rockets' red glare."[38]

British tactics in the Chesapeake mainly consisted of amphibious raids. The Royal Navy could land troops in any number of locations, leaving the Americans hard-pressed to respond. Raids were carried out in force, frequently in battalion strength, with guns and Congreve rockets for fire support. This made it difficult for local militia, if they turned out in time to meet the threat, to repel it. Napier wrote a detailed description of these operations:

> Nothing can be more interesting than our landings, which have always been by moonlight. Numbers of boats filled with armed men gliding in silence over the smooth water, arms glittering in the moonshine, oars just breaking the stillness of night, the dark shade of the woods we are pushing for combining with expectation of danger to affect the mind. Suddenly, Cast off is heard, and the rapid dash of oars begins, with the quick hurrah! hurrah! hurrah! as the sailors pull to shore. Then the soldiers rush into and through the water. Then the soldiers rush into and through the water. We have generally had two or three miles to row, the boats tied together and

moving slowly; but when in reach of shot every boat casts loose, and they pull furiously with shouts; the 102nd excepted, which no shouting hath! I forbid all noise until they can rush on the enemy: then they have leave to give a deadly screech and away! away![39]

As an infantry officer landing on an unknown shore, Napier's concern over noise is understandable. It gives away the element of surprise. Perhaps the British sailors were contemptuous of the Americans and felt it did not matter. Napier's journal and memoirs reveal a decided lack of contempt for the enemy, unlike many of his army and navy colleagues.

The raiders usually removed valuable commodities, such as tobacco, and offered slaves their freedom. They frequently set fire to buildings, both public and private. Napier certainly felt qualms about what his men were expected to do: "much I dislike sacking and burning of towns, it is bad employment for British troops." Napier further described it as "very disgusting," and resolved to personally kill any of his men who indulged in "brutality." He also felt sympathy for poor American farmers, lamenting that "it is hateful to see the poor Yankees robbed, and to be the robber. If we could take fairly it would not be so bad, but the rich escape; for the loss of a few cows and oxen is nothing to a rich man, while you ruin a poor peasant if you take his only cow."[40] But Napier did allow for some plundering, if it was absolutely necessary: "a pair of breeches must be plundered, for mine are worn out, and better it will be to take a pair than shock the Yankee dames by presenting myself as a *sans culotte*."[41]

Many British officers did not share Napier's concerns about plundering. Gleig matter-of-factly recorded pilfering items such as milk and cheese. He recalled some hesitation, but it was due to a rumor that the Americans poisoned foodstuffs and left them for the British. After finding some particularly delicious cream to be untainted, Gleig concluded the rumor was actually propagated by the British high command, to keep their men from plundering.[42]

Gleig was quite possibly incorrect about the origin of the rumor. In fact, some British officers believed permitting their men to loot decreased desertion. This was actually a serious problem for the British, and not just among suspect units like the Independent Companies of Foreigners. British officers frequently referred to their American cousins with contempt and derision, but for seamen and soldiers, the prospect of a new life in America proved a powerful temptation. As early as March 1813, 30 sailors jumped ship and made for Hampton. In August, seven men of a landing party at Cape Henry escaped.[43] Captured deserters were lucky to escape execution, but most were never caught. Under the circumstances, it seemed practical to at least tacitly encourage looting. The lure of plunder possibly encouraged some to remain with the colors. Also, men who robbed the Americans were less likely to seek sanctuary among them. British desertion rates did decline in 1814, so perhaps there was some truth to this assertion. Other British officers believed plundering was justified, due to the craven conduct of some American civilians. Lieutenant Scott of the Royal Navy recalled with horror and disgust a farmer who offered his daughters to his brother officers, if it would preserve his livestock.[44]

Still, it is difficult to read accounts of British raids and not feel outrage at the plundering. At Nomini Church in July 1814, the British stole the silver communion service.[45] At Tappahannock in December, British looters were particularly thorough. From one house, according to a British officer, "a large staircase clock was clapped upon a few geese at the bottom of the boat to keep them quiet; then came a bundle of books and some cabbages, a featherbed, and a small cask of peach brandy."[46] Many houses suffered broken windows and smashed furniture, which was unfortunate but not unexpected vandalism. But the Ritchie family crypt was also burglarized, and the coffins thoroughly searched.[47] Such wanton conduct offends decent people across the span of two centuries.

These were the forces the Virginians faced. Some were gentlemen; others were rogues, while most did their duty as experienced soldiers, sailors, and Marines. Though the Chesapeake remained a secondary theater in an unwanted war, the size of the forces reveals Great Britain's power at the height of the Napoleonic Wars. How did the Virginians fare in mortal combat? Let us now examine the campaigns in which the soldiers of the Old Dominion fought.

6

Virginians in the Northwestern Campaign

The War of 1812 in the Old Northwest was the final act in a struggle begun long ago, when that illustrious Virginian, George Washington, contested French claims to the Ohio Country. That wilderness skirmish sparked a world war. Though the French and Indian War ended in 1763, peace did not come to the Old Northwest. Pontiac's Rebellion, the American Revolution, and the Northwest Indian War—the bloody cycle of violence continued with little interruption for 60 years. Through it all, Virginians such as George Rogers Clark played a major role.

Americans—particularly Westerners—believed that the British incited the tribes to violence. The specter of Colonel Henry Hamilton loomed large. Hamilton served as lieutenant governor of Quebec and Superintendent of Indian Affairs during the American Revolutionary War. Patriots dubbed him "the hair buyer," for it was rumored he paid bounties for frontier settlers' scalps. When Hamilton surrendered to George Rogers Clark, he was taken to Virginia as a prisoner, and held in chains.

After peace with Great Britain, the United States remained at war with the Indians in the Old Northwest. The British still held Canada, and some posts on U.S. territory, before Jay's Treaty. From these posts, British officers exhorted their Native minions, promising them bounties for American scalps. Cartoons even portrayed the grisly transaction for American audiences.

In reality, the British were not such active instigators. They supported the tribes in the Northwest as a buffer against American expansionism, but not at the risk of full-scale war. When the British closed the gates of Fort Miami after Fallen Timbers, and refused to shelter Indian refugees, they proved this point. But the frontier theme of the nefarious British served a purpose. It absolved the Americans of blame. Somehow, this theory ignored the fact that Indians were independent people with their own ambitions who might resent continued encroachment by the land-hungry "long knives."

6. Virginians in the Northwestern Campaign

A British officer buys American scalps from Indian warriors. William Charles cartoon depicting a common belief among Americans—particularly frontiersmen—that the British incited the tribes to raid their settlements (Library of Congress).

From 1801, Virginian William Henry Harrison (1773–1841) served as governor of Indiana Territory. As territorial governor, one of Harrison's greatest ambitions was to make Indiana a state. To accomplish this goal, the population needed to increase. But settlers would not want to move to Indiana if land was scarce. Harrison needed to acquire more land. He did this at the expense of Indians, persuading chiefs to sign over enormous tracts of lands.

Harrison's plan ran into a major obstacle. Two Shawnee brothers, Tecumseh and Tenskwatawa, vehemently opposed further cessions of Indian land. Tecumseh wanted to establish an Indian confederacy as a bulwark against American expansion. Tenswatawa, known to whites as "The Prophet," preached a millennial faith and a return to traditionalism. In 1811, a large group of Indians assembled at Prophetstown (near present-day West Lafayette, Indiana). Harrison demanded the Indians disperse. After the Indians ignored his demands, Harrison led a 1,000-man army to Prophetstown. Before dawn on November 7, the Indians attacked Harrison's camp. The Battle of Tippecanoe was a bloody, closely fought affair, but Harrison emerged victorious.

The Battle of Tippecanoe meant war between the United States and the Indian tribes of the Old Northwest. Historians often view the battle as an overture to the War of 1812, though a confrontation was in the offing regardless of war with Great Britain. Land-hungry Americans demanded something be done about the "Indian problem," and they would not be denied. Naturally, Tecumseh sought an alliance with the British, for they seemed to offer the best chance for the preservation of tribal lands. Also, the British population in Canada was significantly smaller than that of the United States. This made them less of a threat to the Indians.

At the outbreak of the War of 1812, Brigadier General Isaac Hull led an American army into Upper Canada from Detroit. Hull was a distinguished veteran of the Revolutionary War, but by 1812 he had grown old and indecisive. After an abortive invasion of Uppermost Canada—the land between Detroit and Buffalo—he retreated to Detroit. The British and Indians could only muster 1,300 men, but Major General Isaac Brock boldly took the offensive. After a brief bombardment, Hull lost his nerve. He surrendered Detroit and his 2,200-man army.[1]

Americans responded with shock and outrage. They squarely placed the blame for this disaster at the feet of Hull. The *Norfolk Herald* found it incredible "that an army of 2500 should surrender without a battle, probably without firing a gun, to a force not greater perhaps much less than its own."[2] The *Richmond Enquirer* declared that "the disgrace of Gen. Hull has roused every atom of patriotic feeling in their [the people's] bosoms."[3] Jefferson wrote to Madison, declaring, "Hull will of course be shot for cowardice & treachery."[4] A court-martial did find Hull guilty of cowardice, and pronounced a sentence of death, but this harsh sentence was set aside because of his Revolutionary service. At any rate, Hull's military career was at an end.[5]

After Hull's debacle, William Henry Harrison—now a major general—took command of the Northwest army. Today he is chiefly remembered as the first president to die in office, after serving for only one month. But the 40-year-old Harrison was a talented man in his prime. A scion of one of the first families of Virginia (his father signed the Declaration of Independence), young Harrison studied medicine under the preeminent physician Dr. Benjamin Rush. Finding himself unsuited to the medical profession, he took a commission in the U.S. Army, serving as an aide-de-camp to Anthony Wayne at Fallen Timbers. From 1801 to 1812, Harrison served as governor of Indiana Territory. The Battle of Tippecanoe was the first time Harrison led troops into action. It was a closely fought battle, but the resulting victory made Harrison a national hero. It also enhanced his reputation among the hardy frontiersmen. Though he was a classically educated Virginia gentleman, Harrison had the common touch. He inspired affection and respect among the men he commanded.[6]

On September 1, shortly after word reached Richmond of Hull's surrender, Governor Barbour received a communiqué from Secretary of War Eustis, calling for 1,500 Virginia militia to join the Northwestern army for six months of service.[7] A flurry of activity engulfed Richmond as ordinary citizens made equipment for the brigade. Barbour asked for 250 tents and 1,500 knapsacks. With a great deal of pride, Barbour told Eustis that "thousands rallied about the Capitol of all ages and sex to tender their aid." The patriotic citizens exceeded the governor's quota, producing 262 tents and 1,900 knapsacks in the space of a few days.[8]

Barbour named Brigadier General Joel Leftwich as commander of the Virginia Brigade. His younger brother Jabez served on the staff as inspector general, with the rank of major. The Leftwiches are one of the First Families of Virginia, having lived in the Old Dominion since the 1650s.[9] Joel Leftwich was a veteran of the Revolutionary War. He fought at Brandywine, wintered at Valley Forge, and later fought at the bloody battle of Guilford Courthouse. Postwar, he served as an officer in the Bedford County militia. In 1809, he was promoted to the rank of brigadier general. By 1812, Leftwich was a prosperous planter who owned 900 acres and 11 slaves.[10]

William Henry Harrison as he appeared during the War of 1812 (Lossing's *Pictorial Field Book*).

The brigade was divided into two regiments of 12 companies each. The 1st Regiment was commanded by Lieutenant Colonel John Connell. Connell was also a veteran of the Revolutionary War, but had served exclusively in the militia. In the 1790s he served two terms in the Virginia House of Delegates. For almost 30 years, from 1797 to 1825, he was the Brook County clerk of court.[11] Lieutenant Colonel Dudley Evans commanded the 2nd Regiment. He was too young to have served in the Revolutionary War, but was also active in the state militia. He served as the sheriff and justice of Monongalia County, and also many terms in the House of Delegates.[12]

The entire brigade came from west of the Alleghenies, currently within the state of West Virginia. Point Pleasant was designated as the rendezvous point. This was the site of the climactic battle of Lord Dunmore's War. Many of the men journeying to the rendezvous had family members who had fought in the 1774 battle. In 1812, Point Pleasant was a small village of perhaps 20 families, but its location at the junction of the Ohio and Kanawha Rivers made it an excellent point to assemble the Ohio-bound expedition.[13] But reaching Point Pleasant entailed a lengthy journey for many brigade members. Several men required almost a month to reach the rendezvous, traveling by wagon and flatboat.[14] By October 12 just over 1,350 men mustered at Point Pleasant. Six hundred and seventy were assigned to the 1st Regiment, and 685 to the 2nd.[15]

The Virginia Brigade marched into Ohio in mid–October. By October 27 they reached the town of Chillicothe, the state capital in 1812. The local newspaper declared their arrival "highly honorable to the patriotic state from which they come."[16] The brigade spent $1,500 on stores in Chillicothe. After a parade down the main street, the troops resumed their march on October 31. On November 5, they reached the town of Delaware.[17] In the early 19th century, northern Ohio was a sparsely populated wilderness. One veteran of the campaign called the little town of Delaware the *"ultima thule,"* or northernmost point, of civilization.[18]

Most of the brigade remained at Delaware until Christmas, while details built roads and escorted supply convoys. In late December, the Virginians moved 40 miles to Upper Sandusky. This was the site of a new post named Fort Ferree. Fort Ferree was only 40 miles north of Delaware, but it took the brigade one week to complete the journey. Winter had come in earnest to Ohio, making travel that much more difficult. The Virginia brigade remained at Fort Ferree for most of January, waiting for further orders. On January 14, 1813, the men received a welcome surprise. A company of volunteers arrived at the wilderness outpost. They also hailed from the Old Dominion.[19]

The city of Petersburg is 24 miles south of Richmond, at the confluence of the James and Appomattox Rivers. Though far removed from the Northwest frontier, patriotic local citizens responded with shock and outrage to the surrender of Detroit. At a public meeting on September 8, chaired by Mayor Nathaniel Friend, citizens condemned "the imbecile [if not treacherous] conduct of General Hull." They resolved to form a volunteer company "to retrieve the reputation of the republic."[20]

The Petersburg Volunteers formally mustered in on October 16, 1812, under the command of Captain Richard McRae. They pledged to serve for one year. The company comprised four officers, four sergeants, six corporals, two musicians, and 86 privates, for a total strength of 102 men.[21] One of the privates was named Alfred M. Lorrain. He had recently returned to Petersburg after several years at sea, having reached the rank of second mate. Lorrain vividly recalled the surge of patriotism which swept his hometown:

> Promising young men sprung their counters, and fell into the ranks. Students of medicine and law shoved aside their volumes, sufficiently uninteresting before, but now made irksome by the ceaseless din of war, and rushed to the standard. The mechanic threw the uplifted hammer from his hand to swell the train. The placid farmer rode to town to behold the madness of the people, but took the epidemic, and fell in.[22]

The patriotic fervor proved irresistible to the young second mate. He joined his boyhood friends on what promised to be a great adventure.

Virginia newspapers heaped extravagant praise on the newly-raised unit. A Petersburg resident proudly informed readers of the *Virginia Argus* that the citizen soldiers were from the best families in town.[23] Another writer declared the men would become "as celebrated in the war of their country as the immortal band who defended the pass of Thermopylae."[24] Presumably, the writer was merely comparing the volunteers' courage to the gallant Spartans, and not predicting they would be wiped out.

The Volunteers received an enthusiastic welcome in Richmond. Governor Barbour and officers of the 19th Militia Regiment hosted an elaborate banquet, also attended by Revolutionary War veterans. The next day, they received a sermon from the Reverend Jesse Lee, a noted Methodist minister. The preacher exhorted those in attendance who had not enlisted to promptly do so.[25] Lee's sermon was echoed by the press. Thomas Ritchie praised the volunteers, and criticized his fellow citizens for not following Petersburg's example: "Richmond ought to have sent forth a compatriot band to have fought by your side; but *she* sleepeth in inglorious repose. Shame, shame, on the Metropolis of Virginia."[26] The exhortations of Lee and Ritchie led to the formation of the Richmond Washington Volunteers. The company-sized unit mustered in November 1812. They served in the St. Lawrence campaign in 1813, though they did not see action.[27]

On November 2, the company proudly marched forth from Richmond. Their passage through the state often resembled a goodwill tour. Everywhere they went the novice soldiers were treated to food and drink. As the Petersburg Volunteers approached Charlottesville, their line of march took them past Monticello. An old man, plainly dressed, came to greet them. Some callow youths in the company wondered "what old codger that is, with his hair blowing nine ways for Easter Monday." They had just concluded he was the plantation overseer when he introduced himself as Thomas Jefferson. He invited the officers to dine with him, while the enlisted men were treated to dinner in town.[28]

Staunton hosted the Virginia Federalist convention. The *Staunton Republican Farmer*—despite its name—was a Federalist newspaper, and decidedly antiwar. Nevertheless, the *Republican Farmer* requested citizens meet at the courthouse to plan a barbecue for the Petersburg Volunteers.[29] The paper proudly gave an account of the proceedings, which included an escort by the local militia. The next day they were treated to "a handsome Barbecue." The Volunteers departed on Sunday morning, "with the anxious wishes of all for their success."[30]

These items from the *Republican Farmer* are early 19th-century examples of opposing the war, but "supporting the troops." Just days before the barbecue, the *Republican Farmer* attacked the Madison administration for being at war with Britain after the repeal of the Orders in Council, while remaining at peace with France, while the Berlin and Milan Decrees remained in effect. Then again, the Petersburg Volunteers were on their way to the Northwest, where they would fight Indians as well as British. As a town in western Virginia, Staunton residents certainly supported expansion. Perhaps this accounts for the warm reception of the Petersburg Volunteers.

The Petersburg Volunteers enjoyed a fairly pleasant journey all the way to Chillicothe, where they arrived on December 22. The company was quartered in the statehouse, and was treated to dinner by the state legislature. On Christmas Day, the citizens of Chillicothe sponsored another banquet for the much-feted volunteers.[31] The Petersburg Volunteers resumed their march on December 26. After the hospitality in the state capital, life suddenly became much harder. Instead of the hearty, plentiful meals they had hitherto enjoyed, Lorrain and his fellow Volunteers now had to subsist on unappetizing army rations.[32] The fact that the portions were smaller was perhaps a blessing in disguise. A storm also blew up, bringing torrents of rain, ice, and snow. It was 110 difficult miles to Fort Ferree.[33] The novice soldiers completed the journey by mid-January, when they rendezvoused with their comrades in the Virginia Brigade.

On January 21, the Petersburg Volunteers received marching orders. They were ordered to proceed to the Maumee Rapids, approximately 60 miles to the north.[34] The Virginia Brigade followed three days later. The march took both units through the horrific mire known as the Black Swamp. An Ohio historian named Maurer Mauer vividly described the place, calling it "a curse upon the traveler who dared to cross it ... the early pioneers called it Black. It was hard cruel and real.... Certainly it was a forbidding land."[35] In fair weather, the Black Swamp was a difficult place to cross. In wintertime, it was a terrible ordeal.

In a letter home, one of Lorain's comrades described the horrors of the march:

> That day I regretted being a soldier. On that day we marched thirty miles, under an incessant rain; and I am afraid you will doubt my veracity when I tell you, that in 8 miles of the best road, it took us over the knees and often to the middle. The Black

Swamp (4 miles from the Portage river, and 4 miles in extent) would have been considered impassable by all but men determined to surmount every difficulty to accomplish the object of their march. In this swamp you lose sight of *terra firma* altogether—the water was about 6 inches deep on the ice, which was very rotten, often breaking through to the depth of four or five feet.[36]

In this young soldier's words, the difficulties of 19th-century campaigning are graphically revealed. There was a simple reason armies went into winter quarters: the poor state of the roads. Thousands of men marching under such conditions quickly turned rudimentary wilderness roads into quagmires. We also hear the cry of a youth who has suddenly realized that soldiering is not all glory and barbecues.

Under such conditions, men needed something to keep them going. The daily tot of spirits proved essential. Years later, Lorain recalled the "indescribable titillation" produced by a small glass of "high wine," which spread warmth through his fingertips and toes. Though he became a Methodist minister and an avowed temperance man, Lorain pointed to this incident to refute the argument that alcohol never proved beneficial under any circumstances.[37]

The ordeal of the Black Swamp caused tempers to flare among officers of the Virginia Brigade. On the evening of January 28, after another grueling day, Major David Scott of the 1st Regiment verbally abused his commanding officer, Lieutenant Colonel John Connell. Scott felt Connell was pushing the men too hard. "Colonel," said Scott, "you have used us damned ill; you have marched us too late. You are no gentleman." Connell gave Scott an opportunity to retract his intemperate language. Surely he was not in earnest. Scott replied that he was indeed serious, declaring, "You are no officer and no gentleman. You are a damned liar. I can do as I please with you any way you please." Connell, now quite angry, drew his sword and approached Scott. Their fellow officers intervened to prevent bloodshed, and Scott stormed off to his quarters. Scott was later court-martialed at Fort Meigs for insubordination. He was found guilty and dismissed from the service.[38]

While the Virginians struggled through foul weather and over rough terrain, the Northwestern army suffered a severe setback. In mid–January, Brigadier General James Winchester advanced to Frenchtown in Michigan Territory. Though he was under orders to remain at the Maumee Rapids, Winchester decided on January 16 to march to Frenchtown. The citizens of the small village on the Raisin River had stockpiled provisions. They also sent word that they were being threatened by hostile warriors. These factors influenced Winchester's decision to advance.[39]

On January 18, approximately 670 Americans—mostly Kentucky militia—attacked the small British and Indian force that held Frenchtown. Several Frenchtown citizens joined in the assault, and after a brief battle, the redcoats and warriors retreated. Despite the battle's short duration, the Americans lost

12 dead and 55 wounded.⁴⁰ Winchester arrived on January 20 with the rest of his men, save 300 who remained at the Rapids. The American force at Frenchtown now numbered about 1,000 men. The report turned out to be false, but Procter wanted to remove his casualties (23 dead and 161 wounded) from the battlefield. Despite warnings that the British were planning to return, Winchester did not fortify the town or increase the guard.⁴¹

Before dawn on January 22, Procter and 1,300 redcoats, militia, and warriors approached Frenchtown. The lack of guards allowed them to take up positions and wait for dawn.⁴² The assault struck the right flank. The Kentuckians did their best to resist, but Winchester's failure to organize defenses soon led to a rout. Hundreds were cut down as they fled. Winchester himself was captured. Meanwhile, on the left flank, 500 of the Kentuckians held firm behind a fence. Procter persuaded their commander, Major George Madison, to surrender, claiming he could not otherwise be responsible for what the Indians might do.⁴³

Madison's men were running low on ammunition. He agreed to surrender, but only if Procter posted soldiers as guards over the wounded and prisoners. Procter then received word that Harrison was on his way with reinforcements. The report turned out to be false, but Procter wanted to remove his wounded from the battlefield (23 dead and 161 wounded).⁴⁴ He failed to provide the agreed-upon guards. Sixty wounded Americans were massacred by the Indian warriors. Many of the British were horrified; an officer declared the Indians were "monsters in human shape."⁴⁵ Procter certainly did not mean for this to happen, but by his careless indifference, he allowed

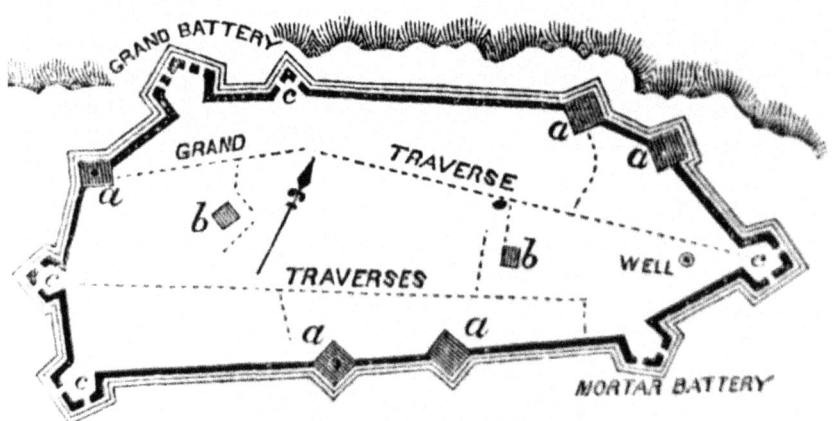

Plan of Fort Meigs, built in early 1813 as a fortified base for Harrison's Northwestern Army. a: blockhouses, b: magazines, c: batteries (Lossing's *Pictorial Field Book*).

it to happen. His name was cursed roundly by Americans and Kentuckians in particular. "Remember the Raisin!" became the battle cry of young men from that state.

The disaster at Frenchtown ground American offensive operations to a halt. Harrison would now consolidate and build up his forces, and wait for spring to take the field. For now, the troops would hunker down and fortify their encampments. The Petersburg Volunteers and Virginia Brigade arrived at the Maumee Rapids in early February. They joined in the construction of a fortified forward base of operations, near the present-day city of Toledo. This fort, called Meigs (after the governor of Ohio, Return Jonathan Meigs), was designed by Captain Eleazar Wood of the U.S. Army Corps of Engineers. It was a massive work, approximately 2,500 yards in circumference, with a 15-foot-high wooden stockade.[46] In front of the stockade was an eight-foot high embankment. Seven two-story blockhouses and six batteries were placed at intervals. The batteries comprised two to four 18-pounder guns.[47]

Soon after their arrival at Fort Meigs, the Petersburg Volunteers saw their first man killed in action. Rangers brought in the body of an American killed and scalped by Indians. An officer of the Virginia Brigade, identified as "Major L." by Lorrain (No major with those initials appears on the brigade roll), stood over the corpse, exhorting his men to "drink in—drink in the spirit of noble revenge! stiffen your sinews, summon up your joints, and nerve your vengeful arms for deeds of mighty daring!"[48] Lorrain saw several men respond with anger, but when he viewed the corpse, he found that he could not bring himself to hate the enemy.[49] Lorrain's reaction reminds us of the ambivalence that soldiers at the front often feel for their enemies.

On February 9, the Petersburg Volunteers formed part of a 600-man expedition. Intelligence reported 200 Indians 15 miles from Fort Meigs. It was a cold march, and a fruitless one. The Indians had already left the area by the time the Americans arrived. A further march of eight miles did not result in contact with the warriors. The detachment returned to the dubious warmth of Fort Meigs.[50]

Life at Fort Meigs settled into monotonous routine, as the men carried out daily fatigues, and struggled to keep warm. The winter of 1812–13 was particularly severe, especially for men from Tidewater Virginia. Lorrain noted one man on sentry post froze after less than two hours on duty. Epidemic diseases also stalked the garrison. Many of the men came from relatively isolated communities, and were not exposed to illnesses commonly experienced in childhood. Now they suffered severely from mumps, measles, and whooping cough. Several times daily, "Roslin Castle" played over shallow graves ("Taps" had yet to be composed).[51] Homesickness depressed the soldiers' spirits.

In early March, with work progressing on Fort Meigs, Captain Wood left to oversee construction of Fort Stephenson. When he returned near the end of the month, Wood was horrified by what he saw. The Virginia Brigade had ceased work on the fort. But that was not all. They were actually dismantling the stockade and burning it for firewood! General Leftwich refused to properly command his men, claiming he could not make the militia follow orders. Wood fumed at the "highly reprehensible" conduct of "this phlegmatic, stupid old granny."[52]

Wood put a stop to the cannibalization of the fort. But a new problem arose. The six month enlistments of the Pennsylvania and Virginia militia would expire in early April. Unless reinforcements arrived, the garrison would shrink to 600 to 700 men. Sickness would reduce this number to no more than 500 men. Wood considered an enemy assault to be imminent. Harrison wrote to the militia generals, asking them to stay until relieved by Kentucky militia. Approximately 150 Pennsylvanians agreed to stay, but the entire Virginia Brigade departed on April 2. In his journal, Wood declared the Virginians had permanently disgraced themselves. He also denounced Leftwich in the harshest terms.[53]

Stuart Butler takes a kinder view of the conduct of the Virginia Brigade. He calls Wood's attitude toward militia "condescending." Perhaps Wood, a

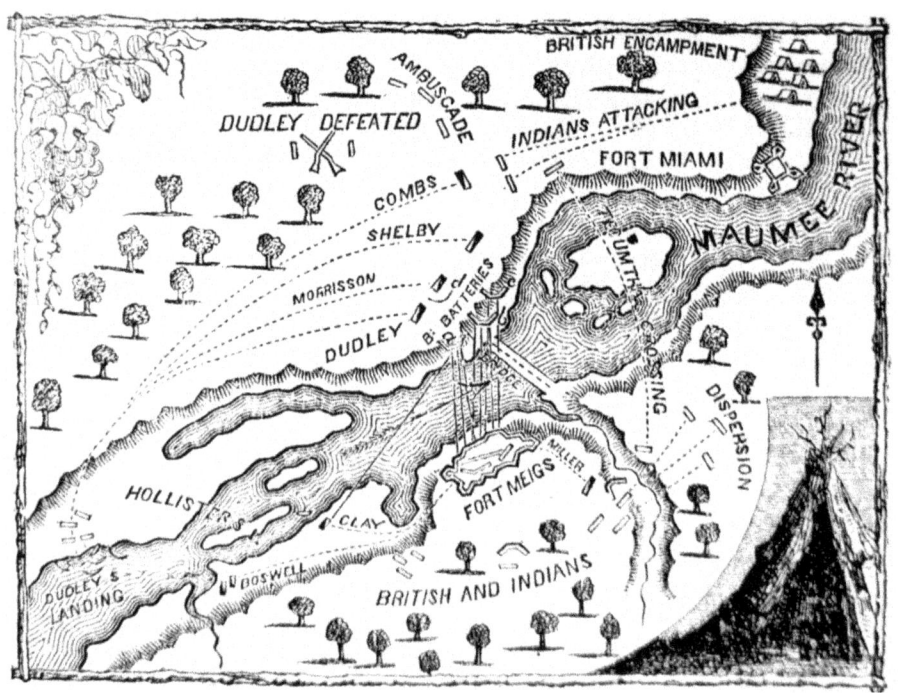

Map of the first siege of Fort Meigs, April-May 1813 (Lossing's *Pictorial Field Book*).

regular, was expecting too much from six month militiamen. But merely staying in place until reinforcements arrived does not seem particularly demanding. Butler does note that the Virginians had not been paid since Point Pleasant. Would money have induced them to remain at Fort Meigs? As for an imminent attack on the fort, Butler cites Harrison's belief that the enemy would not move until the end of April.[54] This is indeed what happened. But Harrison did not arrive at Fort Meigs until April 12. As the man on the spot, Wood certainly viewed the dwindling garrison with alarm. Also Butler was writing in 2008, nearly 200 years after the fact. Wood's journal, written in 1813, does not have the benefit of hindsight.

The Virginia Brigade's service was now concluded. During its six months of service, 44 men died, mostly from disease. Approximately 193 were mustered out early due to medical reasons. Thirty-two men deserted from the 1st Regiment, and 46 from the 2nd Regiment. This is an astonishingly low figure. Perhaps the men realized that in the inhospitable Black Swamp, with hostile warriors about, remaining with the brigade offered the best chance of survival.[55] Leftwich praised his men in a letter to Barbour, declaring his men had displayed "fortitude characteristic of real Patriots and heroic Soldiers."[56] Still, the six-month tour of the Virginia Brigade ended on an anticlimactic note. They marched hundreds of miles through the wilderness and back, but did not engage the enemy. In the parlance of the times, they had not "seen the elephant." It was now springtime in northern Ohio, and the British and Indians were on their way to attack Fort Meigs.

Five hundred thirty-three British regulars and 462 Canadian militiamen boarded ships at Amherstburg on April 23. Tecumseh took 1,300 warriors down Hull's Road. They rendezvoused at the mouth of the Maumee River on April 27. Scouts brought this vital intelligence to Harrison, who ordered General Green Clay's Kentucky militia brigade at Fort Winchester to march as soon as possible.[57] The British dragged their artillery within range of Fort Meigs. It was difficult, backbreaking work, but they reached their destination on April 29.[58]

On the opposite bank of the Maumee across from Fort Meigs, the British constructed siege batteries. They built four positions, containing two 24-pounders, three 12-pounders, one eight-inch howitzer, and a 5½-inch mortar.[59] Harrison countered by ordering the construction of traverses, 12-foot-high earthen mounds that covered the tented encampment. The men worked in three shifts, and completed the traverses before the British opened fire.[60] These works provided a great deal of protection from artillery, reducing the effectiveness of explosive shells and ricocheting solid shot. To counter the traverses, Procter commanded two more batteries built on the American side of the Maumee, 300 yards from the fort. These batteries contained a six-pounder gun, a 5½-inch howitzer, and a 5½-inch mortar.[61] With the opposing forces firmly in place, the siege began in deadly earnest.

The British batteries opened their bombardment on May 1. That day they fired approximately 250 rounds. May 3 saw the heaviest cannonade, with 516 rounds fired at Fort Meigs.[62] By May 8, the British fired 1,676 rounds.[63] These numbers are not particularly impressive for readers familiar with the massive bombardments of World War I. But Procter nearly exhausted his ammunition supply, reflecting the logistical challenges of a wilderness war.

The British artillery fire certainly made life more hazardous at Fort Meigs, but it did little damage. The traverses provided excellent protection, and breaches in the stockade were quickly repaired. The British concentrated much of their fire against the magazines, firing heated shot. If one of these red hot projectiles penetrated the magazine, the resulting explosion would be devastating. A fatigue party was ordered to throw up a protective embankment around the threatened magazines. At first, Colonel Alexander Bourne, commanding the detail, had a difficult time keeping the men from dropping tools and taking cover. When he informed Captain Wood of the men's reluctance, the engineer officer found a novel solution:

> He then gave me an unlimited order on the Commissary for whiskey, and directed me to give it to them every half hour, and make them drink it until they were insensible to fear, but not too drunk to stand and work. He said "There is no other way, it must be done in extreme cases!" And so I did it; the men then kept at their work, reeling and cursing the British and their hot balls, until the work was finished. There were none killed or badly wounded.[64]

During the siege, Harrison kept up the men's spirits by rewarding them with alcohol. Soldiers received a daily ration of one gill, or four ounces of whiskey. For every solid shot or shell retrieved, soldiers would receive an additional gill. This was a dangerous pastime. Retrieving shell meant extinguishing the fuse before ignition. As for solid shot, even at slow speeds the heavy balls had the potential to inflict grievous injuries. Nevertheless, the men were awarded over 1,000 gills.[65] The Americans actually increased their ammunition stocks throughout the siege, returning shot and shell to their original owners.

A brave—or foolhardy—militiaman appointed himself artillery spotter. He would tell his comrades where the British projectiles were headed, and if they needed to take cover. Lorrain recalled,

> In this he became so skillful that he could, in almost every case, predict the destination of the ball. As soon as the smoke issued from the muzzle of the gun he would cry out "shot," or "bomb," as the case might be. Sometimes he would exclaim "Blockhouse No. 1," or, "Look out, main battery"; Now for the meat-house"; "Good-by, if you will pass." In spite of all the expostulations of his friends, he maintained his post. One day there came a shot that seemed to defy all his calculations. He stood silent—motionless—perplexed. In the same instant he was swept into eternity. Poor man! He should have considered that when there was no obliquity in the issue of the smoke,

either to the right or left, above or below, the fatal messenger would travel in the direct line of his vision.⁶⁶

The lack of progress frustrated the besiegers. Tecumseh wrote to Harrison, attempting to goad him into action: "I have with me eight hundred braves. You have an equal number in your hiding place. Come out with them and give me battle; you talked like a brave when we met at Vincennes, and I respected you; but now you hide behind logs and in the earth like a ground hog."⁶⁷ Harrison did not reply to Tecumseh's challenge. Procter also called on Harrison to surrender, to prevent further bloodshed. Not surprisingly, Harrison refused to surrender.

Procter's surrender demand came on May 4. That night, Harrison received welcome news. Brigadier General Green Clay, commanding a brigade of 1,200 Kentucky militiamen, was only two hours' voyage from Fort Meigs. Harrison planned to put these men to immediate good use. Approximately 850, commanded by Colonel William Dudley, would land on the northern bank of the Maumee, and spike the British guns. The rest would land on the southern bank and fight their way into the fort.⁶⁸

To distract the British from the arriving Kentuckians, the garrison planned a sortie against the batteries in the ravine. The sortie, commanded by Colonel John Miller of the 19th U.S. Infantry, comprised 350 regulars and militiamen, including the Petersburg Volunteers.⁶⁹

Lorrain provides a vivid, soldier's-eye-view of the action:

> At last the word was given—the charge made. As we cleared the ravine the whole forest was in a blaze. The continuous roar of the rifles was like the long roll of the drum—no intermission. The balls flew like hailstones—*pish—pish—pish*; now and then *rap—rap*. In our passage to the woods we became exposed to the British battery on the other side of the river. They were not slow in playing their artillery on us; but we heard it not—we felt it not—we saw it not.... Those who were in the fort said it was amazing to see how the balls plowed up the earth about our heels, and with what little effect.⁷⁰

The men eventually reached the troublesome guns and spiked them. Miller's successful sortie cost the Americans 30 killed and 90 wounded. The Petersburg Volunteers lost 17 wounded, three of them mortally.⁷¹

Unfortunately, Dudley's men came to grief. They attacked and successfully spiked the British guns. "But unfortunately," as Lorrain remembered, "the Indian yell was raised in the forest. This was more than a Kentucky ear could bear. Our victors rushed to meet their mortal foe, and a general slaughter ensued."⁷² In the ensuing ambush, Dudley and 50 of his men were killed. Nearly 100 were wounded. Over 600 were captured. The warriors took the captives to the ruins of Fort Miamis. The Kentuckians were guarded by approximately 50 redcoats, including "an old and excellent soldier named

Russell." The Ottawa chief Split Nose arrived on the scene. His warriors began killing American prisoners. When Russell attempted to intervene, he was killed by an Ottawa warrior. Perhaps 40 Kentuckians were massacred before Tecumseh arrived and put a stop to the slaughter. He denounced Split Nose as "a worthless chief." While the killing stopped, the Indians took away other Kentuckians for adoption or other purposes. Many were never seen again.[73]

Clay's other regiment reached Fort Meigs safely. But Dudley's Defeat cast a gloomy pall over the day's events. Captain Wood furiously denounced Colonel Dudley in his journal, condemning the "temerity, folly, ignorance and stupidity of this most unfortunate commander."[74] So enraged was the Engineer officer that he concluded "it was but too just to say that Dudley's conduct merited almost any fate that could possible befall him."[75] Eleazar Wood was obviously a man who did not suffer fools gladly. He also gave praise grudgingly. Nevertheless, he praised the Petersburg Volunteers, who "particularly distinguished themselves by their intrepid and cool conduct while approaching the batteries under a heavy fire of musketry."[76]

During the siege of Fort Meigs, some of the Petersburg Volunteers tried their hands as gunners. Sergeant John Henderson took charge of one of the fort's batteries. According to the *Petersburg Intelligencer*, Henderson was an Irishman, and a veteran of the Royal Navy. Perhaps he learned the artillerist's art as a British tar. At any rate, the novice artillerymen proved up to the task. Harrison himself praised the men's performance, particularly in support of the sortie on May 5. He also recommended Henderson for promotion. On June 20, 1813, he was duly commissioned a lieutenant in the 2nd Regiment of Artillery.[77]

After the victory over Dudley's force, most of the Indian warriors departed with their scalps and loot. A misunderstanding over a flag of truce (to discuss prisoner exchange) also convinced the warriors that Fort Meigs had surrendered, and that Procter was keeping them from a further share of the spoils of victory. Overnight, the number of Indians dwindled to Tecumseh and perhaps 20 warriors. On May 6, the Canadian militiamen presented a petition. The harvest of 1812 was poor. The militiamen—mostly farmers—worried about the harvest of 1813. They asked to return home to plant spring wheat and corn before it was too late. After their officers delivered the petition, at least half of the militiamen departed. Approximately three-quarters of Procter's army had now abandoned the siege. Those who remained were sick and exhausted. Under these circumstances, the British commander felt he had no choice but to raise the siege. By midday on May 9, the British withdrew.[78]

During the siege, the British regulars lost 13 killed, 36 wounded, and 41 captured. The Canadian militia lost one killed and four wounded. Indian losses were low, but a total was never tallied. In contrast, the Americans suffered 81 killed, 270 wounded, and 547 prisoners, though these were just the men held by the British. The Indians also took a significant number of Americans captive.[79] While Harrison's army suffered a greater number of casualties, Fort Meigs held out. It could now be used as a base of operations to regain Detroit and to invade Canada.

In March, Harrison had received orders from Secretary of War Armstrong. This was after news of the Raisin reached Washington. Armstrong ordered Harrison not to march to Detroit; instead, he was to sit tight and wait for the U.S. Navy to win control of Lake Erie. Because of the heavy losses sustained by Kentuckians, the secretary of war also ordered that no more militia from this state would serve in the Northwestern army.[80]

After the raising of the siege, Armstrong's orders imposed a delay on operations. While Harrison waited for the fleet, he embarked on an inspection tour of his Ohio posts. Fort Meigs was now garrisoned by 2,000 men under the command of Major General Green Clay. The operational delay gave Procter time to recover. In late July, he commenced a second invasion of Ohio.[81]

In the predawn darkness of July 21, an American picket was ambushed outside Fort Meigs, losing six men killed or captured. This ambush revealed the British and Indians had returned to besiege the fort a second time. Procter had at his command 350 regulars, up to 4,000 Indian warriors, and a handful of light guns. Actually, it was perhaps an overstatement to say Procter commanded the warriors. At this point, Tecumseh played a large role in determining strategy. Procter wanted to attack an American camp on the Lower Sandusky, which was supposedly not as well defended as Fort Meigs. But Tecumseh refused, insisting Procter attack Fort Meigs. Since Indians now comprised the majority of his force, Procter gave in, for he could not afford to lose so many fighting men.[82]

Over the next several days, the British did not construct siege batteries. Indian warriors approached close to the walls and fired into the fort, but did not inflict serious casualties. Inside Fort Meigs, the well-protected Americans became rather nonchalant, as a letter reveals: "Never did I expect to see men grow so indifferent to the sound of bullets. At home, if a gun is fired at a man a mile off, it is a great concern to the neighborhood. Here, if a man has his glass of grog shattered as he passes it to his lips, it is treated with derision."[83]

On July 25, the defenders observed the British and Indians concentrating on the southern bank of the Maumee. It seemed to indicate an imminent assault on the south wall of Fort Meigs. Before dawn on the 26th, the defenders stood to. Each man had two to three loaded muskets in reserve, to maximize firepower against the anticipated assault.[84]

Nothing happened until late afternoon. Suddenly, the Americans heard heavy firing on the Sandusky Road. Many of the defenders were convinced that reinforcements had been ambushed. According to Lorrain:

At this juncture the troops in the fort became almost unmanageable. "There," said some, "see how they are driving and cutting up our men, our *friends*, our BRETHREN, who have pressed to relieve us, and that right under our guns! Here we are with our hands in our pockets—where is the General? O, if Harrison was only in the fort!" Some could scarcely be restrained by the officers from springing over the picketing, while some wept like children.[85]

Clay did not believe American reinforcements were scheduled to arrive. But he asked his senior officers for their opinion. The majority wanted to send a strong force to the aid of their beleaguered comrades.[86] But Clay ultimately decided that it was a ruse on the part of the enemy, designed to draw out a substantial portion of the garrison. If they were defeated in the open, it would make Fort Meigs easier to carry by storm. Clay's subordinates objected to his decision, but his orders stood.[87]

It was a wise decision. The heavy firing was a clever ruse orchestrated by Tecumseh himself. Perhaps 1,000 warriors engaged in a mock battle with the redcoats. One participant later wrote that the "fighting" was "so animated that we were half in doubt ourselves whether the battle was a sham one or real."[88] According to Lorrain, redcoat prisoners claimed that the Irishmen in their ranks "cherished such a mortal hatred to their red allies that they occasionally dropped in a bullet, and laid some of their finest on the ground."[89] Perhaps this was in retaliation for Russell.

A violent thunderstorm put a stop to the heavy firing. "Tecumseh's sham battle" failed to produce the desired result. After this failure, the British and Indians departed from the vicinity of Fort Meigs. They now turned their attention to Fort Stephenson, on the Sandusky River. This was a small but sturdy fortification, with three blockhouses and an 18-foot-high stockade, topped with bayonets. In front of the stockade was a ditch, six feet wide and six feet deep.[90] However, the fort was relatively weakly garrisoned by seven officers and 160 men of the 17th U.S. Infantry. They had a single six-pounder gun, nicknamed "Old Betsey." Harrison considered Fort Stephenson not worth holding and ordered it evacuated. In his words, it had "nothing of value but 200 barrels of flower."[91]

Harrison's evacuation order arrived too late to be carried out. But Fort Stephenson was in capable hands, under the command of Major George Croghan. Twenty-one years old, and a nephew of George Rogers Clark and William Clark, the youthful Croghan distinguished himself at Tippecanoe and at Fort Meigs.[92] Croghan resolved to hold out, informing his commander, "We are determined to defend this place and by Heaven we will."[93]

On August 1, the British began their bombardment. Their artillery was relatively light, just five six-pounders and one howitzer; therefore, the bombardment caused minimal damage to the fort. On August 2, at Tecumseh's insistence, Procter ordered an assault. Tecumseh's warriors were assigned the southwestern corner. 160 redcoats were to attack the southeastern corner, while 350 redcoats headed for the northwestern corner.[94] Croghan anticipated a heavy assault on the northwestern corner. He had prepared a nasty surprise for the attackers. As the redcoats assembled in the ditch and attacked the walls with axes, a hidden window opened in a nearby blockhouse. From point-blank range, Old Betsey spewed grapeshot into the soldiers.[95]

Grapeshot at close range wrought havoc among the attackers. Procter, distraught at the heavy casualties, cried out, "Good God, what shall I do about the men?"[96] The redcoats trapped in the ditch managed to slip away under cover of darkness. The assault was a complete failure. Casualties were heavy, including 26 killed, 41 wounded, and 29 missing. Most of the missing turned out to be killed.[97] American casualties were light; just one killed and seven wounded.[98] After this dismal failure, Procter abandoned his attempt to capture Fort Stephenson. For his brave stand, Croghan became a national hero. He was immediately promoted to lieutenant colonel. Twenty-two years later Congress further honored him with a gold medal commemorating his gallant conduct on August 2.[99]

The outcome of the campaign ultimately rested upon which side controlled Lake Erie. To achieve this goal, both sides engaged in a naval arms race. At Presque Isle (present day Erie, PA), the Americans opened a shipyard in lakefront wilderness. By summer 1813, the shipyard completed six vessels, including two 20-gun sloops-of-war. These sloops, *Lawrence* and *Niagara*, were built in less than 90 days![100] By early August, the American squadron, under the command of Master Commandant Oliver Hazard Perry, was ready for action.

Manning the American squadron was a challenge. Perry led approximately 500 men into battle, but finding this relatively small number proved a challenge. Drafts of U.S. Navy seamen from ships trapped by British blockading squadrons provided some able hands, but even unskilled landsmen came from far afield.[101] Perry was forced to ask for volunteers among the soldiers of the Northwest army. One hundred men came from Ohio and Kentucky militia regiments.[102] Three men from the Petersburg Volunteers also answered the call: Private John H. Smith, Private William or Nathaniel (the sources are unclear) Harrison, and the irrepressible Sergeant John Henderson. Henderson was now a second lieutenant in the 2nd U.S. Artillery. He armed himself in the fighting tops and served as a marksman.[103]

Surprisingly, Alfred Lorrain did not volunteer. The former second mate was perhaps the most experienced sailor in the entire company. But after the harrowing ordeal of digging the traverses, Lorrain and his messmates made a pact: "*Whereas*, Volunteering is a mere work of supererogation, and commonly founded on animal passions, and moreover, brings no revenue of respect to our judgment; therefore, *Resolved*, That this shall be the last volunteer service with us, come what will."[104]

On September 10, Perry's American squadron met the British, led by Robert Heriot Barclay. The Battle of Lake Erie, also known as Put-in-Bay, was a bloody slogging match, but Perry won a decisive victory, capturing Barclay's entire squadron. Perry wrote a triumphant note to Harrison, declaring, "We have met the enemy and they are ours." Lake Erie was now controlled by the Americans. The way was now open for an amphibious invasion of Uppermost Canada.

Harrison reorganized his army for the invasion. The Petersburg Volunteers were attached to a battalion of 400 "chosen men." This unit was given the honor of spearheading the assault. Morale soared as the men prepared for action. A member of the company wrote home that "our troops, throughout the whole camp, are in high spirits, and pant for the moment when they shall encounter the enemy."[105] The Americans landed a few miles from Amhersburg on September 27. They quietly occupied Fort Malden, for the British had already evacuated.[106]

Procter's force retreated from Harrison's approaching army. The redcoats were demoralized, while the Indians were frustrated that they did not stand and fight. On October 4, the Americans caught up with the British and Indians near Moraviantown in the Thames River valley. The next day, the armies met on the field of battle. Harrison's army won, largely thanks to the Kentucky Mounted Rifles, who shouted, "Remember the Raisin!" as they charged home. Nearly 600 redcoats surrendered, though Procter managed to escape. The Indians fought desperately, but Tecumseh was killed, and the survivors eventually retreated. Harrison's victory was cheaply won, with 15 killed and 20 wounded.[107]

The Petersburg Volunteers, now in the rear of the army, did not reach the field in time to take part in the battle. At this point, their term of service was expired. For his part, Alfred Lorrain "was right glad of it; for our time of service was now expired, and the word 'home sweet home,' seemed to gather additional charms every day."[108] The Volunteers returned to Ohio by way of Lake Erie, and had a close call in stormy weather, when a gun broke loose, unbalanced, and nearly overturned the schooner. Thankfully, the crew was up to the challenge, and the crisis was averted.[109] Lorrain and his comrades arrived safely on dry land, and began their journey home.

In General Orders dated October 17, 1813, General Harrison bid the Petersburg Volunteers "an Affectionate Farewell":

> In granting a discharge to this Patriotic and Gallant Corps, the General feels at a loss for words adequate to convey his sense of their exalted merits. Almost exclusively composed of individuals who had been nursed in the lap of ease, they have, for twelve months, borne the hardships, and privations of Military life in the midst of an inhospitable wilderness, with a cheerfulness and alacrity which has never been surpassed. Their conduct in the Field has been excelled by no other Corps; and whilst in

Camp, they have set an example of Subordination and Respect for Military Authority to the whole Army.[110]

During their 12 months of service, the Petersburg Volunteers withstood two sieges of Fort Meigs. They proved their mettle in the sortie on May 5. Though they did not take part in the Battle of the Thames, the Petersburg Volunteers certainly earned Harrison's affection. They could march home with their heads held high, for they had taken part in a campaign which— from an American point of view—had a satisfactory outcome. Meanwhile, their home state was also experiencing war firsthand. In 1813, British forces arrived in force in the Chesapeake. Let us now return to Virginia, and examine the campaign of 1813.

7

"The guns are roaring at this moment"
The 1813 Campaign

On February 5, 1813, the Royal Navy arrived in Chesapeake Bay, under the command of Admiral Sir John Borlase Warren. This was the start of a two-year blockade. In a letter to St. George Tucker, judge of the U.S. District Court for the District of Virginia, Madison minimized the British presence, likening it to a cat scratch. He declared, "The mode of warfare pursued agst. us, has certainly not the emblem in the character of the Lyon, nor even in the Cunning of the Fox."[1]

The British launched their first raid in the Chesapeake on February 14. A small force landed unopposed at Cape Henry. The raiders attacked the lighthouse keeper's larder. The *Wilmington American Watchman & Delaware Republican* mockingly described how "with the most undaunted heroism [the British] captured his hams, mince pies and sausages, leaving not a link behind." The raiders then returned in orderly fashion to their boats, "with flying colors, without the loss of a ham!"[2] The Wilmington correspondent found humor in this incident, but it was a sign of darker things to come.

For Great Britain, the War of 1812 was a war they would rather have avoided. The British had their hands full in Europe, where the Napoleonic Wars were reaching their climax. Preservation of Canada was Britain's primary goal. As for the Chesapeake, British strategy was succinctly summarized by Secretary of State for War and the Colonies Earl Bathurst, in a memo to Colonel Sir Thomas Sydney Beckwith, commander of army forces assigned to the expedition: "To effect a diversion on the Coasts of the United States of America, in favour of Upper and Lower Canada ... the object of the Expedition is to embarass the Enemy by different attacks, you will, avoid the risk of a general action."[3]

Bathurst ordered Beckwith to destroy American naval and military stores. He gave Beckwith discretion regarding private property; the British colonel could extract payment from American citizens instead of destroying their homes. But if sizeable enemy forces approached, British troops were to destroy military stores and return to their ships as soon as possible.

Clearly, British objectives in the Chesapeake were limited. But for a diversionary operation, the number of ships committed reveals the power of the Royal Navy. Ft. McHenry ranger-historian Scott S. Sheads notes that "183 known British vessels of various rates entered the Chesapeake in the largest extended naval operation of the war."[4] Many of these were ships of the line, armed with 74 or more guns. During this period in history, Fort Monroe, which guards Hampton Roads, did not exist. British warships sat in the roadstead, unchallenged by American coastal artillery. What forces did the U.S. Navy have to meet the British menace?

The USF *Constellation*, a 36-gun frigate, was just off Cape Henry when she ran into the British fleet. Four British frigates gave chase. The *Constellation* managed to reach safety in Norfolk, moored in the Elizabeth River.[5] There she remained for the rest of the war. According to historian William L. Calderhead, while bottled-up in Norfolk, *Constellation* played a role "as an accidental fleet-in-being." Her "share in victory in the War of 1812 was equal to that of any ship in the American Navy."[6] The concept of a fleet-in-being was articulated by sea power theorist Alfred Thayer Mahan. According to this theory, fleets that do not actively seek battle still pose an active threat to the enemy. They can never be certain the opposing fleet will permanently avoid action. This necessitates the allocation of assets to guard against this threat.

On the face of it then, *Constellation* tied up a large British squadron. But was the Royal Navy solely concerned with a single American frigate? Their primary mission in the Chesapeake was to blockade American merchantmen and privateers. If the *Constellation* did come out, it would not be as significant as the French fleet escaping Toulon. *Constellation* would also need a great deal of luck to escape capture or sinking if she did attempt to exit the bay. This does not mean the crew of the frigate did not provide effective service in the war. 150 of her men were detailed to serve the guns on Craney Island. They distinguished themselves in the battle on June 22, 1813.[7]

The U.S. Navy made use of several Jeffersonian-era gunboats. These oar-powered craft were 50 to 75 feet in length, and usually carried a single 24- or 32-pound gun in the bow, and two 12- pound carronades amidships. These were fairly effective in shallow waters—several played an important role in the defense of Norfolk—but helpless in heavy seas.[8] The gunboats were supposed to be more cost effective than frigates, but according to Hickey, "time would prove that gun for gun the American gunboats were more expensive to build and operate than frigates, and they rotted in a year if left unrepaired."[9] Unfortunately for the Americans, many of the gunboats were poorly maintained.

In wartime, both Britain and the United States used privateers to harass merchant shipping. These ships, known as "militia of the seas," were crewed and equipped by private investors. Successful privateers could reap handsome profits for their owners. Several privateers sailed from the Chesapeake during wartime. Baltimore was a major privateering port. The Royal Naval blockade meant privateers had to run the gauntlet to escape into the Atlantic. Several actions against privateers occurred as a result.

At 9 a.m. on February 8, 1813, in Lynnhaven Bay, the Baltimore privateer *Lottery* was spotted by a sharp-eyed lookout aboard the frigate HMS *Maidstone*. Boats launched from two other British frigates gave chase. *Lottery* nearly escaped, but just after 1 p.m., the wind stopped.[10] 250 British sailors swarmed aboard the privateer. *Lottery* had a crew of only 28 men, but inspired by Captain Southcomb, the privateersmen gave stout resistance. After a vicious, close-quarters melee, *Lottery* struck her colors. Her crew suffered 19 casualties, including Captain Southcomb, who was mortally wounded. The British lost 13 men. The British honored the gallant privateer captain, firing guns in salute.[11]

The beginning of April brought a lively action in the Rappahannock River. On April 2, off New Point Comfort, the British sighted four American privateer schooners: *Dolphin*, *Racer*, *Lynx*, and *Arab*. The British launched boats in pursuit. The Americans ran 15 miles up the Rappahannock before the British rowers caught them. *Arab's* captain ran his ship aground and set her alight, but British boarders put the fire out. Local militia tried to recapture *Arab*, but the British drove them off, refloated the schooner, and brought her to the safety of the squadron. *Racer's* crew fought hard, but eventually surrendered. The British then used her guns to force *Dolphin* to submit. *Lynx* surrendered without a fight. For the loss of 13 men, the British took four prizes, 219 prisoners, and 31 guns.[12]

The British attacked ships other than privateers. In June, the revenue cutter *Surveyor* was moored in the York River near Gloucester Point. The small vessel mounted six 12-pounder carronades, and had a crew of 25 men. Captain Samuel Travis believed the British might attack his ship. Accordingly, *Surveyor's* crew remained vigilant, especially after dark. Sure enough, on the night of June 12, 50 British sailors and marines from HMS *Narcissus* approached *Surveyor*, intent on capturing the American cutter.[13]

For reasons which remain unclear, Travis was unable to get his carronades into action. But his men grabbed muskets and met the enemy boarders with a heavy fire. After a desperate battle, in which the issue remained in doubt, *Surveyor* finally surrendered.[14] The Americans suffered six wounded, including Captain Travis. British losses were three killed and seven wounded, or 20 percent of the assault force. Impressed by his gallant resistance, Royal Navy lieutenant John Cririe, who commanded the boarding party, returned

Travis' sword, with an accompanying note, praising the American commander's valiant resistance.[15]

In these actions, the Royal Navy displayed the highest abilities of seamanship, for which it is justly known. But the Americans gave a good account of themselves, displaying a great deal of skill and courage.

The Royal Navy blockade of the Chesapeake had an almost immediate impact on the price of agricultural commodities. In February, flour sold in Richmond for $10 per barrel.[16] Just one month later, the price had fallen below $7.[17] At the end of May, flour now averaged $4 per barrel, though an agent by the name of Robertson managed to sell 50 barrels at $5 apiece.[18] By the middle of August, "flour may be said to be worth nothing."[19]

The British blockade made it nearly impossible for American vessels to exit Chesapeake Bay. This created a surplus in interior Virginia, which drove prices down. Anxious to get their produce to market, farmers found a gap in the blockade. The geography of coastal North Carolina made Royal Navy captains reluctant to keep a close blockade. In stormy weather, ships might be driven onto Cape Lookout or Cape Hatteras. Even when the seas were placid, treacherous shoals proved dangerous to sailors unfamiliar with the area.[20]

By the end of summer, Richmond flour and tobacco now took a circuitous route to Currituck and Pamlico Sounds. From there, the cargo was placed on larger ships. One hundred voyages to Wilmington, NC were made during this period. None of the vessels were captured. From Wilmington, the cargo usually went to Charleston, South Carolina. Only three vessels were captured.[21] This was but a small percentage of prewar commerce, but it promised some hope for farmers that their produce would get to market.

On the night of June 19, Captain Tarbell, now in command of *Constellation*, attacked HMS *Junon*. The 38-gun frigate was becalmed at the mouth of the Elizabeth River. She was also isolated—the nearest British ship was three miles away. Tarbell mustered a scratch force of volunteer soldiers, sailors, and Marines. They embarked in 15 gunboats, and stealthily approached under cover of fog. At 3:30 a.m., the gunboats opened fire on *Junon*. A lively artillery duel commenced which lasted approximately three-quarters of an hour. Then a breeze sprang up, and *Junon* managed to escape, covered by two more frigates which came to her defense. Casualties on both sides were light; one killed and six wounded for the Americans, one killed and three wounded for the British.[22] Historian John M. Hallahan described the action best "as a terrier's bite on the ankle but it brought matters to a head. It convinced Warren that he had to put his plan of attack into action without further delay."[23]

Summer brought a serious British attempt to capture Norfolk and the American frigate *Constellation*. Brigadier General Robert Barraud Taylor commanded the Virginia militia in this sector. Thirty-eight years old in 1813,

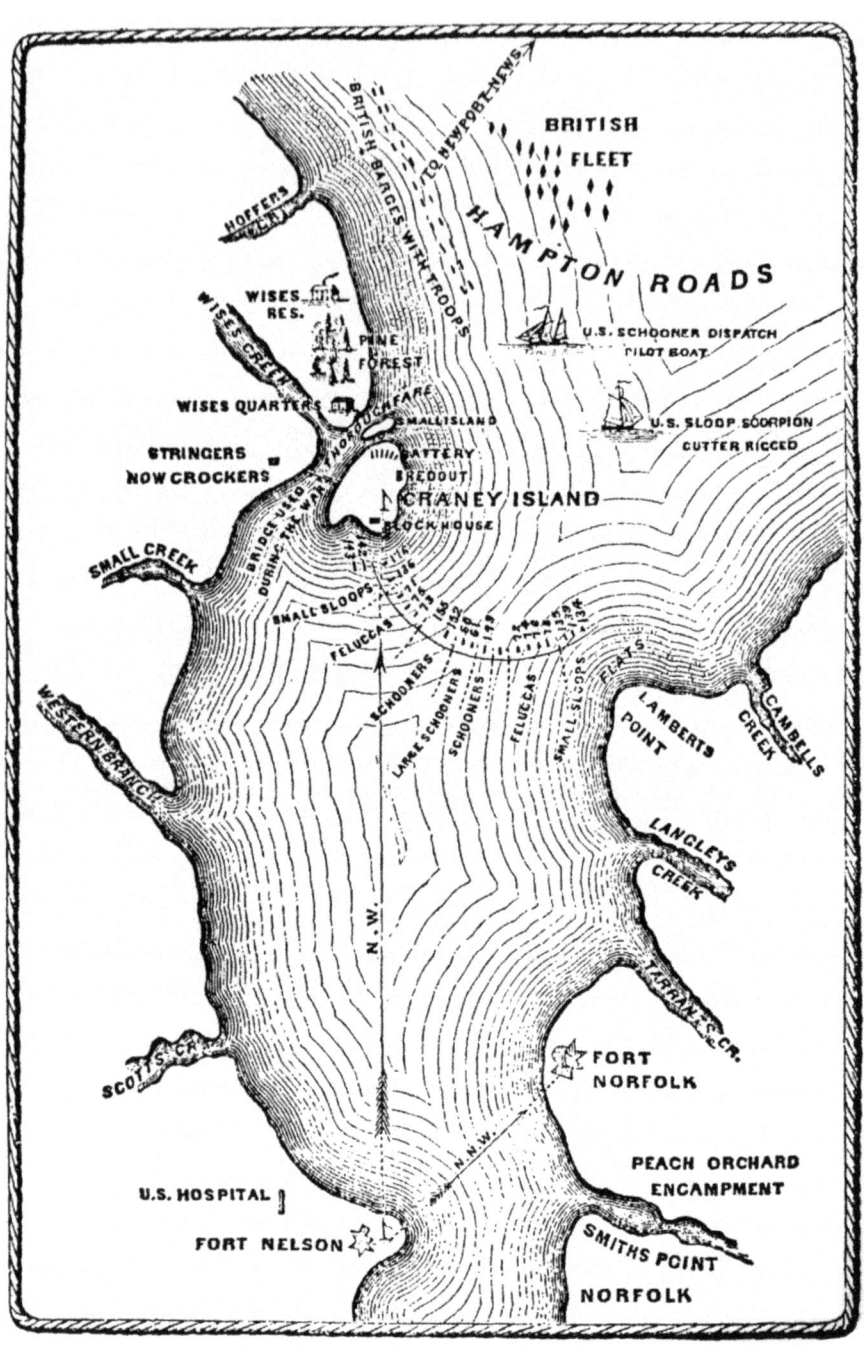

Map of the Battle of Craney Island, June 22, 1813 (Lossing's *Pictorial Field Book*).

Taylor was a gifted lawyer, and a former member of the General Assembly. He was also a Federalist, but put politics aside to defend his city. Taylor was too young to have fought in the Revolution, and had no combat experience.[24] But Taylor possessed common sense and a natural ability to command. To improve discipline, he reformed militia units, so that privates were not commanded by family and friends.[25] Taylor's novel approach produced positive results, though it lead to complaints from displaced officers. For the time being, the general's reorganization remained in effect.

In June 1813, Norfolk was perhaps the best fortified city in the region.[26] Its defenses included four forts: Forts Norfolk, Nelson, Barbour, and Tar. The most important of these was Fort Norfolk, an "asymmetrical and oddly shaped" fort with two bastions, built in 1794. By spring 1813 the fort boasted 27 24-pounders, and two nine-pounders. Fort Norfolk is still in existence today, and "is one of the best preserved examples of pre–1812 fortifications to survive largely unchanged."[27] Norfolk's fortifications were more of an inner defense line, however. As stated earlier, there were no major works covering Hampton Roads (Fort Monroe was built after the war to rectify this). As an outer line of defense, the Americans sunk blockships off Lamberts Point, on the Elizabeth River.[28] Near the mouth of the river sat Craney Island. The Americans did not start fortifying the island until after the British arrived in the Chesapeake. In March 1813, U.S. Navy captain Charles Stewart regretted the absence of strong works.[29] Eventually, the Americans emplaced guns on Craney Island. They were unfinished by the time of the British assault, but comprised seven guns, including two 24-pounders, one 18-pounder, and four six-pounders. Twenty gunboats covered the gap between Craney Island and Lambert's Point.[30]

On June 21, Craney Island's defenses were manned by 557 militiamen: 416 infantrymen, 91 artillerymen, and 50 riflemen. Lieutenant Colonel Henry Beatty was in command.[31] While the performance of militia in the War of 1812 was mixed, the Portsmouth Light Artillery, commanded by Captain Arthur Emmerson, was a well-drilled and -led unit. The 38-man company was established in the summer of 1809, and regularly trained with its guns. They manned the four six-pounders.[32]

Still, the force defending Craney Island was small. Captain Cassin, commanding the navy yard, and General Taylor sent reinforcements. *Constellation* provided 150 sailors and Marines, while the army provided 30 regulars from Fort Norfolk. Another 30 militiamen came from local units. Beatty now had 767 men under his command. It was still a small force, but the bluejackets and leathernecks were particularly welcome, for their experience manning heavy guns. They were assigned to the two 24-pounders and the 18-pounder.[33]

A footbridge over Craney Island Creek led to Stringer's Farm on the mainland. It was too narrow to permit a rapid withdrawal. The 400- to 500-

foot-wide creek was fordable at low tide, but at high tide, when the attack came, it was impossible.[34] The Virginians were unable to retreat, and determined not to surrender. To signal their determination to the enemy, the nailed the American flag to its pole.[35]

The British anticipated an easy victory. At dawn on June 22, 2400 men, led by Colonel Beckwith, with Lieutenant Colonel Napier as his second-in-command, landed at Hoffleur's Creek on the mainland, about two and a half miles from Craney Island. In his journal, Napier wryly criticized the landing, noting it was accomplished "in tolerable confusion."[36] Beckwith tried to bring his command to the footbridge near Stringer's Farm, but they were unable to ford Wise's Creek, which stood in their way and was at high tide. Beckwith's force took up positions on Wise's Farm, particularly in the vicinity of the slave quarters.

Royal Marines brought up Congreve rockets, and opened fire. The ineffectual bombardment caused no damage, and alerted the Virginians to the enemy's presence. Across the narrow water, the British heard American gun chiefs giving orders to return fire.[37] A shot killed a sergeant standing next to Napier. He quickly ordered his regiment to take cover in thick woods. But the Royal Marines failed to take cover in time. Napier described what happened next:

> I ordered the brigade to file into a wood where shot could not strike, and the 102nd executed this instantly and were safe, but the marines could not do it before the battery threw three rounds into the thick of them. Eight or nine were killed and wounded, all that were hurt that day, except two sergeants of the 102nd hit unavoidably. One of these recovered, the other was killed, both his legs being shot off close to his body. Good God! what a horrid sight it was![38]

The American fire—from seven artillery pieces—heavily damaged Wise's slave quarters. Gunboat Number 67 also opened fire on the enemy.[39] The Royal Marines followed their army comrades into the safety of the woods.[40] Beckwith's force was effectively out of the fight. The first phase of the Battle of Craney Island was over.

The British now attempted an amphibious assault directly on the island. At 11 a.m., 50 barges carrying 1,500 men—including the Independent Companies of Foreigners—approached the northern tip of the island in two columns. Captain John Hanchett, an illegitimate son of George III, led one of the columns. He borrowed Admiral Warren's barge for the occasion, a bright green 24-oar craft named *Centipede*. Hanchett sat confidently in the garishly painted boat, holding an umbrella to provide shade from the hot sun.[41]

A small boat preceded the columns of barges, taking soundings under a hail of grapeshot. Approximately 300 yards from the objective, the boat grounded on the shoals.[42] The tide was going out. A sailor thrust a boathook into the water, and discovered "three or four feet of slimy mud at the bottom."⁴³ This would make it extremely difficult for attacking troops to wade ashore. The sounding boat withdrew, signaling the cancellation of the attack, but it was too late many of the following barges. Several grounded on the shoals, including *Centipede*.

The gunners on Craney Island had a field day. At this range, they could not miss. Hanchett was severely wounded by a six-pound round shot. Another shot took off the legs and feet of almost an entire crew.⁴⁴ The survivors of this bloody shambles abandoned their foundered barges, and the seaworthy vessels returned to the fleet.⁴⁵ Jubilant defenders waded out to the barges, capturing those unable to escape. *Centipede* was salvaged and taken into American service.

It was just before noon—the British attack and repulse had taken less than an hour—and the defenders expected another British assault. Suddenly there was a loud explosion. A noncombatant Quaker accidentally blew up the reserve powder supply while lighting his pipe. He was killed in the explosion. Captain Tarbell quickly forwarded replacement powder to Craney Island. General Taylor also dispatched 120 militia infantry reinforcements.⁴⁶ But the British did not attempt a second assault. Beckwith advised Warren that he did not believe he could capture Craney Island without prohibitive losses. His force returned to the fleet.

Beatty estimated the British suffered 200 casualties, a figure which was widely circulated by contemporary newspapers. Napier recorded 71 casualties in his journal entry that evening.⁴⁷ Warren's initial report to the Admiralty tallied three killed, eight wounded, and 52 missing. These numbers were later revised to three killed, 16 wounded, and 62 missing.⁴⁸ Captain Hanchett was transported to Halifax, where he lingered in great pain, before dying of his wounds that November.⁴⁹

These losses were far from crippling, but British operations in the Chesapeake were a diversion to protect Canada. There was no need to capture stoutly defended objectives such as Craney Island, especially if it caused heavy casualties. Napier blamed the British defeat on Cockburn and Beckwith: "Cockburn thinks himself a Wellington, and Beckwith is sure the navy never produced such an admiral as himself—between them we got beaten at Craney."⁵⁰ He also criticized Warren, claiming he lacked "gumption," and conducted operations hastily and without detailed planning.⁵¹ Warren did seem content to leave planning to his subordinates, who were hard-driving and contemptuous of the Americans. Reflecting on the failure at Craney Island, Napier concluded, "We despise the Yankees too much."⁵²

Virginians were jubilant at the British repulse. In Norfolk, Dr. Philip Barraud exclaimed, "The affair is romantic and wonderful."⁵³ Victory was also won at an amazingly low cost. Except for the unfortunate Quaker, the defenders suffered no men killed or wounded in action. Captain Cassin

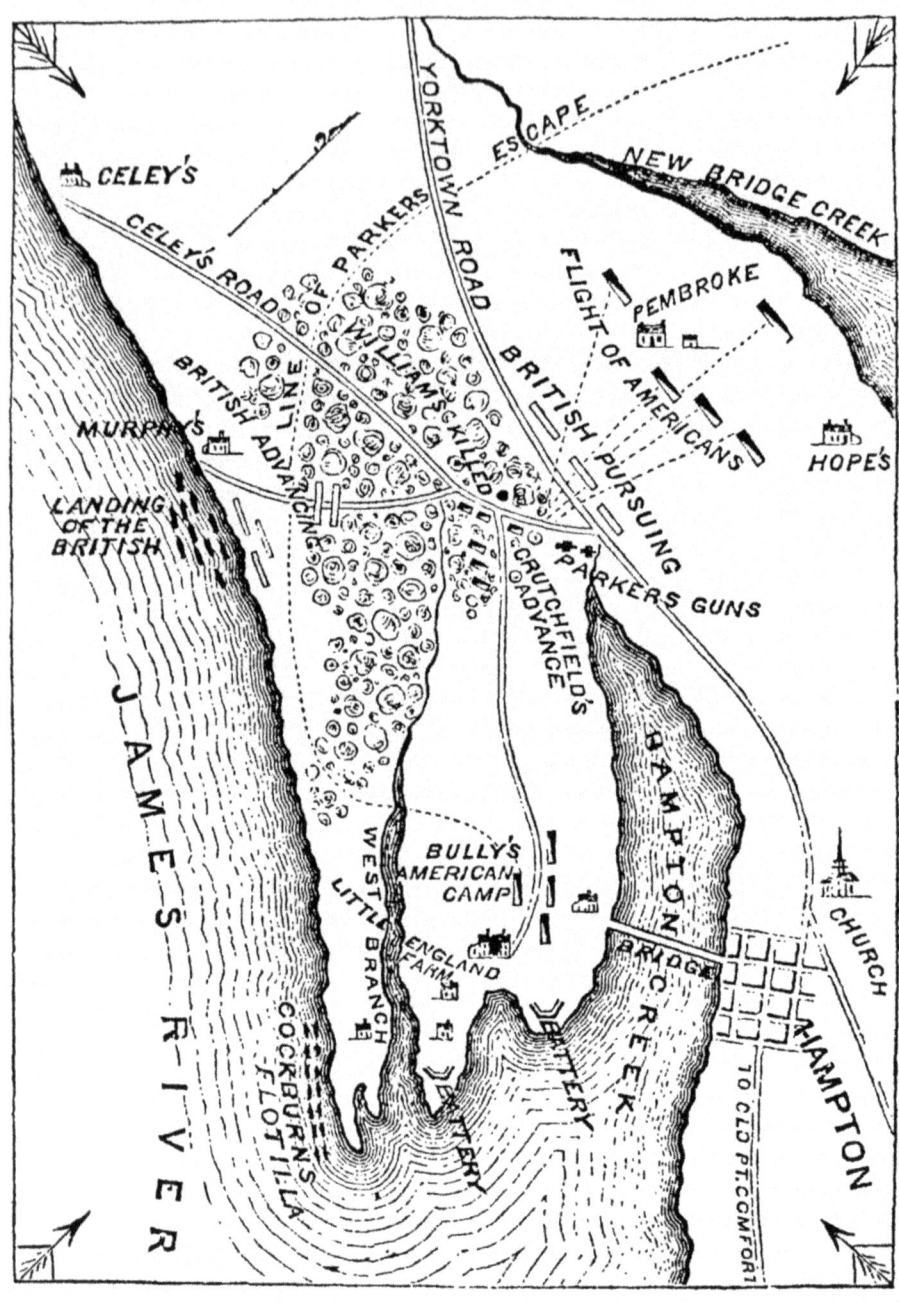

Map of the Battle of Hampton, June 25, 1813 (Lossing's *Pictorial Field Book*).

praised the performance of the sailors from *Constellation*, who "fired their 18-pounder more like rifle men than artillerists."[54] While Cassin clearly wanted to give praise, especially to fellow sailors, this marked the beginning of a controversy over which of the defenders deserved the most credit for the victory. But that was in the future. For the moment, it was enough that Norfolk was saved.

Repulsed at Craney Island, the British attacked the town of Hampton on June 25. Hampton had little military value, but an attack here would serve the British diversionary strategy in the Chesapeake. Hampton was defended by 436 Virginia militiamen, mostly from York County. They had seven guns (four 12-pounders, three six-pounders). The entire force was under the command of Major Stapleton Crutchfield. They camped at Little England Farm, owned by Commodore Barron of the *Chesapeake-Leopard* affair.[55] British warships engaged the Americans, while a force of 2,250 men, who landed upriver, attacked their flank.[56] Crutchfield's force put up a good fight, but was soon forced to retreat. In his report, Crutchfield minimized his losses, while maximizing those of the enemy—20 Americans to 200 British.[57] Actually, the Americans suffered 31 casualties, the British, 48.[58]

During the assault on Craney Island, a boatload of Independent Companies of Foreigners foundered. Sir Sydney Beckwith alleged that the defenders "waded off from the island, and, in the presence of all engaged, fired upon and shot these poor fellows. With a feeling natural to such a proceeding, the men of that corps landed at Hampton."[59] In other words, the Foreigners, enraged that their comrades had been butchered, took their vengeance on the helpless citizens of Hampton. It is possible this was just an excuse, for deserters from the unit claimed that Cockburn himself had promised a thorough sack of Norfolk. He also told the renegade Frenchmen that Norfolk ladies were particularly attractive, and they would have "the disposal of them."[60] Perhaps Cockburn never said such things, but whatever the reason, when the Independent Companies of Foreigners arrived in Hampton; they committed one of the worst atrocities of the war. Naturally, it was widely covered by the American press.

The first mention of atrocities in Hampton appeared in Major Crutchfield's report to his commanding officer, General Taylor. Crutchfield mentioned the murder of a bedridden man named Kirby. He also claimed that the British soldiers were joined by "the unfortunate and infatuated Blacks who were encouraged in their excess."[61] Two American physicians, Philip Barraud and William Grayson, who came to treat the wounded on June 27, confirmed Crutchfield's report.[62] Two more American eyewitnesses, Thomas Griffin and Robert Lively, arrived in Hampton on a prisoner exchange mission. They reported "that, from all the sources we could procure, from sources too respectable to permit us to doubt, we are compelled to believe that acts of violence have been perpetrated, which have disgraced the age in which we live."[63] These various reports soon found their way into Virginia newspapers. On July 1, the *Argus* brought the terrible news to its readers, describing in detail the "wanton excesses of the British."[64]

Lieutenant Colonel Richard E. Parker of Westmoreland County visited Hampton after the British assault. Parker hoped that the reports of atrocities were exaggerated, but sadly, he found them to be true. He recorded what he saw in a lengthy letter printed by the *Richmond Enquirer* on July 16, under the byline "P." One of the most horrifying passages of Parker's report described the gang rape of a young mother:

> This woman was seized by five or six ruffians, some of them *dressed in red* and *speaking correctly the English language*, and stripped naked. Her cries and prayers were disregarded, and her body became the subject of the most abominable indecencies. She at one time made her escape and ran into a creek hard by, followed by a young daughter, whence she was dragged by the monsters in human shape to experience new and aggravated suffering. In this situation she was kept the whole night, whilst her screams were heard at intervals by some Americans in town, who could only clasp their hands in helpless agony.[65]

Parker's specification that the rapists wore red and spoke perfect English is noteworthy. The British claimed the green-coated Independent Companies of Foreigners were the only men who committed atrocities at Hampton. Parker refutes this, and accuses the redcoats of active participation in the shameful events.

Parker recounted several other incidents of rape, robbery, and murder. He concluded his report with a rousing call to arms:

> Men of Virginia! Will you permit all this? Fathers and Brothers and Husbands, will you fold your arms in apathy and only curse your despoilers? No. You will fly with generous emulation to the unfurled standards of your country.... You will neglect for a time all civil pursuits and occupations and devote yourselves to the art and knowledge of all which the enemy has made necessary. You will learn to command and obey and—with Hampton as your watchword, to conquer.[66]

The conclusion of Parker's report is particularly interesting. By covering the atrocities in gruesome detail, patriotic Virginians hoped to whip up support for the war. They seemed to have some success in this endeavor, for the *Argus* reported on July 25 the arrival in Richmond of several hundred militiamen from Botecourt County, which was well removed from immediate danger. The *Argus* praised the selfless patriotism of these gallant men, who rallied to the defense of their fellow Virginians.[67] While the Botecourt men might have been sincere in their patriotism, their arrival in Richmond in late July reflects how slowly news traveled in those times. By the time these reinforcements reached the state capital, the British threat had subsided. Their arrival in Richmond was merely grist for the patriotic propaganda mill.

7. "The guns are roaring at this moment" 111

Not all Virginians believed the stories from Hampton were true. Robert Anderson, a militia captain who actually fought in the battle, expressed skepticism in a letter to a friend:

> There are men who have published to the world Wonders indeed—those men stand high in the estimation of the publick, and what I should say in opposition to their statements would no doubt not only be laughed at, but more when I say to you that I do not believe that a single female was ravished against her will by one of the invading army...[68]

Anderson expressed his doubts in private correspondence, but a Federalist newspaper from the District of Columbia, the *Georgetown Federal Republican*, publicly dismissed reports of atrocities as propaganda "from the highest authority in Virginia, with the laudable view of rousing and exasperating the honest people of the state to the support of a most wicked and dishonorable war."[69] The editor, Jacob Wagner, also printed reports of American soldiers sexually assaulting Canadian women.[70]

Thomas Ritchie, editor of the *Richmond Enquirer*, exploded in righteous fury. He asked incredulously if the eyewitnesses were liars. As for American atrocities, in Canada, these were lies "...trumped up by J. Wagner himself for the purpose of screening the enemy from our just indignation."[71] In the aftermath of the sack of Hampton, partisan rancor reared its ugly head.

American accounts of atrocities were corroborated by a notable British witness. In his memoirs, Lieutenant Colonel Charles Napier related a particularly dastardly deed:

> They [Independent Companies of Foreigners] really murdered without an object but the pleasure of murdering. One robbed a poor Yankee and pretended all sorts of anxiety for him: It was the custom of war he said to rob a prisoner, but he was sorry for him. When he had thus coaxed the man into confidence he told him to walk on before, as he must go to the general; the poor wretch obeyed, and when his back was turned the musket was fired into his brains. This is one of many instances of their killing without any object but murder, and they intended to desert in a body.[72]

At the same time, Napier was quick to absolve his own regiment of misconduct. "Well! Whatever horrible acts were done at Hampton they were not done by the 102nd, for they were never let to quit their ranks, and they almost mutinied at my preventing them joining in the sack of that unfortunate town."[73] Napier also praised the conduct of the Royal Marine Artillery, who maintained discipline and refused to take part in the sack of Hampton.

General Robert B. Taylor, the American commander, was outraged by the British atrocities. In a June 29 communiqué, he put Admiral Warren on notice that such conduct would not be tolerated. It was up to the commanders to ensure their men obeyed the rules of war, lest the conflict degenerate into savagery: "I hope these sentiments will be reciprocated. It depends on you whether the evils inseparable from a state of war in our operations be tempered by the mildness of civilized life or, under your authority, be aggravated by all the fiend-like passions which can be instilled into them..."[74]

Warren replied to Taylor the same day. He acknowledged "some excesses committed by the troops in the late affair at Hampton." Warren assured Taylor that he wished to do all he could to observe the rules of war.[75] Colonel Sir Sidney Beckwith wrote his own reply to Taylor. While he regretted the events at Hampton, Beckwith repeated the rumor that the Americans murdered several men of the Independent Companies of Foreigners at Craney Island. This caused the unit to run amok in Hampton.[76]

Napier felt the Americans were justified in their outrage. He criticized Beckwith for lax discipline. "He ought to have hanged several villains at little Hampton; had he so done, the Americans would not have complained: but every horror was committed with impunity, rape, murder, pillage, and not a man was punished!"[77] After their disgraceful conduct at Hampton, the Independent Companies of Foreigners were withdrawn from the Chesapeake and sent to Halifax. Even in a friendly port, the renegade Frenchmen showed little restraint. Eventually, the unit was disbanded.

After the capture and sack of Hampton, the British went further up the James River. On July 2 they landed near Smithfield, near Fort Boykin. This site was first fortified in 1623. By 1813, Fort Boykin was a substantial work, mounting six guns. The British were driven off after a brief skirmish with local militia.[78] While they did not attack Fort Boykin, they continued upriver, threatening Richmond. Richmond's citizens had cause for alarm—indeed, some of them remembered the dark days of early 1781, when the British burned the city. In July 1813, it seemed as if history was about to repeat itself.

Dr. Thomas Massie, originally from Nelson County, spent much of the war in Richmond. He corresponded regularly with his father, Major Thomas Massie, who remained in Nelson County. Dr. Massie's correspondence frequently mentions the price of wheat, his father's primary crop. But in early July 1813, the good doctor vividly captured the mood in the capital city:

> July 2d. I arrived here on the third day after I left you. I found the inhabitants of this place in a state of considerable alarm in consequence of the arrival of a British land force in the Chesapeake.... On Wednesday last an express arrived here stating that a part of the British force had arrived at Sandy point [on the James in Charles City County]. The Bells were rung, the alarm guns fired, and the town thrown into a state of great consternation.... At present we are here under martial law, the militia of the town parades morning and evening, and nothing else is done. The militia are coming in from the neighboring counties, among whom are many well mounted cavalry.... As a [surgeon's] mate to the Regt, I have two hours every day for the purpose of prescribing for the sick.[79]

Attorney William Wirt was in the market-house when the alarm bell rang. He described utter pandemonium, as frightened men made plans to

7. "The guns are roaring at this moment" 113

evacuate their wives and daughters to safety (they had just received news of the atrocities at Hampton). All men capable of bearing arms rushed to the square, including the elderly silver greys.[80] Wirt quickly assembled a company of flying artillery, but due to the panic, he suspected they might not serve their guns well. He summarized the mood by stating, "There was nothing wanting but composure."[81]

The threat to Richmond led to the formation on June 26 of a Committee of Vigilance. This is interesting, for the term "vigilance committee" has negative connotations of extralegal justice, due to the 19th-century American West. This was not the case with the Richmond committee, which resolved to work closely with civil and military authorities.[82] Richmond's Committee of Vigilance is best characterized as an *ad hoc* crisis management organization.

The members of the Committee included leading citizens such as John Marshall, William Wirt, and Thomas Ritchie. They resolved to consult with Governor Barbour and other members of the state Executive Branch. They also made arrangements for satellite committees to be formed in surrounding counties.[83] It was found that 12,000 pounds of gunpowder was available. Five thousand pounds was immediately measured out into cartridges.[84] As for small arms, the supply was not deemed "plentiful," or of particularly good quality, though there was a "tolerable supply of swords." It was estimated that 5,000 militiamen were "ready to act on short notice on this side [north] of the [James] river."[85] Where these men could make an effective stand was another matter, at the Committee reported on June 28:

> That there is in this City or its immediate vicinity, no particular height or eminence which overlooks and commands the whole town ... nor is it necessary for an invading army to enter the city by any particular route. Any one or more of five or six roads may be used.... The fortifications of any particular spot therefore would afford no protection to the City, nor would the defence of any particular road impede the advance of enemy into the centre of the town.[86]

On the James below Richmond stood Fort Powhatan. This fort occupied eight acres in Prince George's County, on Hood's Point. It was built following the *Chesapeake-Leopard* affair. It was a well-armed, solid work, mounting 22 guns, but it was not well manned. Just a handful of regulars from the 35th Infantry garrisoned this unhealthy spot. This created unease among Richmond's citizens. The *Enquirer* insisted on July 6 that the only ships from Jamestown to Hood's Point were British.[87] Three days later, the paper declared British frigates sat in Pagan Creek, near Smithfield, ready to assault Fort Powhatan at any moment.[88]

Ultimately, Richmond was saved by the limited objectives of the British. Above Fort Powhatan the James has several twists and turns. This would have made an ascent difficult for the British fleet. The infantry and Marines were not about to leave the safety of the fleet on a solo expedition into the interior.

Even if Richmond were captured, they were not willing—or prepared—to hold it.

The threat to Richmond subsided, but the fighting continued. The British turned their attention to the Northern Neck, the peninsula between the Rappahannock and Potomac Rivers. On July 14, British brigs observed the American schooner *Asp* and the sloop *Scorpion* in the Yeocomico River, a tributary of the Potomac. *Scorpion* escaped up the Potomac, but the British brigs launched two cutters in pursuit of *Asp*. The cutters caught up with the American schooner. In the melee that followed, the British boarded and captured *Asp*. British losses were two killed and six wounded. The Americans suffered ten casualties, including the commander, Midshipman James Butler Sigourney, who was killed.[89] Since *Asp* was three to four miles up the Yeocomico, "and the Channel extremely difficult and narrow, with a wind right and a vast number of Troops advancing toward the beach," British commander James Rattray set the schooner on fire and departed.[90]

On July 19, the British attempted to land at Mattox Creek. Militiamen, observing the British movements of the previous days, expected a landing here. Captain Hungerford and a company of light infantrymen stood ready. After a brief skirmish, the British retreated. On July 21, a powerful British squadron of up to 30 ships anchored off Blakistone Island and Ragged Point. They remained in place for a week, while Admiral Warren contemplated an expedition further up the Potomac. The treacherous Kettle Bottom Shoals convinced the admiral not to make the effort.[91] But the British would return to the Northern Neck in October, and again the next year. As for the Potomac passage, a bolder sailor would try his luck in 1814.

While events unfolded in the Potomac, the action continued in Hampton Roads. In July 1813, the Americans made several attempts to destroy HMS *Plantagenet* with a torpedo. This particular explosive device was the brainchild of Robert Fulton, who tried for many years to interest the Royal and U.S. Navies in his invention, without success. The outbreak of war made the U.S. Navy more receptive to new technology. In April 1813 Sailing Master Elijah Mix saw the potential in Fulton's device. Armed with 500 pounds of gunpowder, Mix and a small crew headed to Hampton Roads.[92]

HMS *Plantagenet* was a 74-gun ship-of-the line. In July 1813, she was on station in Lynnhaven Bay, a few miles from Cape Henry. Mix observed that *Plantagenet* often stood alone, which made her a particularly tempting target. With two other men, Mix set out on the night of July 13 in *Chesapeake's Revenge*, a small boat, with Fulton's torpedo at the ready.

When the modern reader thinks of torpedoes, they usually envision the self-propelled "fish" fired from submarines. Fulton's torpedo lacked propulsion. Essentially, it was a naval mine, mounted on a spar. When the boat came close to the target, the crew would lower the spar into the water, releasing the torpedo beneath the hull of the enemy ship. (During the Civil War, Union navy lieutenant Cushing used a similar device to sink the Confederate ironclad ram *Albemarle*.) This meant a difficult approach for *Chesapeake's Revenge* and her stouthearted crew.

Mix's attempt on July 13 was a failure. A sharp-eyed lookout on *Plantagenet* spotted the Americans before they could get into position. Mix made another attempt on July 19, which also failed. On the night of the 20th, *Chesapeake's Revenge* came close to the target, so close that he was just about to lower the spar into the water. A lookout once again spotted the Americans, and opened fire. Rockets screamed into the sky, lighting up the night. The British spotted *Chesapeake's Revenge*, but pulling for all they were worth, the Americans made good their escape.[93]

On July 24, the indefatigable Mix tried once again. This time, he released the torpedo at a range of 100 yards. He hoped the tide would take the weapon to the target. After a brief interval, which seemed much longer, the torpedo reached *Plantagenet* and exploded. Ritchie's *Enquirer* described what happened next:

> The scene was awfully sublime! It was like the conclusion of an earthquake attended with a sound louder and more terrific than the heaviest peal of thunder. A pyramid of water 50 feet in circumference was thrown up to the height of 30 or 40 feet; its appearance was a vivid red tinged at the sides with a beautiful purple. On ascending in its greatest height, it burst at the top with a tremendous explosion and fell in torrents on the deck of the ship which rolled into the yawning chasm below, and had nearly upset.[94]

To Mix's frustration, the torpedo detonated prematurely. It was a near miss. But it was a close call. *Plantagenet* now gave up her solitary habits, and sailed in the company of other British ships. This marked the end of torpedo warfare in the Chesapeake during the War of 1812. Mix later proposed a stationary line of torpedoes in Hampton Roads, a sort of rudimentary minefield. But costs were estimated at over $1,000, and the idea was dropped.[95] In retrospect, Mix's proposal seems quite cost-effective, but it must reluctantly be consigned to the vast collection of historical might-have-beens.

Plantagenet survived Mix's torpedo attack, but earlier in the month, a watering party from the ship-of-the line was not so fortunate. Early on the morning of July 14, 28 sailors and marines landed at Cape Henry, to procure fresh water. Cape Henry was a popular watering spot for the British blockaders. That morning, local militia lay in wait among the dunes. When the British reached the wells, the Virginians opened fire. The sudden volley threw the British into confusion. They suffered three killed and five wounded. The rest surrendered. The Virginians suffered no casualties.[96]

In retaliation, British tenders bombarded the Pleasure House on July 16. The observation post established by William Tatham had been reactivated in February. A tower was also built, providing an excellent view of Lynnhaven Bay. Fortunately, the British bombardment caused no damage. The *National Intelligencer* sarcastically described the ineffectual cannonade: "With their usual accuracy, their balls passed over and under on either side without doing any injury."[97]

Two months later, the British launched a more serious amphibious assault. On September 21, a force of 100-150 men landed. Lookouts on shore raised the alarm. Captain Richard L. Lawson commanded a company of Virginia militia infantry, and about a dozen militia cavalry.[98] According to the *Virginia Argus*, Lawson attempted resistance, but with only 27 men fit for services, retreat was the only realistic option. The British took six Virginians prisoner. In the confusion, the militiamen ran toward the enemy and were captured. Otherwise, there were no casualties on either side.[99] The British burned the Pleasure House and the observation post, and returned to the blockading squadron.

On November 8, Walter Jones, a resident of Kinsale in the Northern Neck, wrote directly to the president. He wanted to alert Madison to the vulnerability of the Northern Neck. This region produced a great deal of grain and timber. These products were mostly sent to Baltimore and the District of Colombia by ship. British ships lying off Smith's Point on the Potomac were in an ideal position to interdict this trade.[100] The British presence also excited "The Spirit of defection among the negroes."[101] In late October and early November, 50 to 60 Northern Neck slaves escaped and joined the British. Jones was afraid that without effective resistance to the British, the remaining slaves might become openly rebellious, threatening the safety of the citizens.[102]

Jones wrote to the Madison because he felt the Northern Neck was neglected by the state government. During the July raids, militia reinforcements from Richmond (known as a "flying camp") finally reached the Northern Neck. According to Jones, the commanding officer, a Colonel McDowell, complained to local militia officers about the number of streams between Richmond and the Northern Neck. McDowell informed these officers "that he should think it a Duty, to represent to the Executive [Barbour], the Impropriety of sending any aid again from that quarter." Based on continued neglect from the capital, Jones concluded that the Northern Neck was considered expendable in comparison to Richmond, Norfolk, and "the hallowed shores of the James."[103]

To combat the British threat, Jones proposed keeping approximately 300 local militiamen permanently on duty. He requested Madison assign a regular officer to instill proper discipline. He also asked for barges to repel the invaders, as gunboats and sloops were ineffective in the shallow tributaries of the Potomac.[104] Jones' letter to Madison reflects the increasing difficulties of mounting a successful defense of Virginia. While McDowell's remarks were tactless, it is not surprising that other points, such as Norfolk and Richmond, would take priority. Feeling neglected by the state government, Jones took his grievances to a higher authority. Of course, Jones' proposals cost money, and the Northern Neck was an even lower priority for the federal government. His requests to the president were unfulfilled.

On December 7 Captain Joseph Tarbell of the U.S. Navy led a gunboat flotilla to Mobjack Bay. His objectives were the British brigs *Armide* and *Sophia*, which were attacking American vessels. Unfortunately, the British spotted Tarbell's gunboats off New Point Comfort. A British frigate and the two brigs chased the Americans into the East River. Fortunately, strong winds from the northwest allowed the Americans to escape the next day. Tarbell's assault accomplished nothing, but all the gunboats and their crews returned to Norfolk safely.[105] This brought an end to offensive operations in the Chesapeake for 1813.

In December, Madison once again proposed an embargo. In a confidential message to Congress, dated December 9, the president noted "the tendency of our commercial and navigation laws in their present state, to favor the Enemy and thereby prolong the war.... Supplies of the most essential kinds find their way, not only to British ports and British armies at a distance, but the armies in our neighbourhood."[106] Madison's solution was to propose an embargo, which effectively confined all ocean-going ships to port. The coasting trade was severely limited. Fishermen had to post expensive bonds before being allowed to leave port. Government agents were granted sweeping enforcement powers. Those who broke the law were subject to severe penalties.[107] Madison felt such extreme measures necessary to shorten the war as much as possible. He believed all good citizens would cheerfully accept the new law in a patriotic display of self-sacrifice.[108] Madison misjudged the people's willingness to sacrifice their livelihoods. Federalists compared the new measures to Britain's Coercive Acts of 1774. Even loyal Republicans hesitated to adopt the president's proposal.[109] But the embargo finally passed Congress.

In Virginia, the passage of the embargo abruptly slammed the door on the route through the North Carolina sounds. Several Norfolk vessels, ready to put to sea, were forced to linger in Charleston. The severe restrictions on the coasting trade forbid grain shipments from Richmond and Petersburg to Norfolk. The official reason given was to prevent capture by the enemy.[110] The *Norfolk Gazette and Publick Ledger* complained bitterly, calling the measures "arbitrary and useless ... since rice and spirits were still permitted to pass from Norfolk up the James, and whiskey, beef, pork, and butter from Baltimore to Norfolk."[111]

At the end of the year, news arrived of Napoleon's defeat at Leipzig. Allied victory at "The Battle of the Nations" was the death knell for the Continental

System. This meant the new embargo lost its effectiveness. By spring 1814, Madison reversed his position, calling for a repeal of the embargo.[112] The rapid policy change created a sensation. In Virginia, the entire exercise imposed needless hardship. Its repeal was greeted with relief.

Shortly after the 12th Congress adjourned (March 1813), Andrei Dashkov, Russian minister to the United States, passed on an offer of mediation from his country. Russia had just entered into an alliance with Great Britain against France. Alexander I did not want his new ally distracted from Continental affairs. Also, American merchantmen carried on a lucrative trade with Russia, bringing tropical fruits to the Baltic. These fruits were sorely missed in northern climes.

Washington quickly accepted St. Petersburg's overture. In Hampton Roads the British and Americans arranged flags of truce for Dashkov and his secretary Sverchkov.[113] For the St. Petersburg delegation, the president appointed Treasury Secretary Albert Gallatin and James A. Bayard, a Federalist from Delaware. The Senate initially balked at Gallatin's appointment, as he was a cabinet member. This caused some delays, but by July 1813, they joined John Quincy Adams, American minister to Russia, in St. Petersburg. By this time, Britain had rejected Russia's offer, but the Russians kept this to themselves, in the hope that they might reconsider. After six months of fruitless waiting, Gallatin and Bayard traveled to London, where they hoped a direct approach might meet with more success.[114]

Samuel Snowden had long ago decided that the administration was insincere about peace negotiations. In April, as another invasion of Canada was in the offing, Snowden declared this was "another evidence of the insincerity of our administration in their pacific professions, and of the fallacy of the hopes which the rumor of a speedy peace, by means of the Russian mediation, had so generally inspired." Snowden further argued that if Madison truly desired peace, he could broker a temporary armistice with Admiral Warren, who had the power to negotiate such ceasefires.[115] But this road was not taken, to the detriment of the citizens of the Old Dominion.

On the last day of November 1813, Jefferson mused to Kosciuszko about the fortunes of war and the dangers of peace:

> I have less fear now for our war than for the peace which is to conclude it. your idea that our line of future demarcation should be from some point in Lake Champlain is a good one: because that would shut up all their scalp-markets. but that of their entire removal from the continent is a better one. while they hold a single spot on it it will be a station from which they will send forth their Henrys upon us to debauch traitors, nourish conspiracies, smuggle in their manufactures, and defeat our commercial laws. unfortunately our peace commissioners left us while our affairs were still under the depression of Hull's treason and it's consequences, and they would as soon learn their revival in the moon as in St. Petersburg. the English newspapers will still fill their ears, as those of all Europe with lies, and induce them to offer peace

under these erroneous impressions: and a peace which does not leave us the Canadas will be but a truce.[116]

After Perry's victory on Lake Erie and Harrison's victory at the Thames, Jefferson might be pardoned for believing American fortunes to be on the upswing. These victories gave the United States control of Lake Erie for the duration of the war and brought an end to war with the Indians for the Northwest. But Harrison's army, mostly Kentucky volunteers, began returning home soon after the Thames. Apart from a raid in late 1814, the Americans made no further advances into Uppermost Canada. Conflict with Secretary of War Armstrong led to Harrison's resignation in early 1814.[117] He further stated that Canada was just compensation for the many outrages committed by the British, "which have degraded them from the rank of ivilized nations."[118]

Jefferson's letter then took a dangerously optimistic tone. He told the Polish revolutionary he actually *wanted* the war to continue, so that American industry, particularly textiles, would grow. War with Britain meant that European imports did not reach the United States, which removed competition from American mills.[119]

Jefferson was not the only prominent Republican to express these sentiments. At the beginning of December, Monroe wrote Madison. The secretary of state was unsure if Great Britain had accepted the offer of Russian mediation. Even if Britain had accepted, Monroe was not optimistic that negotiations would have a satisfactory outcome. According to Monroe, the United States' best option was "to carry the war into the heart of the enemy's territories in the hope of terminating the contest by land." The onset of winter weather necessitated a postponement of operations, "to be resumed when the season will permit."[120] The year 1813 had been difficult for the United States, and for the state of Virginia. But powerful Republicans had no inclination of suing for immediate peace. Under these circumstances, the war would continue.

8

"VIRGINIANS TO ARMS!"
The 1814 Campaign

The year 1814 began on a bright note. In November 1813, the British offered "to enter upon a direct negociation for the restoration of Peace." Madison appointed John Quincy Adams as leader of the peace delegation. The other members were Jonathan Russell, James A. Bayard, and Henry Clay. Clay seems an odd choice; as a prominent War Hawk, he did much to bring about the war. These men rendezvoused with Albert Gallatin, who was still in Europe. The British did not choose their delegation until May, and negotiations did not begin until August.[1] In the interim, Napoleon had abdicated for the first time, and many Britons wanted their government to take a hard line with the Americans, demanding significant territorial concessions as the price of peace. It was felt that America was teetering on the brink, and would have no choice but to accept. The American delegation was not about to make such drastic concessions. The stage was set for several months of acrimonious negotiations in Ghent.

Meanwhile, the war in the Chesapeake continued in earnest. In February 1814, the Richmond Committee of Vigilance reconvened. The members expressed concern over "the present defenceless state" of the capital. They hoped to rectify this before spring, when campaigning would begin in earnest.[2] Particular attention was paid to the sorry state of Fort Powhatan. The Committee resolved it should be "put in a proper situation for defending the passage up James River."[3] But Virginia lacked the funds to carry out such repairs.

Governor Barbour was also concerned about Fort Powhatan. For months, he appealed to Secretary of War John Armstrong to see to its repair. The haughty New Yorker waited several months before replying in the negative. He also attached a report by Colonel John Swift, who concluded Fort Powhatan was "worthless" for "any other purpose than that of affording a point of security to the inhabitants in the vicinity of the Fort in case of the *insurrection of negroes.*"[4]

8. "VIRGINIANS TO ARMS!"

Swift's report offended Virginia's leaders, who did not like to be told their fear was groundless, especially by a Northerner. At the same time, it was rumored that the War Department would not reimburse the state for the costs incurred for calling out the militia.[5] Many Virginians supported the decision to declare war. Now that their state was on the front line, they felt abandoned by the federal government.

The coming of spring filled residents of the Northern Neck with dread. William Lambert, a government clerk, wrote Governor Barbour in February that "the inhabitants of Lancaster and North'land [Northumberland] are in daily expectation of another visit, altho by no means prepared to give them a suitable reception."[6] The beleaguered citizens did not have long to wait. On March 16, a large force landed at the mouth of the Great Wicomico River. They raided the homes of leading citizens. In April, they captured two vessels in the Rappahannock. One of these ships, *Antelope*, was loaded with a valuable cargo of coffee, sugar, and whiskey.[7]

On April 22, the British struck Lancaster County, at the former site of King Carter's Corotoman Plantation. Though Carter's original estate had been subdivided among his heirs, it remained a profitable—and tempting—target. The British met no opposition and liberated 69 slaves. They also captured 60 beeves, which meant fresh meat for men tired of subsisting on salt pork.[8]

Thomas Ritchie inserted propaganda in his account of the raid. While most—if not all—of the slaves joined the British willingly, Ritchie's *Enquirer* claimed they forcefully took a woman in labor. They also took her elderly midwife. Ritchie was quick to highlight the virtues of these slaves: "Let it be known too to the honor of these captive slaves that such was their fidelity to their masters that they did not betray to the enemy some wines, spirits and valuable property which were deposited in their care."[9] Perhaps Ritchie's account provided anxious planters with some solace that despite increasing numbers of runaways, *their* slaves would remain loyal. Virginia slave owners needed all the reassurance they could get. That spring, a unit of escaped slaves in British slaves received its baptism of fire.

On April 14, 1814, the British seized Tangier Island. This small piece of Virginia, in the middle of Chesapeake Bay, would serve as an ideal base of operations for the coming campaign. On the southern tip of the island, the British built Fort Albion. This consisted of two redoubts, armed with eight 24-pounders. Barracks provided shelter for over one thousand men. It was here that the Corps of Colonial Marines learned the art of soldiering, spending many hours on the barracks square, perfecting their craft.[10]

The residents of Tangier Island, a very close-knit group (they continue to speak a dialect reminiscent of Elizabethan English), found themselves at the mercy of a foreign occupier. Though the British treated the islanders with civility, they required all men to register their boats. The Tangiermen's boats were numbered, and could not leave the island without a passport. Not surprisingly, mainland Americans viewed the islanders with suspicion, and often prevented their return.[11]

For their part, the British suffered sickness and privation on Tangier Island. By July, deserters told a tale of woe. Bad water caused many to suffer from dysentery. For two months, the men subsisted on reduced rations. Deserters also reported only three sides of Fort Albion were completed. This information was conveyed to Governor Barbour, but a daring assault on the island was impracticable, for it was well guarded by the Royal Navy.[12]

The Virginians responded to the establishment of Fort Albion by strengthening their defenses around Pungoteague Creek, opposite Tangier Island on the Eastern Shore. They built two barracks, and emplaced a light four-pounder of Revolutionary War vintage. The British attacked the militia encampment at dawn on May 30. Approximately 500 men landed in 11 barges. The newly-organized Corps of Colonial Marines led the way, supported by artillery, including the shrieking Congreve rockets. Poor quality gunpowder forced the defending militiamen to spike their venerable cannon and retreat. The British burned the barracks and plundered the home of John Smith. At 1 p.m. they were hit by a counterattack of up to one thousand militiamen. The British retreated to their boats and departed, having suffered six killed and 14 wounded. No Virginians were killed, but two were wounded.[13]

The action at Pungoteague Creek showed militiamen could perform satisfactorily in combat. Of course, it certainly helped that a British assault was expected. This meant the militia concentrated in sufficient force to meet the threat. As for the British, the action was the combat debut of the Corps of Colonial Marines, who performed well under fire and in retreat. Cockburn and other senior officers were pleased by their conduct.

The first abdication of Napoleon meant thousands of British troops were now available for service in America. British forces were now commanded by Vice Admiral Sir Alexander Cochrane, a much more energetic commander than the elderly Warren. Several regiments, veterans of Wellington's Peninsular army, were deployed to the region. Many Britons felt that the United States had stabbed them in the back by declaring war, when they had their hands full fighting Napoleon. They were eager to see their army and navy teach "Cousin Jonathan" (a derogatory nickname for Americans) a lesson.

In July, British raiders struck the Northern Neck. On July 20, several boatloads of Royal Marines landed at Nomini Creek. Intelligence reported substantial militia forces in the area.[14] The British made contact with the British, but according to Cockburn's report, the Virginians' superior knowledge of the country "enabled him to baffle all my endeavors to bring him to action, though I succeeded in overtaking a few of his Stragglers in the Woods and making them prisoners."[15]

The British remained overnight at Nomini Ferry. They liberated approximately 135 slaves. They also burned several buildings, and took great quantities of tobacco and several head of cattle. They also stole the silver communion service from Nomini Church. British casualties in this operation were light; just one killed and four wounded.[16]

After this raid, the British accused the Virginians of attempting to poison their men. According to the British, a decanter of wine at the home of Mrs. Thompson was found to contain arsenic. Cockburn ordered her house destroyed in retaliation. Virginia militia officers took offense at the poisoning allegations. Such behavior violated their sense of honor. Both General Hungerford and Colonel Parker affirmed they had drunk from the decanter in question. A court of inquiry finally assembled at Yeocomico Church on July 29. The inquiry lasted six days, and the court declared "to the world their most decided opinion that the charge of poisonous matter having been infused into the spirit left in Mrs. Thompson's house on the morning of the 20th of July is utterly without foundation."[17]

Twelve hundred British landed in the vicinity of Machodoc Creek on July 26. The Virginians mustered 250 militiamen in response, but declined to attack such a large force. The ineffective response prompted General Hungerford to ask Governor Barbour for 3,000 men, including cavalry. Barbour was unable to fulfill Hungerford's request. But it is a startling example of the manpower necessary to defend a single Virginia peninsula from a powerful amphibious enemy.[18]

On August 3, approximately 300 British landed at Mundy's Point on the Yeocomico River. Captain William Henderson and 30 Northumberland militiamen guarded the point. They also had a four-pounder gun.[19] The action that followed has gone down in history as the "Battle of Mundy's Point," but it was merely a 15-minute skirmish. But Henderson's men put their four-pounder to good use. Three Royal Marines were killed by artillery fire. One poor man had his head taken off. His brains spattered his comrades. Eventually, the British numerical advantage forced the Virginians to retreat. Perhaps in retaliation for his effective gunnery, the raiders burned Captain Henderson's house.[20]

Later that day, the British learned that Hungerford and 600 militiamen were near the town of Kinsale. Hungerford's force included artillery, cavalry, and riflemen.[21] Cockburn wrote in his report "though the Position of the Enemy ... was extremely strong he had only time to give us an ineffectual Volley or two of musquettry before our People gained the height, when he retired again with precipitation and we saw no more of him."[22] The Virginians lost eight killed and five prisoners, while the British had four wounded.[23]

After driving off Hungerford's militia, the British turned their attention to Kinsale. The *Enquirer* reported all the houses were burned, except for "the hovel of a poor old negro." The raiders took what they could with them and destroyed the rest. Ritchie denounced Cockburn as a buccaneer, and ended with an emotional flourish: "Weep, Briton, weep and blush at the destitution of shame, which marks thy countrymen!"[24] For their part, the British considered themselves avenging angels. Admiral Cochrane, Cockburn's superior, ordered him to carry out these raids "in view [of] the conduct of the American Army towards his Majesty's unoffending Canadian Subjects."[25] Cochrane was referring to incidents such as the burning of Newark, when Americans forced Canadian citizens into subzero temperatures. It was a needless act which led to terrible retribution. Unfortunately, this retribution fell on similarly unoffending Americans, and Cockburn was eager to carry out his orders. Such is the folly and tragedy of war.

The British reinforcements in the Chesapeake caused anxiety among the populace. In Richmond, Dr. Thomas Massie noted in mid-July that the city was in an uproar, and business at a standstill. He was glad his wife and children were not with him, for he did not "think it improbable that Richmond will be a pile of ashes before the fall."[26] In Hampton Roads, the *Norfolk Gazette and Publick Ledger* reassured its readers that preserving Canada was the primary objective. There was little cause for alarm in the Chesapeake:

> It must appear obvious, upon a moment's reflection, that the enemy will make no attempt upon our Atlantic frontier, until all the force destined for Canada shall be arrived; to be of any service in that country, the troops ought to be now there, and no doubt they are. If peace should not take place, we shall not be surprised if we are visited in the fall, not with a force to menace our independence, as the democratick papers more than insinuate, but to distress and harass.[27]

It is difficult to find the logic in the author's argument. If the Chesapeake was a diversion from Canada—and indeed it was—why would the British wait for all of the expected reinforcements before commencing diversionary operations in the Middle Atlantic? The American offensive on the Niagara began in early July. Just two days after this item appeared in the *Gazette and Publick Ledger*, American and British forces fought to a bloody standstill at Lundy's Lane, just one mile from Niagara Falls.

On August 20, the Richmond-based *Virginia Patriot* reported "twenty sail of the enemy heading for what was presumed to be Washington." The editor responded to this news with bellicose defiance:

> Our waters are now literally covered with their fleets, our shores may soon be lined with their troops.—They now have a force sufficient to undertake more of a consequence than mere predatory warfare.—They may think of making a stand in our country—of demolishing some of our cities.—Let them come! The spirit of Virginia is roused—the days of the revolution are revived.[28]

Such militant posturing is surprising from the *Patriot*, for it was well known as an antiwar sheet. These words sound as if they could come straight from Thomas Ritchie of the *Enquirer*.

The Americans made their stand at Bladensburg, four miles outside the capital. This happened to be the site of the Old Dueling Grounds, where Congressman settled arguments outside the legislative chamber. The battle is surely unique in American history, for the number of government officials present, including the president, secretary of state, secretary of war, and the attorney general.

On July 23, the president himself reviewed the troops assembled seven miles from Washington. That evening he dashed off a quick note to the first lady:

> My dearest.... I have passed the forenoon among the troops, who are in high spirits and make a good appearance. The reports as to the enemy have varied every hour. The last and probably truest information is that they are not very strong, and are without avalry and artillery, and of course that they are not in a condition to strike at Washington.[29]

From what source Madison received his intelligence is a mystery, but it was remarkably inaccurate. The American forces outnumbered the British—approximately 7,000 versus 4,200—but the British were veteran troops. While the British lacked cavalry, they most certainly had artillery.

Brigadier General Winder ostensibly exercised command, but as he formed his men for battle, Secretary of State James Monroe decided to test his military talents. Without consulting the generals, Monroe changed the troop dispositions.[30] The American army formed in three lines. Militiamen comprised the first and second lines, while the third line consisted of militia, regular infantry, sailors, and Marines. In the ensuing battle, the militia turned back the first British attack, but gave way after continued attacks on their front and flanks. Finally, the militia could stand no more. They streamed to the rear in droves. The Navy and Marines fought furiously, manning their 18-pounders until the British were upon them. They went for the foe like it was a boarding action, wielding pistols, pikes, and cutlasses.[31] But their commander Barney was wounded, and his men captured or joined the army in its flight.

A Virginia militia regiment from Fairfax County, the 60th, 700 strong under Lieutenant Colonel George Minor, was supposed to take the field at Bladensburg. The 60th reached Washington on the night of August 23, but they carried no arms or ammunition. The colonel asked President Madison himself for orders, who directed Minor to the secretary of war. Armstrong told Minor to report to Colonel Carberry, who would supply the regiment with arms and equipment. On the morning of the 24th, Minor was unable to find Carberry, but did encounter General Winder, who ordered the 60th to the Washington arsenal. At the arsenal, Minor finally met Carberry, and his command was properly armed. By the time the 60th marched, they met the American army in full retreat. Eventually, they received orders for Baltimore. Perhaps it is fortunate that these Fairfax militiamen missed "the Bladensburg races," for the battle offered little chance of distinction for the men of the Old Dominion.[32]

The Battle of Bladensburg is one of the most humiliating episodes in the annals of American military history. The humiliation was multiplied by the British capture of Washington, D.C. The redcoats burned the public buildings, including the White House, the Capitol (which housed the Library of Congress), and the Treasury. The invaders then returned unopposed to their ships, and prepared for their next objective.

Before the embarrassing defeat at Bladensburg and the burning of Washington, the Virginia press was complacent, even confident. All of this rapidly changed. On August 27, the *Argus* reported the news in tones of anger and despair:

> With bitter and indignant feelings we take up the pen to record the triumph of the enemy. They have succeeded, contrary to all expectation, in penetrating to Washington City; and on Wednesday afternoon [August 24] about 4 o'clock the Capitol of the American Republic was blown up, and the Metropolis of the United States consigned to the flames. Fatal, fatal apathy! monstrous, suicidal neglect! Why would not the American government cover their Capital with sufficient defence![33]

In the same issue, the *Argus* called Virginians to arms, emphasizing the desperate nature of the situation: "The time is come, the hour of heroes is arrived—not the *eleventh* but the *twelfth* hour—the very moment of saving and losing all that is dear to the hearts of patriots and of men."[34]

At this point, Governor Barbour showed true leadership, confirming he was the right man to lead the Old Dominion in wartime. He issued a proclamation, informing fellow Virginians of the burning of Washington. He confirmed that the threat to the Old Dominion was very real. At the same time, he earnestly assured "the good people of the Commonwealth, that every effort has been made, and is making, to embody the militia, and by all means, to provide such a force as may be able to repel and chastise the invaders."[35] The governor also encouraged those not called up to volunteer their services. At the same time, Barbour led by personal example. He took the field, joining 2,500 militiamen encamped at Fairfield, about two miles from Richmond.[36] It was a symbolic gesture, perhaps, but it proved the governor took his role as commander-in-chief of the forces of the Commonwealth seriously.

Barbour's proclamation was an appropriate measure. No doubt it reassured frightened Virginians that the state government would handle the crisis. At the same time, the executive's calming words appeared in an issue of the *Argus* which was full of doom and gloom. It offers a strange dichotomy. On one page, we read the governor's reassurances, while on another page, the author hysterically cries, "Oh shame, shame! We burn with grief and rage to record in our day such a stigma on the American name."[37] Such shame was not easily erased. The situation required scapegoats. In President Madison's cabinet, John Armstrong played this role. James Monroe took over as secretary of war, while continuing to serve as secretary of state.

As for Madison, Jefferson reassured him in a sympathetic letter that the fault was not his, for "execution must depend on other & failures be imputable to them alone, yet I know that when such failures happen they afflict even those who have done everything they could to prevent them." Jefferson invoked Washington himself, comparing the burning of Washington to the U.S. Army's defeat at the Battle of the Wabash, the worst defeat suffered at the hands of Native Americans. Like Washington, Madison was not responsible for the current debacle. This seems disingenuous on the part of Jefferson to say the least. Surely Madison shared some of the blame, if only for pushing the nation into war. On a more practical note, Jefferson offered to sell his 10,000-volume book collection to the government, to replenish the Library of Congress destroyed by the British.[38]

Perhaps the president took solace in the elder statesman's words. Jefferson's opinion still carried weight in the Republican Party. It must have been reassuring to know that criticism of Madison's conduct was not likely to originate in the ranks of the party faithful. But Virginians also wanted scapegoats at a local level. The city of Alexandria fit the bill. On August 29, the city capitulated to a British naval squadron without a fight.

On August 17, a British squadron under the command of Captain James Gordon (a battle-scarred veteran of Trafalgar) entered the Potomac. His squadron included two frigates, *Seahorse* (flagship), and *Euryalus*, the rocket ship *Erebus*, and the bomb ships *Etna*, *Devastation*, and *Meteor*. The schooner *Anna Maria* served as a dispatch vessel. Gordon's orders were to keep "the country bordering the river in a state of alarm."[39] The operation was to serve as a diversion from the attack on Washington. It was 100 miles from the mouth of the river to Alexandria, and a difficult passage. The treacherous Kettle Bottom Shoals caused the British ships to run aground—Gordon later estimated that each ship ran aground 20 times.[40] Nevertheless, the British squadron made slow but steady progress toward Alexandria.

By the summer of 1814, Alexandria was part of the 10th Military District, commanded by Brigadier General William Winder. It included Maryland, the District of Columbia, and northern Virginia. The citizens felt that if Washington, D.C., was attacked, their city would also be in danger. A Committee of Vigilance assembled to meet the crisis. They petitioned Winder to fortify Alexandria, but the general demurred, citing lack of funds.[41] Alexandria's militiamen were marched and countermarched across the Potomac, due to a flurry of conflicting orders. When the British approached, they were 19 miles south of the city. With the departure of the city, Mayor Charles Simms—

a Revolutionary War veteran, delegate to the Virginia constitutional ratifying convention, friend of Washington and a pallbearer at his funeral—estimated perhaps 100 able-bodied men remained to defend his city.[42] This left Alexandria solely defended by Fort Washington.

Fort Washington (Fort Warburton until 1809, though the names continued to be used interchangeably) lay six miles below Alexandria on the Maryland side. Its main earthwork mounted two 50-pounders, two 32-pounders, and nine 24-pounders. A separate water battery contained seven 18-pounders, with a further six 18s in an octagonal-shaped brick blockhouse.[43] On the face of it, Fort Washington was a formidable obstacle. But the Baltimore *Federal Republican* expressed doubts as early as July 1813, calling the fort "a mere pig pen."[44]

What is more, Fort Washington was severely undermanned. As the British squadron approached on the evening of August 27, Captain Samuel T. Dyson commanded a mere 49 men, not nearly enough to man all the guns. He did not attempt serious resistance. After a brief British bombardment, Dyson spiked the guns, blew up the fort, and retreated (Dyson was later court-martialed and cashiered for his actions).[45] Simms later wrote that the abandonment of Fort Washington left the way to Alexandria open to the enemy. Seeing no other option, the city's Common Council appointed a delegation to parley with the British.[46]

While the mayor and his delegation visited the British squadron, the Alexandrians received word that General Hungerford was 16 miles from the city, commanding a brigade-sized force of infantry, cavalry, and two pieces of light artillery. But it was deemed "too late to enter into any arrangements with General Hungerford for defence—he was too distant to afford relief."[47] Simms and his delegation returned to the British squadron and asked for terms.

Gordon proposed seven articles of capitulation. First and foremost, he reassured the Alexandrians that their town would not be destroyed, as long as the residents did not offer resistance. In exchange for this guarantee, all naval stores and munitions were to be handed over. All ships at anchor were forfeit to the British. Gordon also demanded the delivery of "merchandize of every description." This undoubtedly meant the large amounts of cotton, tobacco, and flour in waterfront warehouses. Citizens who removed their merchandise after August 19 were required to hand it over to the British. The Royal Navy squadron was to be victualed by the Alexandrians, but Gordon promised they would be reimbursed by the British government. Finally, officers were appointed to see that the articles were strictly enforced. Any deviation on the part of the Alexandrians would render the agreement null and void.[48]

The Alexandria Common Council reviewed Gordon's terms. They agreed and issued the following statement:

Resolved. That the Common Council of Alexandria, in assenting to the conditions offered by the commander of the British squadron now off the town, has acted from the impulse of irresistible necessity, and solely from a regard to the welfare of the town. That it considered the assent given by it as only formal, inasmuch as the enemy already had it in their power to enforce a compliance...[49]

The British remained in Alexandria for three days. They took three ships, four brigs, and ten schooners as prizes. They also seized 150 bales of cotton, 1,000 hogsheads of tobacco, and 16,000 barrels of flour.[50] These seizures amounted to several thousand dollars, but Alexandria itself was spared.

Gordon's squadron did not leave the Potomac unmolested. Four miles below Mount Vernon, at site known as White House, American batteries gave the British a difficult time. Some of the British ships temporarily grounded, causing a great deal of anxiety while they remained stuck. American Commodore Rodgers attempted a fire-ship attack, but contrary winds prevented their employment. The actions around White House lasted from September 2 to September 5. In the course of these engagements, the British suffered seven killed and 35 wounded. The Americans lost 11 killed and 18 wounded. By the morning of September 6, the British squadron cleared the Potomac. Though the ships suffered damage, they were quickly repaired, and took part in the assault on Baltimore.[51]

The capitulation of Alexandria was greeted with widespread outrage. First Lady Dolley Madison declared that the citizens should have allowed the British to destroy the city, instead of surrendering without a fight.[52] Many suspected the British were all too eager to throw in the towel. In a letter dated September 3, 1814, Simms praised the behavior of the enemy forces: "It is impossible that men could behave better than the British behaved while the town was in their power, not a single inhabitant was insulted or injured by them in their person or houses."[53] Although he undoubtedly did not mean to suggest it, for many Americans, Simms' letter suggested too cozy a relationship to the British on the part of the Alexandrians.

The Alexandrians' behavior did seem rather timid, even after the British departed. General Hungergord and his brigade (14th Brigade Northern Neck Militia), who were too far away to defend Alexandria, received orders to proceed to Washington. Ten miles from Alexandria, nervous citizens beseeched him not to enter their city. Hungerford replied that he was under orders, but soon received orders to camp to the west of town, on Shuter's Hill.[54] When the British were 20 miles below the town, Alexandrians still refrained from flying the American flag. This drew the ire of Commodore Rodgers, who threatened to open fire if the national flag was not raised. After Rodgers' threat, the Stars and Stripes were swiftly hoisted.[55]

The conduct of the Alexandrians was sharply criticized by the *National Intelligencer*:

The degrading terms dictated by the Commander of the British squadron below Alexandria, to the civil authority of that town, connected with the offer of the townsmen, *before* the squadron had even reached the fort [Washington], to surrender without resistance, and their singular submission to Admiral Cockburn whilst he was in this city, have everywhere excited astonishment and indignation.[56]

As previously noted, the Common Council actually did not seek terms until after the abandonment of Fort Washington. Also, the Alexandrians submitted to Captain Gordon, and not to Admiral Cockburn. But Cockburn was a hated figure, frequently excoriated in the pages of the *Intelligencer*. By connecting the Alexandrians to the despised admiral, further outrage was justified.

The *National Intelligencer* was the house organ of the Madison administration. It is to be expected that they would give a full-throated condemnation of the Alexandrians. But the *Norfolk Gazette and Publick Ledger*, no friend of the president, also joined the chorus of criticism:

> Since our remarks in the preceding page were written, we have received the terms on which Alexandria was surrendered, which are at once disgraceful, and do not appear to us to have been necessary; much better would it have been to have made no terms, and left the enemy to pursue his own course; this capitulation, if it can be so called, appears to us harder on the inhabitants than a surrender without any terms; but we shall not enlarge on the subject until we are further informed. The people will in this perceive that their best chance is in defending themselves and their property to the last extremity.[57]

At least the *Publick Ledger* promised to reserve further judgment until more information was received. Thomas Ritchie, editor of the vehemently pro-administration *Richmond Enquirer*, printed some of the harshest words on the matter:

> We had some hopes that the disgrace of our country would cease with the disasters at Washington.—But the cup was not yet full.—Fort Warburton was "*disgracefully* surrendered" and Alexandria capitulated "*at discretion*" to the British squadron that went up the Potomac—and after the British forces had retreated from the City of Washington. The disgrace of these last transactions, opens afresh the wounds of every pure American bosom…
>
> In what terms can we express our indignation against the conduct of the citizens of Alexandria? Thanks be to Almighty God! that this degraded town no longer forms a part of the state of *Virginia!* We would scorn to live in the same State with men who would stoop to kiss the feet of a British officer, and throw themselves upon his discretion: —To beg their houses at his hands, to solicit the mercy of the enemy, is such a meanness that none but men deeply contaminated by British Influence would have endured. Let the enemy have come; let him have glutted his cupidity by seizing every thing he could lay his hands on; but let no American compromise for the salvation of his houses by the sacrifice of his honor. If they were unable to have made any effectual resistance, they must submit—but they might at least have said, "Thou must take it if thou choosest; but I will not give it unto thee. We will enter into no compromise with the enemies of our country." How contemptible does the Committee of Vigi-

lance of Alexandria stand in comparison with the inflexible and brave men of Stonington!⁵⁸

The last sentence in Ritchie's tirade referred to the seaside town of Stonington, Connecticut. A few weeks previous, the town was threatened by British blockading ships with bombardment if they did not submit. The citizens bravely refused. Fortunately, the British bombardment was remarkably ineffectual. Stonington even brought an ancient cannon into action. While Ritchie commonly excoriated the "blue light" Federalists of New England, the conduct of this plucky Connecticut town excited his admiration. It also served as further grist for the propaganda mill. If citizens in disloyal Connecticut could bravely resist the British, what excuse did a town in a supposedly loyal section of the county have?

Critics of the capitulation referred to it sarcastically as "The Donation of Alexandria." An 1814 cartoon by William Charles, entitled "Johnny Bull and the Alexandrians," lampooned the conduct of the townsfolk. Two townsmen—in red coats, no less—on bended knee plead with a bull dressed as a British sailor, who brandishes the terms of surrender in one hand, and a cutlass in

"Johnny Bull and the Alexandrians." An 1814 cartoon by Scottish-born engraver William Charles lampoons the surrender of Alexandria to the British. The citizens cravenly cower while a nautically dressed anthropomorphic bull presents a list of British demands (Library of Congress).

another. One of the townsmen simpers, "Pray Mr. Bull, don't be too hard with us—You know we were always friendly, even in the time of our Embargo!"[59]

This statement was not just cartoonish exaggeration. In the years before canals and railroads, Alexandria was the principal port on the Potomac. During the Embargo, Alexandria exported large amounts of grain. Spain and Portugal were two of the biggest customers. Actually, the real customer was Wellington's Allied army. The trade dramatically increased in the years following the *Chesapeake-Leopard* affair, as the British military presence in the Iberian Peninsula also increased. In 1807, of 1,186,000 barrels exported, a mere 115,000 went to Spain and Portugal. By 1811, this had increased to 835,000 of 1,385,000 total exports. In 1813—when the United States and Britain were at war—972,500 barrels were sent to the Peninsula. In that year, Congress cracked down and put a halt to this profitable trade.[60] Wellington himself confirmed the importance of American grain, writing in May 1812, "All this part of the Peninsula has been living this year on American flour."[61]

These are the total figures for exports of American grain. How much did Alexandria contribute? These statistics were examined in 1932 in *The William and Mary Quarterly* by Arthur G. Peterson. Peterson's article actually covers the entire period prior to the Civil War, but his statistics for 1801–15 show the importance of the Iberian grain trade to Alexandria. During these years, Alexandria exported 1,154,778 barrels of flour, 323,920 bushels of wheat, and 592,954 barrels of corn.[62] Fifty-seven percent of the corn, 54 percent of the wheat, and 27 percent of the flour went to Portugal, while an additional 27 percent of the wheat and 24 percent of the corn went to Spain.[63] For 1811 alone, Alexandria's exports totaled $2 million.[64]

Congressional prohibition of the grain trade, combined with the British blockade, reduced Alexandria's exports to a measly $2,500 in 1814. Only 410 barrels of flour were exported that year.[65] The loss of export revenue was deeply felt. At the start of the war, the *Gazette* was a daily paper. Hard times meant fewer advertisements, forcing Snowden to scale back to a thrice-weekly publication from October 1, 1813, to April 13, 1815.[66] It is not surprising that many Alexandrians opposed the war due to economic interests. It is also not surprising they did not go out of their way to antagonize the British, especially when their city was left virtually defenseless.

Not all Virginia newspapers condemned the Alexandrians' conduct. The *Virginia Argus* felt the actions of the leading citizens justified under the circumstances. It reprinted without comment this statement from Simms:

> Against the attack of such an enemy was the town of Alexandria without any means of defence whatever. The people of the town were at his mercy, and compelled to yield to such terms as the "victor" might think fit to prescribe. If the members of the municipal authority and citizens of the town had given loose to the feelings of indignation which the occasion had excited, and had sacrificed the town and exposed

their wives and daughters to the wanton insults of an unrestrained enemy, they would have betrayed their trusts and deplored the consequences.[67]

The example of Hampton surely played a role in the Alexandrians' capitulation. Simms and his colleagues could not bear the thought of a brutal sack of their city. Protecting their families, rather than fighting to the death, was their top priority.

It is unfortunate that Samuel Snowden was unable to print a single issue of the *Gazette* during this period (August 23–September 8, copies from the *Herald* from this period have not survived).[68] When he resumed publication, Snowden initially responded to the attacks on his city with silence. But the continued virulence of the attacks forced Snowden to direct a response to Ritchie's "matchless impudence" and "unparalleled libel." Snowden was particularly concerned about a significant point of honor:

> It was not our intention to have taken any further notice of the falsehoods which are in circulation respecting the late occurrences at this town. In the *Enquirer* of the 10th instant, however, we find a story which we have thought it well enough to contradict.... We can assure the public that the British flag was *not hoisted at all* at Alexandria by any of its inhabitants.[69]

Continued attacks in the *National Intelligencer*, house organ of the Madison administration, prompted an indignant reply from "Impartiality" to the editors of the rival sheet. The anonymous editor criticized Gales and Seaton (co-editors of the *Intelligencer*) for trying the Alexandrians in the court of public opinion. "Impartiality" also reminded them that many Alexandrians—Federalists though they well may be—were also subscribers to the *National Intelligencer*. If their reputation continued to be dragged through the mud, perhaps they would no longer pay for the dubious privilege of reading such libel.[70]

Some felt that Alexandria was scapegoated for its Federalist sympathies. John S. Williams, an officer in the Washington militia, concluded that "reasons of state, therefore, and the good of the [Republican] party required that the people of Alexandria should be vilified as the authors of their own sufferings, and the cause of the enemy's triumph and gain."[71] The Madison administration's reputation was severely tarnished by "The Bladensburg Races" and the burning of Washington. Vilification of Alexandria deflected painful questions about the administration's competence in time of crisis. If political points could be scored for the Republicans by attacking a Federalist stronghold, that was a welcome benefit.

The *Norfolk Herald* confirmed the political motivation of the excoriation of Alexandria. It reminded its readers that from the outbreak of hostilities, Alexandria was "under the spell of British influence," and "the headquarters of Toryism in the southern section of the Union." The *Herald* declared that "had the commander of the British forces stipulated that a certain number of the heads of the town should appear in the most public place, and there lick the dust from his feet, we make no doubt, that it also would have been complied with."[72]

After the burning of Washington, the British returned to Tangier Island to refit. Once resupplied, they planned an amphibious assault on Baltimore. Before departing, the British commanders decided their men might benefit from some words of scripture. They turned to the Reverend Joshua Thomas. The Methodist preacher was already a legendary figure, known affectionately as "The Parson of the Islands." Thomas agreed to deliver a sermon. He stood before thousands of British servicemen, and loudly shouted, "Thou shalt not kill!" Anyone who lived by the sword would "perish by the sword." Thomas concluded that God personally informed him the British would never capture Baltimore. All those listening to his sermon should prepare for death.[73] Whether the British were moved by Thomas' sermon is unclear. It is also incredible they did not immediately clap him in irons. But as a beloved member of the island community, it was probably thought best to ignore the reverend's fire-and-brimstone message. Perhaps overconfidence provided insulation from religious criticism.

After the burning of Washington, Baltimore prepared for a British assault. With a population of 50,000, it was the third largest city in the United States. The majority of the inhabitants were solid Republicans, and it was a thriving privateering port. These facts made Baltimore a likely target. Fortunately, there were residents ready to meet the challenge. One of these was Samuel Smith, Revolutionary War veteran, U.S. senator, ardent Federalist, and no friend of the president. The 61-year-old Smith took command as a major general of the Maryland militia.

Baltimore was part of the 10th Military District, but the federal government did little to assist the beleaguered city. In fact, the War Department asked the Baltimoreans to return 19 artillery pieces, as it was feared the British might return to the burned-out capital. Smith refused, arguing that the guns belonged to the federal government, but the carriages they were mounted upon belonged to the City of Baltimore. When Brigadier General Winder, holding a federal commission, attempted to exert control, Smith defied him and continued to exercise command.[74]

In the absence of federal assistance, the Baltimoreans took matters into their own hands. All white men aged 16 to 50 were liable for militia duty, while older men still capable of shouldering a musket were encouraged to volunteer. All others stood ready to respond to fire alarms and other emergencies. Most Baltimoreans—whites, free blacks, and slaves—turned out to dig entrenchments. They dug a solid line of earthworks centered on Hampstead Hill (in Fells Point).[75]

Neighboring states also came to Baltimore's aid. Pennsylvania sent

8. "VIRGINIANS TO ARMS!"

"John Bull and the Baltimoreans." In contrast to the Alexandrians, William Charles shows the British retiring from the resolute Baltimoreans, with encouragement from their bayonets. General Ross falls mortally wounded from his horse in the background (Library of Congress).

approximately 1,100 militia. Virginia sent two militia brigades, commanded by Brigadier Generals Douglass and Singleton, totaling 2,641 men.[76] Smith now had approximately 14,000 men in the vicinity of Hampstead Hill. Most of these were Marylanders, but they were grateful for the assistance rendered by the Old Dominion and the Keystone State.

On September 12, the British landed ten miles below Baltimore at North Point. The ensuing battle was a draw, but Ross was killed. Colonel Brooke assumed command. The British now turned to the Royal Navy to neutralize the forts defending Baltimore. Fort McHenry now found itself squarely in the crosshairs, on a collision course with immortality.

Fort McHenry was commanded by Major George Armistead, a true son of the Old Dominion. The fort was part of the First System of American fortifications, and built between 1799 and 1805. It was a star-shaped fort with five bastions, armed with 30 guns. Three water batteries built during the war were armed with 36-pounder French naval guns. A 600-yard-wide boom from the fort to Lazaretto Point blocked the entrance to the harbor.[77] Five hundred twenty-one men with three 18-pounders were stationed at the Lazaretto Battery.[78] Behind the boom, 400 seamen in 11 armed barges stood ready.[79] At Fort McHenry, Armistead commanded nearly 600 men—a handful of regular artillerymen, militia artillerymen, sailors, and sea fencibles.[80] The Sea Fencibles were locally-recruited seamen, organized into a federalized militia.

Armistead anticipated an attack on Ft. McHenry as early as 1813. He therefore requested from General Smith "a flag so large that the British will have no difficulty in seeing it from a distance."[81] Armistead's wish was granted; on September 13, 1814, a 30-by-42-foot "garrison flag" waved above the star-shaped fort.

The British bombardment of Ft. McHenry commenced at 6:30 a.m. on September 13, 1814. For the next 25 hours, British vessels pounded the American fort with rockets and mortars. The Americans responded in kind, but their guns lacked the range to strike back effectively. The British ships were firing at extreme range. They did not risk coming closer for fear of running aground. Nevertheless, it was a nerve-wracking experience for the defenders of Ft. McHenry. Captain Joseph Hopper Nicholson of the Baltimore Fencibles later wrote, "We were like pigeons tied by the legs to be shot at."[82]

Meanwhile, the British army made an attempt on the defenses on Hampstead Hill. A gap was discovered on the American right flank. Douglass' Virginia militia brigade covered the gap.[83] Brooke was under orders from Cochrane not to attack unless absolutely certain of success. Seeing his best chance evaporate, Brooke declined to attempt a frontal assault. He made preparations to withdraw.

For the Americans on Hampstead Hill, it was a long, anxious night. Rain and fog obscured the view of Fort McHenry. Rather more ominously, the fort had stopped firing. John Dagg, later a prominent Baptist theologian, was a young Virginia militiaman in Douglass' brigade. He recalled the tension as dawn approached: "At first dawn, every eye was directed towards the Fort, to see whether the American banner still waved there; and when the morning mists had sufficiently dispersed, we were filled with exultation at beholding the stars and stripes still floating in the breeze."[84] The British soldiers returned to their ships, and the last of the enemy fleet left the Patapsco River by September 17. Baltimore was saved!

The ever-aggressive Admiral Cockburn was disappointed that the army did not attempt to storm Hampstead Hill. Colonel Brooke explained to his superiors that while his troops might well have carried the heights and captured Baltimore, the prize would not be worth the heavy losses.[85] In his diary, he was more candid: "If I took the place, I should have been the greatest man in England. If I lost, my military character was gone forever."[86] For a junior officer like George Gleig, the orders to retreat were mortifying. In his memoirs, he bitterly recalled the frustration, as veteran troops were forced to withdraw from unfinished fieldworks. True, the Americans substantially outnumbered the British, but "a compact body of veterans, well-disciplined and orderly, are at all times an overmatch for whole crowds of raw levies."[87] Gleig's words are the opinions of an energetic young subaltern, a veteran of the Peninsular War, who was accustomed to triumph over the French. He had nothing but contempt for Cousin Jonathan, and was certain the small but veteran British force would triumph. As for Brooke, the burden of command is a heavy one. He cannot be faulted for not making the attempt on the American defenses, when it was not a matter of do-or-die.

The majority of the Virginians were passive observers to the dramatic events in Baltimore. But their Maryland compatriots were grateful for their assistance. General Winder praised the men of Douglass' brigade for their patriotism and obedience in the face of the enemy. As for Colonel Taylor's 1st Regiment, "that he only wanted an occasion to prove himself and them the worthy coadjutors of their countrymen.... Those gallant Virginians will have the consolation of believing they have essentially contributed to its safety."[88]

The American defense of Baltimore was a triumph. But it was a state and local victory, rather than a federal one. Militiamen comprised the majority of the forces defending the city. Federal support was decidedly lacking. If the Baltimoreans had not taken the initiative, perhaps their city would have met the same fate as Washington. For the Virginians on the scene, it was a point well taken. In times of crisis, the federal government was not to be relied upon. The states themselves must control their own destiny.

After the failed British attempt to capture Baltimore, many Virginians thought the enemy would make another attempt on Richmond. In fact, Admiral Cochrane had already ruled this out. In mid–July, he noted in a letter to Viscount Dundas, First Lord of the Admiralty, that the trickiness of the riverine approaches to Richmond made it not worth the effort. As for Norfolk, with as many as 10,000 militiamen stationed there, it was too strongly defended, as the British were not waging a war of conquest.[89]

Still, it was felt that Norfolk needed reinforcements. In late September, at least 2,700 men of the Norfolk garrison were on the sick list, confirming the city's reputation as an unhealthy location.[90] Governor Barbour requested assistance from Governor Hawkins of North Carolina, who dispatched two militia regiments of riflemen—nearly 2,000 men—to the beleaguered city. A grateful Barbour exclaimed, "The mingled blood of the heroes of Virginia and North Carolina is the cement of our connexion."[91] These were stirring words, but the fact that Barbour asked for assistance from a sister state indicates the Old Dominion was stretched to the breaking point. The fact that Barbour did not ask for reinforcements from the federal government is also quite revealing. Unfortunately, the North Carolina troops arrived poorly clad and supplied, adding to the burdens borne by the Old Dominion, who had to provide arms and equipment.[92]

The winter of 1814–15 saw the largest number of deaths among the Virginia militia, as hundreds succumbed to disease.[93] By the end of 1814, the number of men defending Norfolk had dwindled to 6,636, with over one-third on the sick list.[94] The North Carolina militia was also hit hard. In the 1st Regiment, ten men died from measles in a single day. By February 1815, this regiment, which entered service 1,000 strong, had lost 212 men from disease.[95] Bacteria proved a greater menace than British bullets, but the hundreds of men laid low from illness left senior officers wondering how they would resist a determined British assault.

During the early 19th century, armies routinely went into winter quarters, to renew the conquest in fairer weather. The Potomac froze, but the British continued raiding. The first week of December brought a series of amphibious assaults on the Rappahannock. On December 2, 500 British landed at Tappahannock. The heavily outnumbered militia retreated, sped on their way by Congreve rockets. The British burned the courthouse, jail, custom house, and a granary. They also plundered several homes, and departed the next day.[96]

The British landed at in Lancaster County on December 6. Royal Navy captain Robert Barrie commanded approximately 360 men, including a detachment of Colonial Marines. He received intelligence that 600 Virginia militiamen with two guns were seven miles away, at Farnham Church. As the British came within range, they received "several ineffectual Shot" from the cannons. A small force kept the Virginians occupied while the main body moved left through thick woods. The British hit the Virginians' left flank. The militia fired a volley and took to their heels, but their "superior speed and knowledge of the Country enabled him to escape." The Virginians lost two wounded and 13 missing. The British suffered no casualties, but 12 men got "beastly Drunk" and disappeared in the woods. They were left behind. Seventy slaves—valued at $31,500—took the opportunity to escape to freedom.[97] Twenty of them were rescued by the Colonial Marines, who found them handcuffed by their masters to a large tree.[98]

Meanwhile, on the opposite side of the Rappahannock, Captain John Sheridan led a smaller raid on Jones Point in King and Queen County. During this raid, two British stole a barge and deserted. They warned the inhabitants that the British planned to attack Urbanna, downriver from Jones Point in Middlesex County. The next morning, the British attempted to recover their barge. The Virginians anticipated such a move. Thirty-eight militiamen sprang from ambush. They kept up a lively fire, but British reinforcements arrived. As their ammunition dwindled, the militia withdrew. The British presumably retrieved the stolen barge and departed. The Virginians suffered no casualties, and reported several British killed and wounded, though there is no mention of losses in British sources.[99] Militiamen mustered to defend Urbanna, but the expected assault did not occur.[100]

8. "VIRGINIANS TO ARMS!"

The troops on duty that last winter of the war did not see the end in sight. They did not expect positive results from the peace negotiations. On February 11, 1815, Virginia militia lieutenant colonel Armistead Thomson Mason wrote his brother Jack from Norfolk. The young officer expected hard fighting that summer. He excoriated Congress, accusing them of shirking their responsibilities, leaving the country "at the mercy of the enemy." In contrast, the state governments had "acted with more firmness and taken upon themselves its [the nation's] defence."[101] Mason did not look forward to the coming of fair weather, but grimly resolved to do his duty.

The year 1814 was momentous, full of minor triumphs and major tragedies. Severe cracks in the national foundation appeared which threatened to tear the Republic apart. As 1815 began, Americans—especially Virginians—expected hard fighting against an experienced opponent. Would the beleaguered state and the young nation survive?

9

The Aftermath

Unbeknownst to Major Mason and his comrades, the peace commissioners signed the Treaty of Ghent on Christmas Eve 1814. It took several weeks for word to reach America. Also, the treaty would not become binding until ratified by the U.S. Senate. When news of the treaty reached the United States, the Senate quickly ratified it.

Most Virginia newspapers carried an official announcement of the end of hostilities on February 20, 1815.[1] The news was greeted with joy and relief. In Richmond, citizens celebrated by holding an Illumination on March 2 (the delay was due to inclement weather). The *Virginia Patriot* described the joyous occasion:

> The Illumination for the return of peace, which took place in this city, on Thursday evening last, was by far the most general and brilliant, we ever witnessed, on any occasion.—To attempt to give an account of the various transparent buildings which graced the windows of the different houses in the Brick-Row, would be vain indeed; nor will we mention a few, because discrimination would appear invidious, where all united *"heart and soul"* in the celebration. Among the transparencies, many were emblematic of peace; and the return of the *"golden days"* of commerce and general prosperity.[2]

The report also mentions several transparencies of notable military and political figures, but it is the heartfelt wishes for peace and prosperity which stand out the most. British objectives in the Chesapeake may have been limited, but Virginians certainly felt the impact of the war.

What were the costs of the War of 1812 for Virginia? It is appropriate to address the human costs first. According to Butler, approximately 65,000 men served at least one tour in the Virginia militia during the war. Perhaps 50 died in combat, but between 500 and 600 died of disease. (These figures do not include the Petersburg Volunteers and the Virginia Brigade.)[3] While the total number of battle deaths was low, these citizen soldiers saw a significant amount of active service. Eshelman, Sheads, and Hickey identify three battles (Craney Island, Hampton, and White House), 27 skirmishes, and 11 raids on

9. The Aftermath   141

Virginia soil.⁴ Virginians also served outside the state, notably at the sieges of Fort Meigs and in the defense of Baltimore. Overall however, the performance of Virginia's militia was mediocre. Time and again, the shortcomings of militia was revealed, but in the years following the war, the size of the regular U.S. Army remained small, with many wartime regiments disbanded. The Battle of New Orleans created what scholars call the "militia myth." Jackson's army of ragtag militiamen achieved a lopsided victory over some of the finest soldiers in Europe.⁵ Politicians saw little need to maintain a large regular army, when patriotic citizens would answer their country's call in times of need.

Continued inclement weather delayed the British departure from the Chesapeake, but by spring, they were leaving. British forces left the Chesapeake in the spring. In March, they abandoned their base on Tangier Island. Under orders from Cockburn, all ordnance and stores were removed. All escaped slaves who reach the island prior to the ratification of the treaty on February 17 were also entitled to free passage. For many years, Fort Albion remained as a reminder of the British occupation. In the 20th century, rising sea levels submerged the fort and its adjoining cemetery.⁶ After Waterloo, Cockburn brought Napoleon to his place of final exile, the island of St. Helena. He remained in the Royal Navy, and was promoted to Admiral of the Fleet in 1851. Cockburn died in 1853 after a long and distinguished career.⁷ Though vilified by Americans, he remained proud of his exploits in the Chesapeake. The most enduring image of Cockburn is a full-length portrait in front of a burning Washington, D.C.

Charles Napier returned to command the 50th Foot. From 1819 to 1830, he served as a colonial administrator in the Ionian Islands. Though popular with the inhabitants, disagreements with his superiors led to his dismissal. After a temporary retirement, Napier commanded the Northern District of England. In 1839, this region was in ferment, due to the Chartist movement. Napier diffused the crisis, displaying a great deal of compassion in the process. In the 1840s, Napier fought the warlike Baluchi in Sind, and emerged victorious.⁸ Napier died in 1853. There is a fine statue of him in Trafalgar Square, which stands a short distance from Nelson's Column.

After the Battle of Baltimore, Lieutenant George Gleig took part in the New Orleans campaign, where he was wounded. Postwar, he resumed his divinity studies at Oxford, taking holy orders in 1820. While serving as a priest, Gleig also wrote several books, including *A subaltern in America*. Gleig was appointed chaplain-general of the forces in 1844. This was the top chaplain's post in the British army, a position he held until 1875. Gleig died in 1888, at the age of 92.

Defeat at the Battle of the Thames put Major General Henry Procter's career in jeopardy. In late 1814 he was court martialed in Montreal. The court acknowledged Procter faced "extraordinary circumstances," but found him "erroneous in judgment and deficient in energy." The court recommended a suspension of six months without pay and a public reprimand. The verdict was read before all the regiments of the British army. This effectively ended Procter's career.[9] In 1822, Procter published an article in the London *Quarterly Review*, entitled "Campaigns in the Canadas." In this article, Procter told the truth as he saw it, claiming he was scapegoated by his commanding officer, Sir George Prevost. Prevost, whose career had also ended under a cloud, was unable to respond, having passed away in 1816. Procter died soon after publication of the article, at the age of 59.[10] Pierre Berton characterized Procter best when he wrote:

> To the Americans he remains a monster, to the Canadians a coward. He is neither— merely a victim of circumstances, a brave officer but weak, capable enough in moments of stress, a man of modest pretensions, unable to make the quantum leap that distinguishes the outstanding leader from the run-of-the-mill: the quality of being able in moments of adversity to exceed one's own capabilities. The prisoner of events beyond his control, Procter dallied and equivocated until he is crushed. His career is ended.[11]

In August 1813, Brigadier General Robert Barraud Taylor declined a brigadier general's commission in the regular army. He resigned his militia commission in February 1814, after one year in command at Norfolk. In January 1815, Taylor was promoted to major general in the Virginia militia, but he did not see active service. When Lafayette visited Yorktown in 1824, Taylor delivered a speech. An observer wrote, "In all my time I have never heard such eloquence [nor] saw so many men in tears." In 1831, Taylor received an appointment as judge of the General Court and Superior Court of Law and Chancery for the 1st Virginia Circuit. He died April 13, 1834, aged 60.[12]

The Battle of Craney Island was a proud moment in the defense of Virginia. The successful defense saved the city of Norfolk. It was also characterized by effective cooperation between the Virginia militia, regular army, and navy. Unfortunately, during the postwar period an ugly battle was waged over who deserved the greatest credit for the victory. The lingering bitterness became a controversy in print. Over the next 30 years, various participants of the battle squabbled over the laurels. In 1848, the Virginia General Assembly appointed a select committee to examine the evidence.[13] In its concluding remarks, the committee's report declared:

> The repulse of the British forces, therefore, at Craney Island on the 22d of June 1813, was the result of the united skill and gallantry of Virginia volunteers and of American sailors, and let each enjoy the proud satisfaction of having contributed to the glory and defense of our common country without seeking to detract from each other their just shares in the triumphs of that eventful day.[14]

These were fair-minded words, but as the years passed, the Navy received sole credit for victory at Craney Island. Both Alfred Thayer Mahan and Theodore Roosevelt followed this interpretation in their works on the War of 1812. In 1986, retired army officer John H. Hallahan set the record straight in *The Battle of Craney Island: A Matter of Credit*.

Postwar, a Congressional committee investigated the burning of Washington and the capitulation of Alexandria. The committee did not issue a final report.[15] Why did the committee withhold its verdict, when public feeling against the Alexandrians was running high? The simple answer is that condemnation of the Alexandrians' conduct was not politically expedient. With the return of peace, anger among the populace rapidly dissipated. The successful defense of Baltimore and the stunning victory at New Orleans ended the war on a triumphant note. Furthermore, the committee investigated *both* the burning of Washington *and* the capitulation of Alexandria. The committee might well condemn the Alexandrians, but in the process, it might also expose mismanagement on the part of the Madison administration.

One might argue that by censuring the Alexandrians, the Republicans would score political points against the Federalists. But the Federalists largely discredited themselves by holding the Hartford (Connecticut) Convention (December 1814–January 1815). The most radical of the delegates actually proposed secession from the Union. The Hartford Convention almost singlehandedly destroyed the Federalists, leaving the Democratic-Republicans ascendant. The period that followed—roughly coinciding with Monroe's Presidency—is known as the Era of Good Feelings, partisan rancor was relatively absent.

What of the allegations that the Alexandrians traded with the enemy? The city certainly profited by the grain trade with the Iberian Peninsula, but they were far from alone in subverting the Embargo. During the war itself, some Americans sold goods directly to the British. In the Chesapeake, the Royal Navy received much of its victuals from American farmers. Some of these unscrupulous individuals were actually in the local militia! A British officer described a typical transaction:

> The plan agreed on was this: they were to drive [their cattle] down to a certain point, where we were to land and take possession; for the inhabitants were all militiamen, and having too much patriotism to sell food to "King George's men," they used to say, "put the money under such a stone or tree," pointing to it, "and then we can pick it up, and say we found it."[16]

Exposing such collaboration would bring nothing but grief and recriminations. In time, resentment against the Alexandrians faded. Popular historian Benson Lossing, who was not afraid to give his opinion, was sympathetic to the Alexandrians' plight. In his *Pictorial Field Book of the War of 1812* (1868), Lossing stated that the British allowed the citizens only one hour to submit to "hard and humiliating terms.... They were powerless, and were compelled to submit."[17]

Postwar, Samuel Snowden continued as editor and publisher of the *Alexandria Gazette*, which resumed as a daily. In 1829, he proudly looked back on a long and distinguished career, noting that perhaps three or four other men had "continued so long as active members of the editorial corps."[18] Snowden continued as editor until his death in 1831. His family continued to run the paper until 1911. The *Alexandria Gazette* remained in publication until 1974. It is one of the oldest continuously published newspapers in the United States.

Thomas Ritchie, founder and editor of the *Richmond Enquirer*, continued to be an influential journalist, and a great favorite of Thomas Jefferson. He died on July 3, 1854. His funeral was attended by President Franklin Pierce, cabinet secretaries, and many senators and representatives.[19] His biographer, Charles Henry Ambler, wrote that "Regardless of party affiliations the press of the whole country hastened to pay tribute to the venerable dead. His political enemies ... had never hated him personally."[20] Ambler published his biography in 1913. He was one century removed from the political strife of 1812–15, so perhaps he minimized the animosity Ritchie generated. He certainly thought himself a great patriot. Through the pages of the *Enquirer*, Ritchie excoriated enemies of the Republic—and the Republican Party—which in his mind were one in the same.

One of the highest priorities among Virginians was filing compensation claims with the federal government. Virginians filed $1.8 million in claims, the most among all the states in the Union.[21] William Wirt, the attorney/artillerist, and John Chew were appointed on December 23, 1815, by Governor Wilson Cary Nicholas (elected December 1, 1814) as claims commissioners. Though Wirt and Chew worked diligently, the claims issue dragged on throughout the century, and was not finally resolved by Congress until the passage of an Omnibus Claims Bill in 1903![22] The frustration caused by decades of delay must have been considerable.

Virginians also sought the return of runaway slaves. During the war, approximately 5,000 slaves from the Chesapeake escaped to freedom. Several hundred served honorably in the British Corps of Colonial Marines. James Monroe actually sent three agents in spring 1815 to Bermuda and Halifax. The agents sought British cooperation in returning the former slaves. The British, to their credit, refused to cooperate. Not surprisingly, the runaways responded negatively to direct appeals from the agents to return to their former masters. The agents returned home empty-handed.[23] A rumor was spread that the British resold the runaways into slavery in the West Indies. This rumor was repeated as fact by Benson Lossing in his *Pictorial Field Book of the War of 1812*. In reality, most found a new life in the maritime provinces of Canada, where their descendants can be found to this day.[24]

Virginia veterans of the Northwestern campaign waited 40 years for full

9. The Aftermath

compensation for their service. When they mustered out in fall 1813, the Petersburg Volunteers marched to Cleveland. They expected to meet paymaster James G. Chalmers, who would distribute the company's back pay. After a week, when Chalmers had not arrived, most of the volunteers journeyed to Pittsburgh, in the hope that Chalmers was there. After another ten days of fruitless waiting, the uncompensated veterans headed home. It was later learned that Chalmers lost the company's pay gambling. Apparently, he was not punished for his crime. On March 3, 1853, Congress earmarked $10,334.31 for surviving volunteers or for next of kin for the dead.[25]

Alfred M. Lorrain returned to Petersburg, but felt a spiritual calling. He joined the Methodist Church, and became a minister, first in New Orleans. Eventually, he returned to Ohio, where he became a circuit rider of some renown. At the end of his life, he wrote his memoirs, entitled *The Helm, the Sword, and the Cross*. Though he experienced many adventures at sea and as a member of the Petersburg Volunteers, it is his life as a preacher that comprises the bulk of Lorrain's narrative.

Brigadier General Joel Leftwich returned to his plantation in Bedford County in spring 1813. Despite criticism from Captain Wood, Barbour retained confidence in the militia general. In July 1814, Barbour asked Leftwich to command a brigade in the defense of Richmond, declaring that "the confidence which will be inspired by your leading the forces now called out will be equal to any army in itself."[26] It would be impossible to reject command after receiving such a ringing endorsement. Leftwich reported to Richmond, but in October his brigade headed to Maryland, for British raiders were still a threat. Leftwich's brigade remained in Maryland until November, when they returned home. This concluded Leftwich's service in the War of 1812. Postwar he continued his militia career, and was promoted to major general on January 10, 1822.[27] Leftwich lived a long, satisfying life as a country gentleman. He also won many shooting contests, and competed well into his 70s. Joel Leftwich passed away on October 20, 1846, at the age of 86.[28]

As for Leftwich's Virginia Brigade, a federal law passed in 1850 allowed veterans (at least four months of service) to apply for bounty land warrants. A law passed in 1855 entitled veterans to 160 acres.[29] From surviving evidence, it appears that several applicants had settled in Ohio, though the total number of claims is unclear. It is frustrating to read that it took Congress 40 years to properly reward veterans. To be sure, many men did not survive to receive this compensation.

Term limits meant James Barbour had to leave office in December 1814. But Virginia's war governor found immediate employment as a U.S. senator. He served for ten years, including one year (1819) as president pro tempore. In 1825, President John Quincy Adams appointed him secretary of war. He served in this capacity until 1828, when he became U.S. minister to the United

Kingdom. In 1829, he retired from public life. The "war governor" died in 1842 at the age of 66.

Poor William Tatham never realized his ambitions. By the end of the war, he bitterly reflected that at the age of 64 he had nothing to show for his efforts "but a cold public countenance." The government rewarded lesser men, and seemed determined to "keep back my long and painful exertions, investigations, and discoveries."[30] He took to drink, and hectored state legislators to support his projects. They did their best to ignore him. President Monroe eventually appointed him director of a new U.S. arsenal near Richmond, but Tatham was too far gone. On February 22, 1819, during Washington's Birthday celebrations, he stepped in front of a cannon, and was blown to pieces.[31] But Tatham received postwar vindication. His plans for canals became a part of the Intracoastal Waterway.

The return of peace led to a postwar boom. Cash crops such as tobacco sold for record prices. In Richmond, flour sold for $15 a barrel. Speculation abounded, as consumer confidence soared. Real estate prices went through the roof. In the capital, Samuel Mordecai reported a tenfold increase in property values. "Corn-fields, Slashes, and Piney thickets were laid out into streets and squares," as Richmond's population dramatically increased.[32]

The boom received a sharp check in 1816. The eruption of Mount Tambora in the Dutch East Indies led to "the year without a summer." Americans experienced hard frosts and even snowfalls during the summer months. At Monticello in September, Jefferson wrote to Albert Gallatin:

> We have had the most extraordinary year of drought & cold ever known in the history of America. In June, instead of 3¾ I. our average rain for that month, we had only ⅓ of an inch, in Aug. instead of 9⅙ I. our average, we had only 8/10 of an inch. and it still continues. the summer too has been as cold as a moderate winter. in every state North of this there has been frost in every month of the year; in this state we had none in June and July. but those of Aug. killed much corn over the mountains. the crop of corn thro' the Atlantic states will probably be less than ⅓ of an ordinary one, that of tobo [tobacco] still less, and if mean quality. the crop of wheat was middling in quantity, but excellent in quality. but every species of bread grain taken together will not be sufficient for the subsistence of the inhabitants; and the exportation of flour, already begun by the indebted and the improvident, to whatsoever degree it may be carried, will be exactly so much taken from the mouths of our own citizens.[33]

Jefferson's plantations had a poor harvest that year, which drove him further into debt.

When examining statistics on U.S. exports, much of the impact of 1816 is not apparent until 1817. In 1816, U.S. exports totaled $81,920,452. Virginia accounted for $8,212,860 of this total. In 1817, U.S. exports actually increased to $87,671,569, but Virginia's share dropped to $5,621,442. This is a 31.6 percent decline.[34]

9. The Aftermath

There was some recovery in 1817; with U.S. wheat exports totaling 7,492,000 bushels. Despite the impact of "the year with no summer," from June 1816 to June 1817, Alexandria managed to export 209,000 barrels of flour. According to economic historian Arthur G. Peterson, this was "the highest recorded until 1831." But Peterson also notes that Alexandria's flour exports perhaps never again reached the level attained just before and just after the War of 1812."[35] This is a reference to the Panic of 1819, in which the Old Dominion was particularly hard hit.

After the Napoleonic Wars, Great Britain and the nations of Europe drastically reduced military spending. They also put tighter controls on their supply of specie. The United States, in the meantime, was moving to increase credit. Foreign demand for American agricultural products also decreased. American agricultural exports sharply declined; from 1818 to 1821, the nation's exports declined by 42 percent. Virginia was particularly hard hit, experiencing a 56 percent decline.[36] Many farmers were ruined, but the effects were felt beyond the agricultural sector. Businesses also suffered from the economic downturn.

In May 1819, Richmond resident Benjamin Brand wrote his friend George Caskaden, a former retailer who left the capital for Alabama. Brand vividly captured the Panic's impact on business in Richmond:

> You have been lucky in removing from this place.... We have gloomy times here—many protests [failures] have taken place since I last saw you, and many more soon expected.... Many have backed out of business ... at this time there is very little credit business done. Confidence in each others ability to pay is very slight.[37]

In Norfolk that June, John Cowper painted a similarly gloomy picture. He wrote that "The failures here have been as bad as possible."[38] Many businesses went bankrupt or drastically scaled back operations, causing unemployment to soar.

In western Virginia, Jefferson reported auctions of debtors' farms for owing a single year's worth of rent. To pay off debts, property sold at rock bottom prices. Slaves were included in this property. The former president expressed shock when he heard of "good slaves selling for one hundred dollars, good horses for five dollars."[39] He anticipated "local insurrections against these horrible sacrifices of property."

Eighteen twenty did not see much improvement in Virginia. In Richmond, Francis Walker Gilmer observed, "Things here grow worse & worse—the merchants all failed—the town ruined—the banks broke—the Treasury empty—commerce gone, confidence gone, character gone."[40] In Norfolk, commerce was strangled by Congress, in an attempt to open the British West Indies to American trade. This move was supported by mercantile interests in the North, but the Virginia Tidewater was already doing a profitable trade, with grain and naval stores for West Indian rum, molasses, and sugar. As Thomas J. Wertenbaker, chronicler of Norfolk put it, "The only way to secure reciprocity was to retaliate with prohibitive duties or with non-intercourse, and Norfolk had had its fill of both."[41]

Congress—including Virginia representatives—approved the new restrictions. As many feared, the Tidewater felt the negative effects. By late 1821, a visitor to Norfolk reported that the citizens were unanimous in their demands to repeal the restrictive legislation. By December, the city government passed formal resolutions against the policy, declaring it "highly injurious to Norfolk and this district."[42] But the restrictive measures remained in place.

Economic historian Clyde A. Haulman summarized the political impact of the Panic of 1819 on the Old Dominion: "Thus, the Panic of 1819 provided additional rationale for disengagement from an interventionist role for the state and cemented Virginia's opposition to nationalist policies."[43] Alan Taylor noted that Virginia "narrowly and reluctantly" ratified the Constitution. They did so largely based on Madison's assurances that the Old Dominion would increase its status in the new federalist system. It was especially galling that under Madison, the federal government failed to defend the state of Virginia. If a president from Virginia could not provide for his home state, what would happen when the White House was occupied by a man from another section of the country?[44] Taylor concludes:

> While Virginians began the war as champions of the Union, they ended it with powerful new doubts. Feeling betrayed for their wartime nationalism, the Virginians sought support from the other southern states against the distrusted northerners, who seemed poised to seize control of the Union. The South began to become Virginia's nation during the War of 1812, but this was a slow process that did not fully mature until the secession of 1861.[45]

While it was a slow process, it indeed seems a logical progression, when one recalls the origins of the Principles of '98. Also known as the Kentucky and Virginia Resolutions, they were co-authored by Thomas Jefferson and James Madison. These men are revered as Founding Fathers, and proponents of "a more perfect Union." But the Principles of '98 sowed the seeds of disunion. They argued that individual states could judge the constitutionality of federal legislation. This concept is often associated with South Carolina due to the nullification crisis of the early 1830s. But the roots of disunion proceeded from the minds of two men who did so much to unite the states.

Postwar, Virginia lost its position as a leader in national politics. While this was partly due to changing demographics, it was also a voluntary abdication, as Virginians became increasingly insular in their allegiances. When President Monroe left office, it spelled the end of the Virginia Dynasty. It also marked a decline in the influence of the Tidewater elite, as western Vir-

9. The Aftermath

ginians achieved universal white male suffrage. While Harrison, Tyler, and Taylor were scions of the First Families of Virginia, they made a minimal impression during their terms. Harrison died after one month in office. His Vice President, John Tyler, jumped parties when he joined the Whig ticket. This made his erstwhile Democratic colleagues reluctant to work with him. Zachary Taylor spent his life in the army. It is said he never voted until the Election of 1848. As for the Compromise of 1850, that was brokered by the titans of the Legislative Branch: Clay, Calhoun, and Webster. Taylor also died in office after serving 18 months. It was not until Woodrow Wilson that Virginia once again saw a native son elected to the Presidency who made a major mark on the national—and international—stage.

On February 18, 1815, President Madison announced the signing of the Treaty of Ghent to Congress. He declared that the treaty brought to an end "with peculiar felicity, a campaign signalized by the most brilliant successes."[46] Madison declared that the successful outcome was "the natural result of the wisdom of the Legislative Councils, of the patriotism of the people, of the public spirit of the militia, and of the valor of the military and Naval forces of the country."[47] When considering the evidence, Madison's assertions appear grossly unfounded.

How could the president claim with a straight face that the war was characterized by brilliant successes? Had he forgotten the embarrassing attempts to conquer Canada? What about the burning of Washington? Surely the ruins of the White House and the Capitol gave Madison pause. The successful defense of Baltimore owed more to its citizens than to assistance from the federal government. The great victory at New Orleans came after the signing of the treaty. By 1816, *Niles' Register* boasted that the United States "did virtually dictate the treaty of Ghent."[48] Apparently the president was not the only man capable of self-delusion.

As for the argument that the war was won thanks to the wisdom of government, Federalists and many Republicans would argue otherwise. The acrimonious debates in Congress and the war of words waged in the newspapers bore witness to opposition to the war and criticism of its conduct.

In his February 18 announcement to Congress, Madison declared that "the late war, although reluctantly declared by congress, had become a necessary resort, to assert the rights and independence of the nation."[49] These rights were often declared to be "seamen's rights and fair trade." When he examined the articles of the Treaty of Ghent, Thomas Jefferson, though glad for peace, noted "no provision being made against the impressment of our seamen, it is in fact but an Armistice, to be terminated by the first act of impressment committed on an American citizen."[50] The lack of an article dealing with impressment is telling. When the Treaty of Ghent was signed, Napoleon was in exile on Elba. Though he returned in 1815, Napoleon suffered ultimate defeat at Waterloo in June. At the end of the Napoleonic Wars, the Royal Navy drastically reduced the numbers of ships and seamen. During the so-called "long peace" that followed, impressment was no longer needed. This meant that American sailors could ply their trade without fear of forcible removal.

The lack of an article on impressment in the Treaty of Ghent signalizes this change. It also makes one wonder if war over this issue was truly necessary, with the alleged *casus belli* disappearing overnight. For political opponents as well as historians, it also raises the question if this was the true reason for war.

The "golden days" of peace and prosperity longed for by the *Virginia Patriot* proved short-lived. Many Virginians surely longed for the halcyon days before the Embargo and the war.

Conclusion

Works of history often reflect the period in which they are written. Historians view the past through the lens of the present; though "presentism" is to be avoided when making judgments, current events often influence the choice of topic. That is certainly the case with this book. Its origins date from the presidency of George W. Bush. Did 9/11 and the Second Iraq War bear any similarities to past events in American history? If parallels could be drawn between the past and the present did any of these lines pass through the state of Virginia (the place of residence of this writer)? While the present never exactly mimics the past, even a cursory examination identified similarities between the early 19th and 21st centuries; chiefly, the War of 1812. This prompted further research on the subject.

The response to the *Chesapeake-Leopard* affair bears striking similarities to September 11, 2001. While a far greater number of Americans died on 9/11, both events were greeted with widespread shock and outrage. In 1807, as in 2001, American citizens stood united. In Virginia, even the opposition press supported President Jefferson. They even offered strategic advice in the event of war with Britain.

Presidents Thomas Jefferson and George W. Bush squandered the political capital generated by their respective traumas. Bush pushed for war with Iraq, which had nothing to do with 9/11. Jefferson decided against war in 1807, and pursued a policy of economic embargo. The Embargo hurt the United States more than Great Britain or France. Virginians certainly felt the negative effects. Many ignored the restrictions; Alexandrians profited by exporting grain to Spain and Portugal, where the principal customer was Wellington's army.

When the United States finally declared war in 1812, many Americans questioned the official line of "sailors' rights and free trade." If these issues were so important, why did the United States not go to war in 1807? The *Chesapeake-Leopard* affair offered a simple, straightforward reason for war. Five years of delay damaged the American economy, and did nothing to improve the nation's military strength. The opposition declared that the United States was serving the cause of Napoleonic France. In 1812, the Napoleonic Wars were reaching their climax. Britain had its hands full, and the United States stabbed them in the back, doing the bidding of a tyrant.

James Madison hailed from the Old Dominion. It might be safely assumed that fellow Virginians enthusiastically supported their President. In fact, there was significant opposition in the state to "Mr. Madison's war." Many among the opposition called themselves Federalists, who were given a new lease on life thanks to wrongheaded Republican policies such as the Embargo. But a significant number of Madison's opponents were dissident Republicans, who did not feel constrained by party loyalty. In the early 21st century, one might be inclined to declare Virginia a red state, but the reality is more complex. Significant portions of the state, especially the cities, are quite blue. In 1812 Virginia (including present-day West Virginia) was a patchwork of differing political allegiances.

Despite significant opposition among Virginians, James Madison won a second term in 1812. But the election in Virginia was characterized by low voter turnout, a familiar concept in the present day. Many Virginia Federalists felt that rules such as the General Ticket Law gave an unfair advantage to Republicans, making the contest hopeless. At the same time, Virginia Federalists did not rally to the support of dissident Republican DeWitt Clinton, Madison's primary opponent in the election. Madison did not defeat Clinton by a particularly wide margin (128 to 89 electoral votes). Perhaps the support of Virginia Federalists, combined with voters from other states (such as Pennsylvania), would have resulted in a Clinton victory. But Virginia Federalists nominated their own candidate, Rufus King of New York. To them, Clinton was just another Republican who pushed for a war of territorial expansion at Britain's expense. King was closer to their principles, but was unlikely to defeat Madison. Present-day voters often face the same dilemma. Which candidate is the lesser of two evils? Is a third party candidate running, and do they have a realistic chance of victory? Low voter turnout, even with more citizens eligible to vote, unlike 1812, reflects widespread frustration with the electoral system.

Though stymied at the polls, opponents of the War of 1812 in Virginia expressed their discontent in print. At the same time, editors of papers loyal to Madison launched vigorous counterattacks. These newspapers made no pretense at objectivity. They engaged in a lively war of words, reflecting the importance of journalism in the early Republic. Unlike the present day, which is dominated by media conglomerates selling prepackaged consensus, early 19th-century newspapers operated on a shoestring budget (In the pre-electronic age, it is incredible how quickly news traveled. Newsworthy events in Norfolk commonly appeared in Richmond papers within the next day or two.) In edition, Virginia editors did not know the meaning of "sound bites." They reprinted Congressional speeches verbatim, at a time when brevity was not considered a virtue. Virginia editors loyal to the Madison administration labeled dissent as unpatriotic, though they previously protested attempts to censor the press by the Adams administration. To their credit, opposition editors refused to be cowed. They did not feel that their dissenting views gave aid and comfort to the enemy. They reveal the value of a truly free press.

In the 21st century, the percentage of the budget devoted to defense is staggering. When researching the War of 1812, it is striking to discover how little was devoted to military expenditures. The U.S. Army during the War of 1812 remained very small; incentives meant to attract recruits were unsuccessful. The small size of the regular army meant Virginia militia bore most of the responsibility for the defense of their state.

At first glance, it would appear that few comparisons on military matters can be made between the Iraq War and the War of 1812; however, the researcher is rewarded by persistence. In the present day, and in 1812, the United States did not resort to conscription. In both cases, Washington used state militias, or the National Guard, to augment the regular forces. In Virginia during 1812–15, as in the present day, this led to complaints that state forces were bearing an unfair burden. Virginia militiamen were also poorly equipped, similar to recent concerns about the combat readiness of Guard and Reserve units.

In 1812, unlike the war in Iraq, the war was fought on Virginia's very doorstep. British operations in the Chesapeake were intended as a diversion, to ease American pressure on Canada. Nevertheless, the British maintained a two-year blockade of the Chesapeake. The size of this "diversion" speaks volumes about the awesome power of the Royal Navy. It would be ludicrous to even imagine such a thing in the present day. Hampton Roads is home to the world's largest naval base. A single nuclear submarine has more destructive power than all of Britain's wooden walls combined, to say nothing of the carrier battle groups.

In 1812–15, Hampton Roads was practically undefended. Fort Monroe, a mighty coastal fortification covering the roadstead, was not built until the 1820s. The defenses of Norfolk were merely an inner line covering the city. Tidewater Virginia is characterized by numerous rivers and inlets. There were not enough militiamen to guard the entire coast. The British were highly experienced in amphibious operations. They could—and did—raid the coast at will. This was a tremendous tactical advantage. British forces controlled the pace of operations, forcing the Virginians into a reactionary posture.

In contrast, the United States fought in Iraq "to fight them there instead of here." Critics pointed to the lack of evidence that Iraq possessed weapons of mass destruction, or had anything to do with 9/11. Iraq did not seem like a significant threat to the United States, the preeminent military power of our times. During the War of 1812, Great Britain was a formidable opponent. They took the fight to American soil. Several actions were fought in Virginia. Noncombatants were not spared—the sacking of Hampton was one of the war's worst atrocities. General Taylor's letter to Admiral Warren insisting both sides observe the rules of war stands in sharp contrast to Bush administration attempts to subvert the Geneva Convention.

When one looks at the opposing forces, the British were undoubtedly stronger than the Americans. War with Great Britain seems like the epitome of recklessness. Fortunately for the Americans—and Virginians in particular—the young Republic avoided total defeat, for British objectives in the War of 1812 were strictly limited. Preservation of Canada was their top priority, while the Chesapeake remained a secondary theater. Virginians certainly suffered from the war—hundreds of militiamen died, mostly from disease. If the British were truly attempting to re-conquer the United States, the toll would have been higher. Virginians died in a war that did not have to be fought. A significant number of Virginians—and West Virginians, as it was part of the Old Dominion in 1812—served in Iraq. According to icasualties.org, from 2003 to 2014, 134 Virginians and 24 West Virginians died in Iraq. 679 and 218 were wounded. These soldiers were also casualties of an avoidable war.

In 1812 and 2003, war was not in the best interest of most Virginians. Examination of the past provides clarity to present-day events. Though the past is not a mirror image of the present, there are certainly many similarities. Identifying similarities and points of convergence make the past relevant to the present. This is particularly important in the case of forgotten or neglected events. It is hoped that this book will generate interest in the War of 1812 and its effect on the state of Virginia, leading to further research on this important subject. If it succeeds in this respect, it will more than fulfill the author's ambitions.

Chapter Notes

Introduction

1. Victor Sapio, *Pennsylvania and the War of 1812* (Lexington: University Press of Kentucky, 1970).
2. Sarah McCulloh Lemmon, *Frustrated Patriots: North Carolina and the War of 1812* (Chapel Hill: University of North Carolina Press, 1973).
3. Lemmon, *North Carolina and the War of 1812* (Raleigh: North Carolina Department of Cultural Resources, 1971).
4. Benson J. Lossing, *Lossing's Pictorial Field Book of the War of 1812* (1869; reprint, Gretna, LA: Firebird Press, 2003).
5. A.J. Langguth, *Union 1812: The Americans Who Fought the Second War of Independence* (New York: Simon & Schuster, 2006).
6. Albert Marrin, *1812: The War Nobody Won* (New York: Atheneum, 1985).
7. Donald R. Hickey, *Don't Give Up the Ship! Myths of the War of 1812* (Urbana: University of Illinois Press, 2006).
8. Donald R. Hickey, "The Federalists and the War of 1812," Ph.D. diss. (University of Illinois, 1972).
9. Donald R. Hickey, *The War of 1812: A Forgotten Conflict*, Bicentennial ed. (Urbana: University of Illinois Press, 2012).

Chapter 1

1. Benson J. Lossing, *Lossing's Pictorial Field Book of the War of 1812*, Vol. 1 (1868; reprint, Gretna, LA: Firebird Press, 2003), 156–57.
2. Pierre Berton, *The Invasion of Canada: 1812-1813* (1980; reprint, Toronto: Anchor Canada, 2001), 35.
3. Berton, 37.
4. Berton, 36.
5. Lossing, V. 1, 157.
6. Lossing, V. 1, 158.
7. Lossing, V. 1, 158.
8. Edwin M. Gaines, "The *Chesapeake* Affair: Virginians Mobilize to Defend National Honor," *VMHB* 64, no. 2 (April 1956): 135.
9. *Virginia Argus*, July 1, 1807.
10. "BRITISH OUTRAGE!" *Alexandria Daily Advertiser*, June 27, 1807.
11. "A Proclamation," *Norfolk Gazette and Publick Ledger*, July 8, 1807.
12. Gaines, 135.
13. Gaines, 136.
14. Gaines, 136.
15. William Tatham, *The Defence of Norfolk in 1807*, edited by Norma Lois Peterson (Norfolk, VA: Norfolk County Historical Society, 1970), 18.
16. *The Complete Jefferson: Containing His Major Writings, Published and Unpublished, Except His Letters*, edited by Saul K. Padover (New York: Tudor Publishing, 1943), 171.
17. Padover, 172.
18. Padover, 172.
19. *Virginia Argus*, June 27, 1807.
20. *Norfolk Gazette and Publick Ledger*, June 26, 1807.
21. Ralph Eshelman, Scott S. Sheads, and Donald R. Hickey, *The War of 1812 in the Chesapeake: A Reference Guide to Historic Sites in Maryland, Virginia, and the District of Columbia* (Baltimore: Johns Hopkins University Press, 2010), 248.
22. *Norfolk Gazette and Publick Ledger*, July 3, 1807.
23. *Norfolk Gazette and Publick Ledger*,

July 6, 1807.
24. *Norfolk Gazette and Publick Ledger*, July 6, 1807.
25. *Norfolk Gazette and Publick Ledger*, July 8, 1807.
26. *Norfolk Gazette and Publick Ledger*, July 6, 1807.
27. *Norfolk Gazette and Publick Ledger*, July 6, 1807.
28. *Norfolk Gazette and Publick Ledger*, July 8, 1807.
29. "INSULT ON INSULT!" *Alexandria Daily Advertiser*, July 7, 1807.
30. *Norfolk Gazette and Publick Ledger*, June 29, 1807.
31. Gaines, 135.
32. "Naval Despotism," *Virginia Argus*, June 27, 1807.
33. Gaines, 139.
34. "British Amity!" *Virginia Argus*, July 8, 1807.
35. *Virginia Argus*, July 8, 1807.
36. Gaines, 137.
37. William Wirt, *Memoirs of the Life of William Wirt, Volume 1*, edited by John Pendleton Kennedy (1856; reprint, Lexington, KY: ULAN Press, 2014), 198.
38. Wirt, 202.
39. "Hints on the Event of a War," *Alexandria Daily Advertiser*, July 16, 1807.
40. *Alexandria Daily Advertiser*, July 13, 1807.
41. *Virginia Argus*, July 18, 1807.
42. "Some Retaliation," *Alexandria Daily Advertiser*, July 18, 1807.
43. Winfield Scott, *Memoirs of Lieut.-General Scott, LL.D.*, Vol. 1 (1864; reprint, London: Forgotten Books, 2015), 20.
44. *Norfolk Gazette and Publick Ledger*, July 24, 1807.
45. Tatham, 51.
46. *Virginia Argus*, July 25, 1807.
47. Tatham, 50.
48. *Virginia Argus*, July 25, 1807.
49. *Virginia Argus*, July 18, 1807.
50. *Alexandria Daily Advertiser*, July 18, 1807.
51. Gaines, 138.
52. "General Orders," *Virginia Argus*, July 17, 1807.
53. *Norfolk Gazette and Publick Ledger*, July 3, 1807.
54. *Norfolk Gazette and Publick Ledger*, July 27, 1807.
55. Gaines, 141.
56. Lossing, V. 1, 158.
57. Spencer C. Tucker and Frank T. Reuter, *Injured Honor: The Chesapeake-Leopard Affair* (Annapolis: Naval Institute Press, 1996), 114.
58. Donald R. Hickey, *Don't Give Up the Ship! Myths of the War of 1812* (Urbana: University of Illinois Press, 2006), 23.
59. Lossing, V. 1, 158.
60. Lossing, V. 1, 157.
61. Tucker and Reuter, 196–97.
62. Lossing, V. 1, 159.
63. Tucker and Reuter, 194.
64. Tucker and Reuter, 193.

Chapter 2

1. *Thomas Jefferson: Writings*, edited by Merrill D. Peterson (New York: Library of America, 1984), 1006.
2. Donald R. Hickey, *The War of 1812: A Forgotten Conflict*, Bicentennial ed. (Urbana: University of Illinois Press, 2012), 6.
3. Hickey, *Forgotten Conflict*, 6.
4. Hickey, *Forgotten Conflict*, 14.
5. Hickey, *Forgotten Conflict*, 15.
6. Hickey, *Forgotten Conflict*, 17.
7. Hickey, *Forgotten Conflict*, 17.
8. Donald R. Hickey, *Don't Give Up the Ship! Myths of the War of 1812* (Urbana: University of Illinois Press, 2006), 29.
9. James H. Broussard, *The Southern Federalists, 1800–1816* (Baton Rouge: Louisiana State University, 1978), 128–29.
10. *Staunton Political Censor*, August 10, 1808.
11. *The Papers of James Madison: Presidential Series*, Vol. 2: 1809–1810, edited by J.C.A. Stagg (Charlottesville: University of Virginia Press, 1992), 183.
12. Madison, 2, 183.
13. Madison, 2, 185–86.
14. Hickey, *Don't Give Up the Ship*, 29.
15. Hickey, *Forgotten Conflict*, 20.
16. Thomas J. Wertenbaker, *Norfolk: Historic Southern Port*, edited by Marvin W. Schlegel, 2d ed. (Durham: Duke University Press, 1962), 105.
17. Wertenbaker, 105.
18. Broussard, 107.
19. Hickey, *Forgotten Conflict*, 21.

20. Hickey, *Don't Give Up the Ship*, 30.
21. *The Papers of James Madison: Presidential Series*, Vol. 1: 1809, edited by Robert A. Rutland and Thomas A. Mason (Charlottesville: University of Virginia Press, 1984), 16.
22. *Virginia Gazette*, May 19, 1809.
23. Madison 1, 117.
24. *Norfolk Gazette and Publick Ledger*, August 14, 1809.
25. Madison 1, 312.
26. Broussard, 125.
27. Madison 2, 179n.
28. Broussard, 126.
29. Hickey, *Forgotten Conflict*, 21.
30. Madison 2, 463n.
31. Madison 2, 460.
32. Broussard, 130.
33. Madison 2, 612–13.
34. Broussard, 130.
35. J.C.A. Stagg, "James Madison and the 'Malcontents': The Political Origins of the War of 1812," *WMQ* 33, no. 4 (October 1976): 561.
36. Stagg, 561–62.
37. *The Papers of James Madison: Presidential Series*, Vol. 3: 1810–1811, edited by J.C.A. Stagg (Charlottesville: University of Virginia Press, 1996), xxx–xxxi.
38. Madison 3, 230.
39. Madison 3, 230.
40. Madison 3, 235.
41. Madison 3, 235–36.
42. Madison 3, xxxii.
43. Stagg, 584.
44. *The Papers of James Madison: Presidential Series*, Vol. 4: 1811–1812, edited by J.C.A. Stagg (Charlottesville: University of Virginia Press, 1999), 235.
45. Madison 4, 263.
46. Hickey, *Forgotten Conflict*, 35.
47. Hickey, *Forgotten Conflict*, 35–36.
48. *The Papers of Thomas Jefferson: Retirement Series*, Vol. 4: 1811–1812, edited by J. Jefferson Looney (Princeton: Princeton University Press, 2007), 611–12.
49. Jack Cassin-Scott, *Scandinavian Armies in the Napoleonic Wars* (1976; reprint, Oxford: Osprey, 2005), 3.
50. Cassin-Scott, 7.
51. *Martinsburgh Gazette*, July 10, 1811.
52. Madison 4, 287.
53. *The Papers of Thomas Jefferson: Retirement Series*, Vol. 5: 1812–1813, edited by J. Jefferson Looney (Princeton: Princeton University Press, 2008), 186.
54. Jefferson 5, 186–87.
55. William Appleman Williams, *The Tragedy of American Diplomacy*, 50th anniv. ed. (New York: Norton, 2009), 19.
56. Williams, 18.
57. Broussard, 136.
58. Broussard, 127–28.
59. Hickey, *Forgotten Conflict*, 36.
60. Madison 4, 280n.
61. Hickey, *Forgotten Conflict*, 37.
62. Madison 4, 432.
63. Madison 4, 437.
64. Stuart L. Butler, *Defending the Old Dominion: Virginia and Its Militia in the War of 1812* (Lanham, MD: University Press of America, 2013), 30.
65. Madison 4, 272.
66. Madison 4, 273.
67. Butler, *Defending the Old Dominion*, 35.
68. William Tatham, *The Defence of Norfolk in 1807*, edited by Norma Lois Peterson (Norfolk, VA: Norfolk County Historical Society, 1970), 99.
69. Tatham, 24.
70. Madison 3, 199.
71. John R. Elting, *Swords Around a Throne: Napoleon's Grande Armee* (1988; reprint, Boston: Da Capo Press, 1997), 104.
72. Tatham, 100.
73. Tatham, 36.
74. Tatham, 100.
75. Tatham, 102.

Chapter 3

1. Myron F. Wehtje, "Opposition in Virginia to the War of 1812," *VMHB* 78, no. 1 (January 1970): 82.
2. Donald R. Hickey, *Don't Give Up the Ship! Myths of the War of 1812* (Urbana: University of Illinois Press, 2006), 40.
3. Hickey, *Don't Give Up the Ship*, 41.
4. Wehtje, 78.
5. Daniel McCarthy, "Liberty and Order in the Slave Society," *The American Conservative* (August 1, 2005).
6. Hickey, *Don't Give Up the Ship*, 36.
7. Wehtje, 78.
8. John Taylor, "Letters of John Taylor of Caroline County, Virginia," *John P. Branch Historical Society Papers* 2 (June 1908): 327.

9. Taylor, 328.
10. Taylor, 328.
11. Taylor, 329.
12. *The War of 1812: Writings from America's Second War of Independence*, edited by Donald R. Hickey (New York: Library of America, 2013), 30.
13. *The War of 1812: Writings from America's Second War of Independence*, 34–35.
14. *The War of 1812: Writings from America's Second War of Independence*, 35.
15. Taylor, 341.
16. Taylor, 341–42.
17. Wehtje, 85.
18. Taylor, 342–43.
19. Taylor, 343.
20. Taylor, 343.
21. Taylor, 292.
22. James H. Broussard, *The Southern Federalists, 1800–1816* (Baton Rouge: Louisiana State University, 1978), 146.
23. Broussard, 147.
24. Broussard, 147.
25. Broussard, 23.
26. Broussard, 25.
27. Wehtje, 66.
28. Broussard, 406.
29. Wehtje, 66.
30. Broussard, 279.
31. Virginius Dabney, *Virginia, The New Dominion: A history from 1607 to the Present* (New York: Doubleday, 1971), 203–04.
32. "War With England," *Virginia Argus*, April 23, 1812.
33. *Virginia Argus*, May 14, 1812.
34. "Rags," *Virginia Argus*, May 21, 1812.
35. Wehtje, 75.
36. "A Change Is Necessary," *Norfolk Gazette and Publick Ledger*, May 13, 1812.
37. Carrol H. Quenzel, *Samuel Snowden, A Founding Father of Printing in Alexandria* (Charlottesville: University of Virginia Press, 1952), 3.
38. Quenzel, 2.
39. Quenzel, 5.
40. Quenzel, 5.
41. Quenzel, 14.
42. Philo-Laos, "On the Folly and Wickedness of War," *Alexandria Daily Gazette*, January 28, 1812.
43. *Alexandria Daily Gazette*, May 15, 1812.
44. *Alexandria Daily Gazette*, October 5, 1812.
45. Wehtje, 69.
46. *Alexandria Daily Gazette*, May 15, 1812.
47. "Senex No. I," *Alexandria Daily Gazette*, June 4, 1812.
48. *Alexandria Daily Gazette*, June 20, 1812.
49. *Alexandria Herald*, July 1, 1812.
50. *Alexandria Herald*, July 1, 1812.
51. *Alexandria Herald*, July 1, 1812.
52. True-Blue, "Federalism of the Boston Stamp," *Alexandria Herald*, August 9, 1813.
53. "Communication," *Alexandria Herald*, March 16, 1814.
54. *Alexandria Daily Gazette*, November 9, 1812.
55. *Alexandria Daily Gazette*, January 1, 1814.
56. *Virginia Patriot*, January 7, 1814.
57. "From a Little Man to a tall Man," *Virginia Patriot*, April 30, 1814.
58. "Marcellus," "Essays on the Liberty of the Press" (Richmond, 1804).
59. *Virginia Argus*, September 7, 1812.
60. "The Conduct of the War," *Virginia Argus*, July 15, 1813.
61. *Staunton Republican Farmer*, November 19, 1812.
62. *Staunton Republican Farmer*, December 10, 1812.
63. Wehtje, 84.
64. Taylor, 343.
65. Wehtje, 84.
66. *Alexandria Daily Gazette*, June 22, 1812.
67. Quenzel, 17.
68. Wehtje, 84.
69. Christopher T. George, *Terror on the Chesapeake: The War of 1812 on the Bay* (Shippensburg, PA: White Mane Books, 2000), 14.
70. George, 16–18.
71. George, 20.
72. Henry Lee and George Beckwith, "Major-General Henry Lee and Lieutenant-General Sir George Beckwith on Peace in 1813," *The American Historical Review* 32, no. 2 (January 1927): 284.
73. Lee and Beckwith, 285.
74. "Cadwallader," *Virginia Argus*, September 3, 1812.

Chapter 4

1. *Norfolk Gazette and Publick Ledger*, June 2, 1813.
2. Gregory J.W. Urwin, *The United States*

Infantry: An Illustrated History 1775–1918 (1988; reprint, Norman: University of Oklahoma Press, 2000), 44.

3. *The Papers of James Madison: Presidential Series*, Vol. 7: 1813–1814, edited by J.C.A. Stagg (Charlottesville: University of Virginia Press, 2012), 22.

4. *Memoirs of Lieut.-General Scott, LL.D.*, Vol. 1 (1864; reprint, London: Forgotten Books, 2015), 35.

5. Urwin, 41.

6. Urwin, 41.

7. Jarvis Hanks, Amasiah Ford, and Alexander McMullen, *Soldiers of 1814: American Enlisted Men's Memoirs of the Niagara Campaign*, edited Donald E. Graves (Youngstown, NY: Old Fort Niagara Association, 1995), 8.

8. Donald R. Hickey, *Don't Give Up the Ship! Myths of the War of 1812* (Urbana: University of Illinois, 2006), 297.

9. James L. Kochan, *The United States Army 1812–1815* (Oxford: Osprey, 2000), 16.

10. Urwin, 42.

11. An Old Federalist, "For the Consideration of Congress and the People of the United States," *Virginia Argus*, June 1, 1814.

12. "To Arms! To Arms!" *Richmond Enquirer*, August 31, 1814.

13. Urwin, 42.

14. Stuart L. Butler, *Defending the Old Dominion: Virginia and its Militia in the War of 1812* (Lanham, MD: University Press of America, 2013), 554.

15. Butler, *Defending the Old Dominion*, 84.

16. Butler, *Defending the Old Dominion*, 85.

17. "A PROCLAMATION," *Staunton Republican Farmer*, February 14, 1812.

18. Butler, *Defending the Old Dominion*, 86.

19. Butler, *Defending the Old Dominion*, 84.

20. Butler, *Defending the Old Dominion*, 83.

21. Butler, *Defending the Old Dominion*, 85.

22. Butler, *Defending the Old Dominion*, 54.

23. Butler, *Defending the Old Dominion*, 39–40.

24. Butler, *Defending the Old Dominion*, 59.

25. Jonathan Cropper, Jr., "Letters from Old Trunks." *VMHB* 45, no. 1 (January 1937): 42.

26. Alan Taylor, *The Internal Enemy: Slavery and War in Virginia, 1772–1832* (New York: Norton, 2013), 150.

27. Taylor, 151.

28. William Wirt, *Memoirs of the life of William Wirt*, edited by John Pendleton Kennedy (1856; reprint, Lexington, KY: ULAN Press, 2014), 337.

29. "Return of our Citizens," *Richmond Patriot*, October 5, 1814.

30. Pleasants Murphy, "Pleasants Murphy's 'Journal and Day Book," *William and Mary Quarterly*, Second Series, 3, no. 4 (October 1923): 234.

31. Murphy, 235.

32. Murphy, 236–37.

33. Murphy, 238.

34. Pierre Berton, *The Invasion of Canada: 1812–1813* (1980; reprint, Toronto: Anchor Canada, 2001), 95.

35. Ed Gilbert, *Frontier Militiaman in the War of 1812: Southwestern Frontier* (Oxford: Osprey, 2008), 32.

36. "Orderly Book of Virginia Militia War of 1812," *VMHB* 46, no. 3 (July 1938): 249.

37. "Orderly Book," 250.

38. "Orderly Book," 253.

39. "Orderly Book, 253.

40. "Orderly Book," 252–53.

41. "Orderly Book," 252.

42. *Norfolk Gazette and Publick Ledger*, June 2, 1813.

43. C. Edward Skeen, *Citizen Soldiers in the War of 1812* (Lexington: University Press of Kentucky, 1999), 45.

44. Skeen, 46.

45. Skeen, 47.

46. *Virginia Argus*, August 5, 1813.

47. "Notice to Delinquent Troopers," *Virginia Argus*, September 3, 1814.

48. Butler, *Defending the Old Dominion*, 538.

49. Butler, *Defending the Old Dominion*, 539.

50. Butler, *Defending the Old Dominion*, 539.

51. Cropper, 45.

52. Butler, *Defending the Old Dominion*, 156.

53. Butler, 487.

54. Taylor, 166.

55. Taylor, 167.

56. Taylor, 167.

57. Taylor, 168.

58. Butler, *Defending the Old Dominion*, 554.

59. Cropper, 42–43.

60. Taylor, 162.
61. Taylor, 162.
62. Skeen, 153.
63. Urwin, 25.
64. Hickey, *The War of 1812: A Forgotten Conflict*, Bicentennial ed. (Urbana: University of Illinois Press, 2012), 264–65.
65. Butler, *Defending the Old Dominion*, 201.
66. Taylor, 161.
67. Butler, *Defending the Old Dominion*, 198–99.
68. Taylor, 161.
69. "WASHINGTON BURNT!!" *Virginia Argus*, August 27, 1814.
70. "A PROCLAMATION," *Virginia Argus*, August 27, 1814.
71. Skeen, 150.
72. "Act of Jan. 18, 1815," *Acts Passed at a General Assembly of the Commonwealth of Virginia* (Richmond, 1815), 40–51.
73. Butler, *Defending the Old Dominion*, 488.
74. Skeen, 148.
75. Hickey, *Forgotten Conflict*, 283.
76. Skeen, 156.

Chapter 5

1. Bryan Fosten, *Wellington's Infantry (1)* (1981; reprint, London: Osprey, 1989), 6.
2. *Wellington's Infantry*, 10.
3. *Wellington's Infantry*, 16.
4. *Wellington's Infantry*, 6.
5. *Advice to the Officers of the British Army* (1783; reprint, Schenectady, NY: United States Historical Research Service, 1992), 34.
6. Philip Haythornthwaite, *British Napoleonic Infantry Tactics 1792–1815* (Oxford: Osprey, 2008), 4–5.
7. Scott S. Sheads, *The Chesapeake Campaigns 1813–15: Middle Ground of the War of 1812* (Oxford: Osprey, 2014), 24
8. Sheads, 13.
9. Sheads, 13.
10. Alan Taylor, *The Internal Enemy: Slavery and War in Virginia, 1772–1832* (New York: Norton, 2013), 196.
11. John K. Mahon, *The War of 1812* (Gainesville: University of Florida Press, 1972), 301.
12. Sheads, 14–15.
13. Sheads, 15.
14. Christopher T. George, *Terror on the Chesapeake: The War of 1812 on the Bay* (Shippensburg, PA: White Mane Books, 2000), 42.
15. General Sir Charles Napier, *The life and opinions of General Sir Charles James Napier, Volume 1*, ed. William Francis Patrick Napier (1857; reprint, Lexington, KY: ULAN Press, 2014), 180.
16. Gareth A. Newfeld, "Anatomy of an Atrocity: Crimes of the Independent Companies of Foreigners in North America, 1813," *War of 1812 Magazine* 10 (October 2008): 3.
17. Newfeld, 11.
18. Napier, 369–70.
19. Napier, 370.
20. Napier, 370.
21. Taylor, 284.
22. Taylor, 283.
23. Donald R. Hickey, *Don't Give Up the Ship! Myths of the War of 1812* (Urbana: University of Illinois, 2006), 189.
24. Benson Lossing, *Lossing's Pictorial Field Book of the War of 1812*, Vol. 2 (1868; reprint, Gretna, LA: Firebird Press, 2003), 684n.
25. Sandy Antal, *A Wampum Denied: Procter's War of 1812* (Ottawa: Carleton University Press, 1998), 67.
26. Antal, 72.
27. Antal, 72.
28. Antal, 148.
29. Richard M. Ketchum, *Saratoga: Turning Point of America's Revolutionary War* (New York: Henry Holt and Company, 1997), 91
30. George Gleig, *A Subaltern in America* (1833; reprint, Middletown, DE: New York Public Library Collection, 2016), 24–25.
31. *Advice to the Officers of the British Army*, 76–77.
32. Donald E. Graves, *Field of Glory: The Battle of Crysler's Farm, 1813* (Toronto: Robin Brass Studio, 2005), 347.
33. Mike Chappell, *British Infantry Equipments, 1808–1908* (London: Osprey, 1980), 11–13.
34. Gleig, 9–10.
35. Ralph E. Eshelman and Burton K. Kummerow, *In Full Glory Reflected: Discovering the War of 1812 in the Chesapeake* (Baltimore: Maryland Historical Society, 2012), 53.
36. Philip Haythornthwaite, *Nelson's Navy* (1993; reprint, Oxford: Osprey, 1999), 49.

37. Sheads, 24.
38. Sheads, 19.
39. Napier, 224–25.
40. Napier, 225.
41. Napier, 212.
42. Gleig, 8.
43. Taylor, 198.
44. Taylor, 294.
45. Ralph E. Eshelman, Scott S. Sheads, and Donald R. Hickey, *The War of 1812 in the Chesapeake: A Reference Guide to Historic Sites in Maryland, Virginia, and the District of Columbia* (Baltimore: Johns Hopkins University Press, 2010), 248.
46. Eshelman, Sheads, and Hickey, 264.
47. Eshelman, Sheads, and Hickey, 263.

Chapter 6

1. Rene Chartrand, *Forts of the War of 1812* (Oxford: Osprey, 2012), 33.
2. *Norfolk Herald*, September 6, 1812.
3. *Richmond Enquirer*, September 8, 1812.
4. *The Papers of James Madison: Presidential Series*, Vol 5: 1812–1813, edited by J.C.A. Stagg (Charlottesville: University of Virginia Press, 2004), 440.
5. Stuart L. Butler, *Defending the Old Dominion: Virginia and Its Militia in the War of 1812* (Lanham, MD: University Press of America, 2013), 122.
6. Sandy Antal, *A Wampum Denied: Procter's War of 1812* (Ottawa: Carleton University Press, 1998), 131.
7. Butler, *Defending the Old Dominion*, 124–25.
8. Stuart L. Butler, *Real Patriots and Heroic Soldiers: General Joel Leftwich and the Virginia Brigade in the War of 1812* (Westminster, MD: Heritage Books, 2008), 18.
9. Butler, *Real Patriots*, 22.
10. Butler, *Real Patriots*, 23–24.
11. Butler, *Real Patriots*, 38.
12. Butler, *Real Patriots*, 40.
13. Butler, *Real Patriots*, 30.
14. Butler, *Defending the Old Dominion*, 128.
15. Butler, *Real Patriots*, 37.
16. Butler, *Defending the Old Dominion*, 131.
17. Butler, *Defending the Old Dominion*, 132.
18. Alfred M. Lorrain, *The Helm, the Sword and the Cross: A Life Narrative* (1862; reprint, London: Forgotten Books, 2012), 108.
19. Butler, *Defending the Old Dominion*, 133.
20. *Virginia Argus*, September 17, 1812.
21. Lee M. Wallace, Jr., "The Petersburg Volunteers, 1812–1813," *VMHB* 82, no. 4 (October 1974): 460–61.
22. Lorrain, 98.
23. *Virginia Argus*, October 12, 1812.
24. *Virginia Argus*, September 14, 1812.
25. Wallace, 462–63.
26. *Richmond Enquirer*, October 23, 1812.
27. Wallace, 464.
28. Lorrain, 103–04.
29. *Staunton Republican Farmer*, November 7, 1812.
30. *Staunton Republican Farmer*, November 19, 1812.
31. Wallace, 467.
32. Lorrain, 109.
33. Wallace, 467–68.
34. Wallace, 468.
35. Butler, *Defending the Old Dominion*, 135.
36. Wallace, 469.
37. Lorrain, 116–17.
38. Butler, *Real Patriots*, 84.
39. Larry L. Nelson, *Men of Patriotism, Courage & Enterprise! Fort Meigs in the War of 1812* (1985; reprint, Westminster, MD: Heritage Books, 2007), 21.
40. Nelson, 21–22.
41. Nelson, 23.
42. Nelson, 23.
43. Nelson, 25.
44. John F. Winkler, *The Thames 1813: The War of 1812 on the Northwest Frontier* (Oxford: Osprey, 2016), 38–39.
45. Winkler, 40.
46. Eleazar D. Wood, *Wood's Journal of the Northwestern Campaign of 1812–1813*, edited by Robert B. Boehm and Randall L. Buchman (Defiance, OH: The Defiance College Press, 1975), 8.
47. Chartrand, 33.
48. Lorrain, 121.
49. Lorrain, 121–22.
50. Wallace, 471.
51. Lorrain, 124–25.
52. Wood, 13.
53. Wood, 12–13.
54. Butler, *Real Patriots*, 108–09.
55. Butler, *Real Patriots*, 122–23.
56. Butler, *Defending the Old Dominion*, 142.
57. Winkler, 42.

58. Antal, 222.
59. Antal, 11.
60. Nelson, 69.
61. Antal, 223.
62. Wallace, 474.
63. Winkler, 44.
64. Nelson, 71.
65. Nelson, 70.
66. Lorrain, 129–30.
67. Antal, 222–23.
68. Winkler, 43.
69. Wallace, 475.
70. Lorrain, 134.
71. Wallace, 476.
72. Lorrain, 134–35.
73. Winkler, 44.
74. Wood, 23.
75. Wood, 25.
76. Wood, 26.
77. Wallace, 477.
78. Antal, 229–31.
79. Antal, 231.
80. Winkler, 41.
81. Winkler, 46.
82. Nelson, 102.
83. Nelson, 103.
84. Nelson, 103.
85. Lorrain, 168.
86. Nelson, 104.
87. Nelson, 111.
88. Winkler, 46.
89. Lorrain, 168.
90. Chartrand, 34.
91. Antal, 255.
92. Winkler, 46.
93. Antal, 255–56.
94. Winkler, 47.
95. Winkler, 48.
96. Antal, 259.
97. Antal, 259.
98. Winkler, 48.
99. Benson Lossing, *Lossing's Pictorial Field Book of the War of 1812*, Vol. 1 (1868; reprint, Gretna, LA: Firebird Press, 2003), 504–05.
100. Mark Lardas, *USS Lawrence vs. HMS Detroit: The War of 1812 on the Great Lakes* (Oxford: Osprey, 2017), 20–21.
101. Lardas, 41.
102. Lardas, 48.
103. Wallace, 480.
104. Lorrain, 131–32.
105. Wallace, 479.
106. Wallace, 480.
107. Winkler, 88.
108. Lorrain, 153.
109. Lorrain, 153–54.
110. Wallace, 481.

Chapter 7

1. *The Papers of James Madison: Presidential Series*, Vol 6: 1813, edited by J.C.A. Stagg (Charlottesville: University of Virginia Press, 2008), 143.
2. Ralph E. Eshelman and Burton K. Kummerow, *In Full Glory Reflected: Discovering the War of 1812 in the Chesapeake* (Baltimore: Maryland Historical Society, 2012), 29.
3. *The War of 1812: Writings from America's Second War of Independence*, edited by Donald R. Hickey (New York: Library of America, 2013), 211–12.
4. Scott S. Sheads, *The Chesapeake Campaigns 1813–15: Middle ground of the War of 1812* (Oxford: Osprey, 2014), 28.
5. *The War of 1812 in the Chesapeake: A Reference Guide to Historic Sites in Maryland, Virginia, and the District of Columbia* (Baltimore: Johns Hopkins, 2010), 249.
6. William L. Calderhead, "U.S.F. *Constellation* in the War of 1812—An Accidental Fleet-in-Being," *Military Affairs* 40, no. 2 (April 1976): 80.
7. Calderhead, 81.
8. Christopher T. George, *Terror on the Chesapeake: The War of 1812 on the Bay* (Shippensburg, PA: White Mane Books, 2000), 6.
9. Hickey, *The War of 1812: Forgotten Conflict*, Bicentennial ed. (Urbana: University of Illinois, 2012), 9.
10. Sheads, 33.
11. Eshelman, Sheads, and Hickey, 249–50.
12. Eshelman, Sheads, and Hickey, 257–58.
13. Stuart L. Butler, *Defending the Old Dominion: Virginia and Its Militia in the War of 1812* (Lanham, MD: University Press of America, 2013), 221–22.
14. Butler, *Defending the Old Dominion*, 222.
15. Eshelman, Sheads, and Hickey, 269.
16. Thomas Massie, "Richmond During the War of 1812," *VMHB* 7, no. 4 (April 1900): 406.
17. Massie, 407.
18. Massie, 408.

19. Massie, 409.
20. Thomas J. Wertenbaker, *Norfolk: Historic Southern Port*, edited by Marvin W Schlegel, 2d ed. (Durham: Duke University Press, 1962), 113–14.
21. Wertenbaker, 114.
22. John M. Hallahan, *The Battle of Craney Island: A Matter of Credit* (Portsmouth, VA: St. Michael's Press, 1986), 59–60.
23. Hallahan, 61.
24. Hallahan, 48–49.
25. Hallahan, 50.
26. Eshelman, Sheads, and Hickey, 18.
27. Eshelman, Sheads, and Hickey, 252.
28. Eshelman, Sheads, and Hickey, 252.
29. Eshelman, Sheads, and Hickey, 226.
30. Sheads, 41.
31. Hallahan, 61.
32. Hallahan, 61–62.
33. Hallahan, 63.
34. Hallahan, 62.
35. Butler, *Defending the Old Dominion*, 245.
36. General Sir Charles Napier, *The life and opinions of General Sir Charles James Napier*, Vol. 1, edited by William Francis Patrick Napier (1857; reprint, Lexington, KY: ULAN Press, 2014), 217.
37. Hallahan, 69.
38. Napier, 224.
39. Hallahan, 70.
40. Hallahan, 69.
41. Eshelman and Kummerow, 36.
42. Butler, *Defending the Old Dominion*, 247.
43. Hallahan, 72.
44. Butler, *Defending the Old Dominion*, 247.
45. Hallahan, 72
46. Hallahan, 74–75.
47. Napier, 217.
48. Hallahan, 76.
49. Hallahan, 104.
50. Alan Taylor, *The Internal Enemy: Slavery and War in Virginia, 1772–1832* (New York: Norton, 2013), 194.
51. Napier, 218.
52. Napier, 217.
53. Taylor, 248.
54. Hallahan, 81.
55. George, 48.
56. Sheads, 43.
57. *Virginia Argus*, June 28, 1813.
58. George, 50.
59. Butler, *Defending the Old Dominion*, 253–54.
60. Butler, *Defending the Old Dominion*, 249.
61. Butler, *Defending the Old Dominion*, 264.
62. Butler, *Defending the Old Dominion*, 265.
63. Butler, *Defending the Old Dominion*, 266.
64. "Operations at Hampton," *Virginia Argus*, July 1, 1813.
65. "P," *Richmond Enquirer*, July 16, 1813.
66. "P," *Richmond Enquirer*, July 16, 1813.
67. "Spirit of the Interior of Virginia," *Virginia Argus*, July 25, 1813.
68. Butler, *Defending the Old Dominion*, 270.
69. Butler, *Defending the Old Dominion*, 270.
70. "Barefaced and Profligate Falsehood," *Richmond Enquirer*, July 27, 1813.
71. "Barefaced and Profligate Falsehood," *Richmond Enquirer*, July 27, 1813.
72. Napier, 224.
73. Napier, 222.
74. Parke Rouse, Jr., "The British Invasion of Hampton in 1813: The Reminiscences of James Jarvis, *VMHB* 76, no. 3 (July 1968): 329.
75. Rouse, 330.
76. Rouse, 330–31.
77. Napier, 221.
78. Eshelman, Sheads, and Hickey, 252.
79. Massie, 408–09.
80. William Wirt, *Memoirs of the life of William Wirt*, edited by John Pendleton Kennedy (1856; reprint, Lexington, KY: ULAN Press, 2014), 318.
81. Wirt, 320.
82. "The Vigilance Committee," *VMHB* 7, no. 3 (January 1900): 228.
83. "The Vigilance Committee," 228–29.
84. "The Vigilance Committee," 230.
85. "The Vigilance Committee," 231.
86. "The Vigilance Committee," 235.
87. *Richmond Enquirer*, July 6, 1813.
88. *Richmond Enquirer*, July 9, 1813.
89. Eshelman, Sheads, and Hickey, 267.
90. Eshelman, Sheads, and Hickey, 268.
91. Butler, *Defending the Old Dominion*, 303.
92. Butler, *Defending the Old Dominion*,

298.
93. Butler, *Defending the Old Dominion*, 299.
94. *Richmond Enquirer*, July 30, 1813.
95. Butler, *Defending the Old Dominion*, 299.
96. Eshelman, Sheads, and Hickey, 222–23.
97. Butler, *Defending the Old Dominion*, 300.
98. Eshelman, Sheads, and Hickey, 244.
99. *Virginia Argus*, September 27, 1813.
100. *The Papers of James Madison: Presidential Series*, Vol. 7: 1813–1814, edited by J.C.A. Stagg (Charlottesville: University of Virginia Press, 2012), 21.
101. Madison 7, 21.
102. Madison 7, 21–22.
103. Madison 7, 23.
104. Madison 7, 23.
105. Butler, *Defending the Old Dominion*, 328–29.
106. Madison 7, 94.
107. Hickey, *Forgotten Conflict*, 174.
108. Madison 7, 95.
109. Hickey, *Forgotten Conflict*, 174.
110. Wertenbaker, 114.
111. *Norfolk Gazette and Publick Ledger*, March 14, 1814.
112. Hickey, *Forgotten Conflict*, 175.
113. Butler, *Defending the Old Dominion*, 191.
114. Hickey, *Forgotten Conflict*, 286–87.
115. Alexandria *Daily Gazette*, April 10, 1813.
116. *The Papers of Thomas Jefferson: Retirement Series*, Vol. 7: 1813–1814, edited by J. Jefferson Looney (Princeton: Princeton University Press, 2010), 11.
117. John F. Winkler, *The Thames 1813: The War of 1812 on the Northwest Frontier* (Oxford: Osprey, 2016), 89.
118. Jefferson 7, 11.
119. Jefferson 7, 11–12.
120. Madison 7, 73.

Chapter 8

1. Donald R. Hickey, *The War of 1812: A Forgotten Conflict*, Bicentennial ed. (Urbana: University of Illinois, 2012), 287–89.
2. "The Vigilance Committee," *VMHB* 7, no. 3 (January 1900): 235.
3. "The Vigilance Committee," 236.
4. Alan Taylor, *The Internal Enemy: Slavery and War in Virginia, 1772–1832* (New York: Norton, 2013), 394.
5. Taylor, 394.
6. Stuart L. Butler, *Defending the Old Dominion: Virginia and Its Militia in the War of 1812* (Lanham, MD: University Press of America, 2013), 398.
7. Butler, *Defending the Old Dominion*, 398.
8. Butler, *Defending the Old Dominion*, 398.
9. "British Humanity," *Richmond Enquirer*, April 30, 1814.
10. Ralph E. Eshelman, Scott S. Sheads, and Donald R. Hickey, *The War of 1812 in the Chesapeake: A Reference Guide to Historic Sites in Maryland, Virginia, and the District of Columbia* (Baltimore: Johns Hopkins University Press, 2010), 261.
11. Eshelman, Sheads, and Hickey, 262.
12. Eshelman, Sheads, and Hickey, 262.
13. Eshelman, Sheads, and Hickey, 257.
14. Eshelman, Sheads, and Hickey, 247.
15. Eshelman, Sheads, and Hickey, 248.
16. Eshelman, Sheads, and Hickey, 248.
17. Butler, *Defending the Old Dominion*, 403.
18. Butler, *Defending the Old Dominion*, 405.
19. Butler, *Defending the Old Dominion*, 405.
20. Eshelman, Sheads, and Hickey, 268.
21. Butler, *Defending the Old Dominion*, 506.
22. Eshelman, Sheads, and Hickey, 268.
23. Eshelman, Sheads, and Hickey, 269.
24. *Richmond Enquirer*, August 10, 1814.
25. Butler, *Defending the Old Dominion*, 398.
26. Thomas Massie, "Richmond During the War of 1812," *VMHB* 7, no. 4 (April 1900): 414.
27. *Norfolk Gazette and Publick Ledger*, July 23, 1814.
28. *Virginia Patriot*, August 20, 1814.
29. *The Papers of James Madison: Presidential Series*, Vol. 8: 1814–1815, edited by Angela Kreider (Charlottesville: University of Virginia Press, 2015), 133.
30. Benson J. Lossing, *Lossing's Pictorial Field Book of the War of 1812*, Vol. 2 (1868; reprint, Gretna, LA: Firebird Press, 2003),

926.
31. Scott S. Sheads, *The Chesapeake Campaigns 1813–15: Middle Ground of the War of 1812* (Oxford: Osprey, 2014), 63–64.
32. Butler, *Defending the Old Dominion*, 423.
33. "WASHINGTON BURNT!" *Virginia Argus*, August 27, 1814.
34. "VIRGINIANS TO ARMS!" *Virginia Argus*, August 27, 1814.
35. "A PROCLAMATION." *Virginia Argus*, August 27, 1814.
36. *The Papers of Thomas Jefferson: Retirement Series*, Vol. 7: 1813–1814, edited by J. Jefferson Looney (Princeton: Princeton University Press, 2010), 632.
37. "VIRGINIANS TO ARMS!" *Virginia Argus*, August 27, 1814.
38. Jefferson 7, 692.
39. Sheads, 66.
40. Butler, *Defending the Old Dominion*, 431.
41. Charles Simms, "Alexandria in the War of 1812," *Alexandria History* VI (1984): 18.
42. Simms, 19.
43. Eshelman, Sheads, and Hickey, 122.
44. Eshelman, Sheads, and Hickey, 122.
45. Eshelman, Sheads, and Hickey, 122.
46. Simms, 20.
47. Simms, 21.
48. Simms, 21–22.
49. Simms, 23.
50. Eshelman, Sheads, and Hickey, 214.
51. Butler, *Defending the Old Dominion*, 425–31.
52. Eshelman, Sheads, and Hickey, 219.
53. Eshelman, Sheads, and Hickey, 214.
54. Eshelman, Sheads, and Hickey, 214–15.
55. Eshelman, Sheads, and Hickey, 219.
56. Eshelman, Sheads, and Hickey, 214.
57. *Norfolk Gazette and Publick Ledger*, September 3, 1814.
58. "CAPITULATION OF FORT WARBURTON AND ALEXANDRIA," *Richmond Enquirer*, August 31, 1814.
59. Sheads, 66.
60. G.E. Watson, "The United States and the Peninsular War, 1808–1812," *The Historical Journal* 19, no. 4 (December 1976): 870.
61. Watson, 869.
62. Arthur G. Peterson, "The Alexandria Market Prior to the Civil War," *WMQ*, Second Series, Vol. 12, no. 2 (April 1932): 105.
63. Peterson, 105.
64. Peterson, 105.
65. Peterson, 105.
66. Carrol H. Quenzel, *Samuel Snowden, A Founding Father of Printing in Alexandria* (Charlottesville: University of Virginia Press, 1952), 17.
67. *Virginia Argus*, September 14, 1814.
68. Quenzel, 17.
69. *Alexandria Gazette*, September 15, 1814.
70. "Impartiality," *Alexandria Gazette*, October 6, 1814.
71. Butler, *Defending the Old Dominion*, 422.
72. Butler, *Defending the Old Dominion*, 421.
73. Ralph E. Eshelman and Burton K. Kummerow, *In Full Glory Reflected: A Reference Guide to Historic Sites in Maryland, Virginia, and the District of Columbia* (Baltimore: Johns Hopkins University Press, 2010), 127.
74. John K. Mahon, *The War of 1812* (Gainesville: University of Florida Press, 1972), 307.
75. Mahon, 307–08.
76. Sheads, 24.
77. Rene Chartrand, *Forts of the War of 1812* (Oxford: Osprey, 2012), 23.
78. Sheads, 23.
79. Sheads, 84.
80. Sheads, 23.
81. Eshelman, Sheads, and Hickey, 115.
82. Eshelman and Kummerow, 140.
83. Butler, *Defending the Old Dominion*, 467.
84. Eshelman, Sheads, and Hickey, 64.
85. Eshelman and Kummerow, 139.
86. Eshelman and Kummerow, 137.
87. George Gleig, *A Subaltern in America* (1833; reprint, Middletown, DE: New York Public Library Collection, 2016), 158–59.
88. Butler, *Defending the Old Dominion*, 468.
89. Butler, *Defending the Old Dominion*, 450.
90. Butler, *Defending the Old Dominion*, 450.
91. Sarah McCulloh Lemmon, *Frustrated Patriots: North Carolina and the War of 1812* (Chapel Hill: University of North Carolina Press, 1973), 51–52.
92. Lemmon, 54.
93. Butler, *Defending the Old Dominion*,

505.
94. Butler, *Defending the Old Dominion*, 447.
95. Butler, *Defending the Old Dominion*, 509.
96. Eshelman, Sheads, and Hickey, 262.
97. Eshelman, Sheads, and Hickey, 230–31.
98. Butler, *Defending the Old Dominion*, 496.
99. Butler, *Defending the Old Dominion*, 496.
100. Eshelman, Sheads, and Hickey, 265.
101. Kate Mason Rowland, "Letters of Armistead Thomson Mason: 1812–1818," *WMQ* 23, no. 4 (April 1915): 231.

Chapter 9

1. Stuart L. Butler, *Defending the Old Dominion: Virginia and its Militia in the War of 1812* (Lanham, MD: University Press of America, 2013), 514.
2. "The Illumination, For the Return of Peace," *Virginia Patriot*, March 4, 1815.
3. Butler, *Defending the Old Dominion*, 554.
4. Ralph E. Eshelman, Scott S. Sheads, and Donald R. Hickey, *The War of 1812 in the Chesapeake: A Reference Guide to Historic Sites in Maryland, Virginia, and the District of Columbia* (Baltimore: Johns Hopkins University Press, 2010), 216.
5. C. Edward Skeen, *Citizen Soldiers in the War of 1812* (Lexington: University Press of Kentucky, 1999), 172.
6. Eshelman, Sheads, and Hickey, 262.
7. John M. Hallahan, *The Battle of Craney Island: A Matter of Credit* (Portsmouth, VA: St. Michael's Press, 1986), 104.
8. Michael Barthorp, *Queen Victoria's Commanders* (Oxford: Osprey, 2000), 7.
9. Sandy Antal, *A Wampum Denied: Procter's War of 1812* (Ottawa: Carleton University Press, 1998), 375.
10. Antal, 393.
11. Berton, *Flames Across the Border: 1813–1814* (1981. Reprint, Toronto: Anchor Canada, 2001), 207–08.
12. Hallahan, 100.
13. Hallahan, 95.
14. Hallahan, 97.
15. Butler, *Defending the Old Dominion*, 422.
16. Alan Taylor, *The Internal Enemy: Slavery and War in Virginia, 1772-1832* (New York: Norton, 2013), 182–83.
17. Benson Lossing, *Lossing's Pictorial Field Book of the War of 1812*, V. 2 (1868; reprint, Gretna, LA: Firebird Press, 2003), 940.
18. Carrol H. Quenzel, *Samuel Snowden, A Founding Father of Printing in Alexandria* (Charlottesville: University of Virginia Press, 1952), 2.
19. Charles Henry Ambler, *Thomas Ritchie: A Study in Virginia Politics* (1913; reprint, London: Forgotten Books, 2015), 298.
20. Ambler, 299.
21. Butler, *Defending the Old Dominion*, 552.
22. Butler, *Defending the Old Dominion*, 553.
23. Taylor, 360.
24. Taylor, 360.
25. Lee Wallace, "The Petersburg Volunteers, 1812–1813," *VMHB* 82, no. 4 (October 1974): 481.
26. Butler, *Real Patriots and Heroic Soldiers: General Joel Leftwich and the Virginia Brigade in the War of 1812* (Westminster, MD: Heritage Books, 2008), 128.
27. Butler, *Real Patriots*, 129.
28. Butler, *Real Patriots*, 130.
29. Butler, *Real Patriots*, 139.
30. William Tatham, *The Defence of Norfolk in 1807*, edited by Norma Lois Peterson (Norfolk, VA: Norfolk County Historical Society, 1970), 105.
31. Tatham, 106.
32. Samuel Mordecai, *Richmond in by-gone days; being reminiscences of an old citizen* (1856; reprint, Lexington, KY: ULAN Press, 2017), 219.
33. *The Papers of Thomas Jefferson: Retirement Series*, Vol. 10: 1816–1817, edited by J. Jefferson Looney (Princeton: Princeton University Press, 2013), 379.
34. Clyde A. Haulman, *Virginia and the Panic of 1819* (London: Pickering & Chatto, 2008), 67.
35. Arthur G. Peterson, "The Alexandria Market Prior to the Civil War," *WMQ*, Second Series, 12, no. 2 (April 1932): 106.
36. Taylor, 407.
37. Haulman, 73.

38. Haulman, 73.
39. Charles Sellers, *The Market Revolution: Jacksonian America, 1815–1846* (Oxford: Oxford University Press, 1991), 138.
40. Taylor, 407.
41. Thomas J. Wertenbaker, *Norfolk: Historic Southern Port*, edited by Marvin W. Schlegel, 2d ed., (Durham: Duke University Press, 1962), 146.
42. Wertenbaker, 148–49.
43. Haulman, 18–19.
44. Taylor, 395–96.
45. Taylor, 396.
46. *The Papers of James Madison: Presidential Series*, Vol. 8: 1814–1815, edited by Angela Kreider (Charlottesville: University of Virginia Press, 2015), 599.
47. Madison 8, 600.
48. Donald R. Hickey, *The War of 1812: A Forgotten Conflict*, Bicentennial ed. (Urbana: University of Illinois Press, 2012), 316.
49. Madison 8, 599.
50. *The Papers of Thomas Jefferson: Retirement Series*, Vol. 8: 1814–1815, edited by J. Jefferson Looney (Princeton: Princeton University Press, 2011), 260.

Bibliography

WMQ = *William and Mary Quarterly*
VMHB = *Virginia Magazine of History and Biography*

Primary Sources

Newspapers

Alexandria Daily Advertiser
Alexandria Daily Gazette
Alexandria Herald
Martinsburgh Gazette
Norfolk Gazette and Publick Ledger
Richmond Enquirer
Staunton Political Censor
Staunton Republican Farmer
Virginia Argus
Virginia Patriot

Journals, Letters, Orderly Books

Cropper, Jonathan, Jr. "Letters from Old Trunks." *VMHB* 45, no. 1 (January 1937): 40–45.
Lee, Henry, and George Beckwith. "Major-General Henry Lee and Lieutenant-General Sir George Beckwith on Peace in 1813." *American Historical Review* 32, no. 2 (January 1927): 284–92.
"Marcellus." "Essays on the Liberty of the Press." Richmond, 1804.
Mason, Armistead Thomson. "Letters of Armistead Thomson Mason: 1813–1818." Edited by Kate Mason Rowland. *WMQ* 23, no. 4 (April 1915): 228–39.
Massie, Thomas. "Richmond During the War of 1812." *VMHB* 7, no. 4 (April 1900): 406–18.
Murphy, Pleasants. "Pleasants Murphy's 'Journal and Day Book.'" *WMQ*, Second Series 3, no. 4 (October 1923): 231–38.
"Orderly Book Virginia Militia War of 1812." *VMHB* 46, no. 3 (July 1938): 246–53.
Simms, Charles. "Alexandria in the War of 1812." *Alexandria History*, Vol. VI (1984): 17–23.
Taylor, John. "Letters of John Taylor of Caroline County, Virginia." *John P. Branch Historical Society Papers* 2 (June 1908): 271–353.
"The Vigilance Committee." *VMHB* 7, no. 3 (January 1900): 225–41.

Books

Advice to the Officers of the British Army. 1783. Reprint, Schenectady, NY: United States Historical Research Service, 1992.

Gleig, George. *A Subaltern in America.* 1833. Reprint, Middletown, DE: New York Public Library Collection, 2016.

Hanks, Jarvis, Amasiah Ford, and Alexander McMullen. *Soldiers of 1814: American Enlisted Men's Memoirs of the Niagara Campaign.* Edited by Donald E. Graves. Youngstown, NY: Old Fort Niagara Association, 1995.

Lorrain, Alfred M. *The Helm, the Sword and the Cross: A Life Narrative.* 1862. Reprint, London: Forgotten Books, 2012.

Mordecai, Samuel. *Richmond in by-gone days; being reminiscences of an old citizen.* 1856. Reprint, Lexington, KY: ULAN Press, 2017.

Napier, Charles. *The life and opinions of General Sir Charles James Napier.* Vol. 1. Edited by William Francis Patrick Napier. 1857. Reprint, Lexington, KY: ULAN Press, 2014.

Scott, Winfield. *Memoirs of Lieut.-General Scott, LL.D.* Vol. 1. 1853. Reprint, London: Forgotten Books, 2015.

Tatham, William. *The Defence of Norfolk in 1807.* Edited by Norma Lois Peterson. Norfolk, VA: Norfolk County Historical Society, 1970.

The War of 1812: Writings from America's Second War of Independence. Edited by Donald R. Hickey. New York: Library of America, 2013.

Wirt, William. *Memoirs of the life of William Wirt.* Vol. 1. Edited by John Pendleton Kennedy. 1856. Reprint, Lexington, KY: ULAN Press, 2014.

Wood, Eleazar D. *Wood's Journal of the Northwestern Campaign of 1812-1813.* Edited by Robert B. Boehm and Randall L. Buchman. Defiance, OH: The Defiance College Press, 1975.

Presidential Papers

The Complete Jefferson: Containing His Major Writings, Published and Unpublished, Except His Letters. Edited by Saul K. Padover. New York: Tudor Publishing, 1943.

The Papers of James Madison: Presidential Series Volume 1: 1809. Edited by Robert A. Rutland & Thomas A. Mason. Charlottesville: University Press of Virginia, 1984; Volume 2: 1809-1810. Edited by J.C.A. Stagg, Charlottesville: UVA, 1992; Volume 3: 1810-1811. Edited by J.C.A. Stagg. Charlottesville: UVA, 1996; Volume 4: 1811-1812. Edited by J.C.A. Stagg. Charlottesville: UVA, 1999; Volume 5: 1812-1813. Edited by J.C.A. Stagg, Charlottesville: UVA, 2004; Volume 6: 1813. Edited by J.C.A. Stagg. Charlottesville: UVA, 2008; Volume 7: 1813-1814. Edited by J.C.A. Stagg. Charlottesville: UVA, 2012; Volume 8: 1814-1815. Edited by Angela Kreider. Charlottesville: UVA, 2015.

The Papers of Thomas Jefferson: Retirement Series Volume 4: 1811-1812. Edited by J. Jefferson Looney. Princeton: 2007; Volume 5: 1812-1813. Edited by J. Jefferson Looney. Princeton: 2008; Volume 7: 1813-1814. Edited by J. Jefferson Looney. Princeton: 2010; Volume 8: 1814-1815. Edited by J. Jefferson Looney. Princeton: 2011; Volume 10: 1816-1817. Edited by J. Jefferson Looney. Princeton: 2013.

Thomas Jefferson: Writings. Edited by Merrill D. Peterson. New York: Library of America, 1984.

Secondary Sources

Journal Articles

Calderhead, William L. "U.S.F. *Constellation* in the War of 1812—An Accidental Fleet-in-Being." *Military Affairs* 40, no. 2 (April 1976): 79-83.

Gaines, Edwin M. "The *Chesapeake* Affair: Virginians Mobilize to Defend National Honor." *VMHB* 64, no. 2 (April 1956): 131–42.

McCarthy, Daniel. "Liberty and Order in the Slave Society." *The American Conservative*, August 1, 2005. Accessed October 24, 2014. www.theamericanconservative.com/articles/liberty-and-order-in-the-slave-society/.

Newfield, Gareth A. "Anatomy of an Atrocity: Crimes of the Independent Companies of Foreigners in North America, 1813." *War of 1812 Magazine*, Issue 10 (October 2008). Accessed November 15, 2014. http://www.napoleon-series.org/military/Warof1812/2008/Issue10/.

Peterson, Arthur G. "The Alexandria Market Prior to the Civil War." *WMQ*, Second Series, 12, no. 2 (April 1932): 104–14.

Rouse Jr., Parke. "The British Invasion of Hampton in 1813: The Reminiscences of James Jarvis." *VMHB* 76, no. 3 (July 1968): 318–36.

Stagg, J.C.A. "James Madison and the 'Malcontents': The Political Origins of the War of 1812." *WMQ* 33, no. 4 (October 1976): 557–85.

Wallace, Lee A., Jr. "The Petersburg Volunteers, 1812–1813." *VMHB* 82, no. 4 (October 1974): 458–85.

Watson, G.E. "The United States and the Peninsular War, 1808–1812." *The Historical Journal* 19, no. 4 (December 1976): 859–76.

Wehtje, Myron F. "Opposition in Virginia to the War of 1812." *VMHB* 78, no. 1, Part One (January 1970): 65–86.

Books

Ambler, Charles Henry. *Thomas Ritchie: A Study in Virginia Politics*. 1913. Reprint, London: Forgotten Books, 2015.

Antal, Sandy. *A Wampum Denied: Procter's War of 1812*. Ottawa: Carleton University Press, 1998.

Barthorp, Michael. *Queen Victoria's Commanders*. Oxford: Osprey, 2000.

Berton, Pierre. *Flames Across the Border: 1813–1814*. 1981. Reprint, Toronto: Anchor Canada, 2001. Berton, Pierre. *The Invasion of Canada: 1812–1813*. 1980. Reprint, Toronto: Anchor Canada, 2001.

Broussard, James H. *The Southern Federalists, 1800–1816*. Baton Rouge: Louisiana State University, 1978.

Butler, Stuart L. *Defending the Old Dominion: Virginia and Its Militia in the War of 1812*. Lanham, MD: University Press of America, 2013.

Butler, Stuart L. *Real Patriots and Heroic Soldiers: General Joel Leftwich and the Virginia Brigade in the War of 1812*. Westminster, MD: Heritage Books, 2008.

Cassin-Scott, Jack. *Scandinavian Armies in the Napoleonic Wars*. 1976. Reprint, Oxford: Osprey 2005.

Chappell, Mike. *British Infantry Equipments 1808–1908*. London: Osprey, 1980.

Chartrand, Rene. *Forts of the War of 1812*. Oxford: Osprey, 2012.

Dabney, Virginius. *Virginia: The New Dominion*. New York: Doubleday, 1971.

Elting, John R. *Swords Around a Throne: Napoleon's Grande Armee*. 1988. Reprint, Boston: Da Capo Press, 1997.

Eshelman, Ralph E., and Burton K. Kummerow. *In Full Glory Reflected: Discovering the War of 1812 in the Chesapeake*. Baltimore: Maryland Historical Society, 2012.

Eshelman, Ralph E., Scott S. Sheads, and Donald R. Hickey. *The War of 1812 in the Chesapeake: A Reference Guide to Historic Sites in Maryland, Virginia, and the District Of Columbia*. Baltimore: Johns Hopkins University Press, 2010.

Fosten, Bryan. *Wellington's Infantry (1)*. 1981. Reprint, London: Osprey, 1989.

Fredriksen, John C. *War of 1812 Eyewitness Accounts: An Annotated Bibliography*. Westport, CT: Greenwood Press, 1997.

Bibliography

George, Christopher T. *Terror on the Chesapeake: The War of 1812 on the Bay.* Shippensburg, PA: White Mane Books, 2000.

Gilbert, Ed. *Frontier Militiaman in the War of 1812: Southwestern Frontier.* Oxford: Osprey, 2008.

Graves, Donald E. *Field of Glory: The Battle of Crysler's Farm, 1813.* Toronto: Robin Brass Studio, 2005.

Grodzinski, John R. *The War of 1812: An Annotated Bibliography.* New York: Routledge, 2008.

Hallahan, John M. *The Battle of Craney Island: A Matter of Credit.* Portsmouth, VA: St. Michael's Press, 1986.

Haulman, Clyde A. *Virginia and the Panic of 1819.* London: Pickering & Chatto, 2008.

Haythornthwaite, Philip. *British Napoleonic Infantry Tactics 1792–1815.* Oxford: Osprey, 2008. *Nelson's Navy.* 1993. Reprint, Oxford: Osprey, 1999.

Hickey, Donald R. *Don't Give Up the Ship! Myths of the War of 1812.* Urbana: University of Illinois, 2006.

Hickey, Donald R. *The War of 1812: A Forgotten Conflict.* Bicentennial Edition, Urbana: University of Illinois, 2012.

Ketchum, Richard M. *Saratoga: Turning Point of America's Revolutionary War.* New York: Henry Holt and Company, 1997.

Kochan, James L. *The United States Army 1812–1815.* Oxford: Osprey, 2000.

Lardas, Mark. *USS Lawrence vs. HMS Detroit: The War of 1812 on the Great Lakes.* Oxford: Osprey, 2017.

Lemmon, Sarah McCulloh. *North Carolina and the War of 1812.* Raleigh: North Carolina Department of Cultural Resources, 1971.

Lossing, Benson J. *Lossing's Pictorial Field Book of the War of 1812.* 2 vols. 1868. Reprint, Gretna, LA: Firebird Press, 2003.

Mahon, John K. *The War of 1812.* Gainesville: University of Florida Press, 1972.

Nelson, Larry L. *Men of Patriotism, Courage & Enterprise! Fort Meigs in the War of 1812.* 1985. Reprint, Westminster, MD: Heritage Books, 2007.

Quenzel, Carrol H. *Samuel Snowden, A Founding Father of Printing in Alexandria.* Charlottesville: University of Virginia, 1952.

Sellers, Charles. *The Market Revolution: Jacksonian America, 1815–1846.* Oxford: Oxford University Press, 1991.

Sheads, Scott S. *The Chesapeake Campaigns 1813–15: Middle ground of the War of 1812.* Oxford: Osprey, 2014.

Skeen, C. Edward. *Citizen Soldiers of the War of 1812.* Lexington: University Press of Kentucky, 1999.

Taylor, Alan. *The Internal Enemy: Slavery and War in Virginia, 1772–1832.* New York: Norton, 2013.

Tucker, Spencer C., and Frank T. Reuter. *Injured Honor: The Chesapeake-Leopard Affair.* Annapolis: Naval Institute Press, 1996.

Urwin, Gregory J.W. *The United States Infantry: An Illustrated History 1775–1918.* 1988. Reprint, Norman: University of Oklahoma, 2000.

Wertenbaker, Thomas J. *Norfolk: Historic Southern Port.* Edited by Marvin W. Schlegel, 2d ed. Durham: Duke University Press, 1962.

Williams, William Appleman. *The Tragedy of American Diplomacy,* 50th anniv. ed. New York: Norton, 2009.

Winkler, John F. *The Thames 1813: The War of 1812 on the Northwest Frontier.* Oxford: Osprey, 2016.

Index

Numbers in **_bold italics_** indicate pages with illustrations

Adams, John Quincy 118, 120, 145
Agricultural commodities 4, 103, 117, 118, 122–23, 129, 132, 146, 147
Alexandria, VA 4, 47, 130; capitulation 127–29, **_131_**, 132–34; as Federalist bastion 46; postwar investigation 143
Alexandria Daily Advertiser 11, 14, 16–17, 19
Alexandria Daily Gazette 44, 46–47, 133, 144
Alexandria Herald 44, 48
Alien and Sedition Acts 6, 50
Ambler, Charles Henry 144
Anderson, Robert 111
HMS *Anna Maria* 127
Antelope (ship) 121
Armistead, George 135–36
Armstrong, John 29, 95, 119, 120, 125, 127
Asp (schooner) 114

Baltimore, MD 4; British attack **_135_**, 135–37; defenses 134–35, 143; 1812 riot 52–53
Baltimore Federal Republican 20, 52–53, 128
Barbour, James **_36_**, 36–37, 39, 65, 83, 85, 120, 122, 123, 126, 137; later career 145–46
Barclay, Robert Heriot 98
Barney, Joshua 125
Barraud, Philip 107, 109
Barrie, Robert 138
Barron, James 9, 10, 20
Bathurst, Earl 53, 100
Bayard, James A. 118, 120
Beatty, Henry 105, 107
Beckwith, Sir George 53
Beckwith, Sir Thomas Sydney 70, 100, 106–07
HMS *Bellona* 14
Berlin and Milan Decrees 23–24, 29, 117–18
Berton, Pierre 142
Bladensburg, MD 4, 65, 125–26

Bonaparte, Napoleon 3, 23, 29, 117, 120, 122, 141, 149–50
Boston, MA 20
Brand, Benjamin 147
British Army 3, 4, 67, 68, 71, 78–79, 95–96, 98; Baltimore 135–37; Bladensburg and D.C. 125–26; Craney Island 106–07; Fort Stephenson 96–97; 41st Foot 73; at Frenchtown 87–88; Hampton 109–13; Independent Companies of Foreigners 71; 102nd Foot 70–71; Royal Artillery 76; siege of Fort Meigs 91–94; uniforms and equipment 75–76
Brock, Isaac 72, 82
Brockenbrough, John 44
Brooke, Arthur 135–37
Broussard, James H. 43
Burr, Aaron 16
Bush, George W. 151
Butler, Stuart L. 1, 56, 61, 63, 90–91, 140

Cabell, William H. 11, 17, 18, 19
Cambell, John 65
Canada 3, 16–17, 54, 98, 100, 119, 124, 144, 154
Canadian militia 73–74, 88, 91, 94
Cape Henry, VA 17, 37, 100, 101, 114, 115
Carberry, Colonel 125
Caskaden, George 147
Cassin, John 105, 107, 109
Charles, William **_81_**, **_131_**, **_133_**
Charles City, VA 18
USS *Chesapeake* 9, 19, 20
Chesapeake Bay 3, 77, 100–03
Chesapeake-Leopard Affair 2, 9, 10, 132
Chew, John 144
Chillicothe, OH 84, 86
Claiborne, Nathaniel H. 65
Clark, George Rogers 80, 96

173

174 Index

Clay, Green 91, 93, 95, 96
Clay, Henry 35, 120
Clinton, DeWitt 42, 43
Clinton, George 15, 151
Cobb, Elijah 126
Cochrane, Sir Alexander Forrester Inglis 68, 70, 122, 124, 136, 137
Cockburn, Sir George *69*, 70, 72, 109; Baltimore 136; Craney Island 107; 1814 raids 122–23, 124, 130; later career 141
Confederate States of America 7, 66
Congreve rockets 76, 77, 106, 122, 138
Connell, John 83, 87
USS *Constellation* 101, 103
Corse, J. 47–48
Cowper, John 147
Craney Island, VA 38, 61, 101, 109, 142–43; battle *104*, 105–07
Cririe, John 102–03
Croghan, George 96–97
Cropper, Jonathan, Jr. 57, 62, 63
Crutchfield, Stapleton 109
Cynthia Ann (schooner) 15–16

Dagg, John 136
Daniel, Peter V. 65
Dashkov, Andrei 118
Davis, Augustine 52
Decatur, Stephen 19, 20
Declaration of Independence 6
Defense Force Act 64–65
Democratic-Republicans 2, 22, 117, 127; postwar ascendancy 143; scapegoat Alexandrians 133–34; sensitivity to British insults 24–25
Denmark 32; captures American ships 33
Detroit, MI 82, 84, 95
HMS *Devastation* 77, 127
Douglas, John Erskine 13, 14, 17
Dudley, William 93–94
Dundas, Sir David 68
Dyson, Samuel T. 128

Eastern Shore: isolation from rest of VA 57, 63
Eddins, Langley B. 62
Election of 1808 26–27
Election of 1812: low voter turnout 43
Embargo Act 3, *25*, 132, 151; repeal 27; unpopularity 26
England, Joseph 59
HMS *Erebus* 77, 127
Erskine, David M. 27, 28
Eshelman, Ralph 140
Essex (Richmond) Junto 44
HMS *Etna* 127
HMS *Euryalus* 127
Evans, Dudley 83

Farnham Church, VA 138
Federalists 2, 15, 22, 64–66, 117, 131, 133–34; attempt to prevent war 34; extent of support in VA 43; hostility to France 24, 46; postwar decline 143
Fort Albion 121–22, 141
Fort Boykin 112
Fort Ferree 84, 86
Fort Malden 98
Fort McHenry 135–36
Fort Meigs *88*, 89, *90*, 91–94, 95–96
Fort Miami 80
Fort Monroe 105, 153
Fort Norfolk 14, 105, 153
Fort Powhatan 113, 120
Fort Stephenson 96–97
Fort Washington 128
Foster, Augustus 35
Fox, Josiah 19
Frayly, Reuben 60
Frenchtown, MI 87–88
Friend, Nathaniel 84
Fulton, Robert 114

Gaines, Edwin M. 11
Gallatin, Albert 30, 118, 120, 146
General Ticket Law 43
George III 6, 15
Georgetown Federal Republican 111
Ghent, Belgium 3, 120
Giles, William Branch 28, 29, 66
Gleig, George 74, 75–76, 78; Baltimore 136–37; later career 141
Gordon, Charles 9, 20
Gordon, James 127–29, 130
Grayson, William 109
Griffin, Thomas 109

HMS *Halifax* 10, 20
Halifax, Nova Scotia 9, 19, 107, 144
Hallahan, John H. 103, 143
Hamilton, Henry 80
Hamilton, John 13
Hampton, VA 3, 59, 71; atrocities 109–13; battle *108*, 109; population 4
Hanchett, John 106–07
Harrison, Nathaniel (or William) 97
Harrison, William Henry 81, 82, *83*, 88, 90, 95, 96, 98–99; at Fort Meigs 91–94; presidency 149; resigns commission 119; Thames 98
Hartford Convention 2, 39, 66, 143
Haulman, Clyde A. 148
Hay, George 46
Henderson, John 94, 97
Henderson, William 123
Henry Affair 31–32
Hickey, Donald R. 2, 23–24, 27, 101, 140
Hudgins, Houlder 62
Hughs, Isaac 59–60
Hull, Isaac 51, 59, 82, 84
Humphreys, Salusbury Pryce 9, 10, 20
Hungerford, John P. 123, 128–29

Index

Jackson, Francis James 28
Jay Treaty 15, 22
Jefferson, Thomas 6, 22, 36, 33, 51, 85; attempts to avoid war 26; consoles Madison 127; on debtors 147; 1816 harvest 146; on fortunes of war 118–19; Hull's surrender 82; response to *Chesapeake-Leopard* Affair 11–12, *12*, 17, 18; Treaty of Ghent 149
Jones, Walter 63, 116–17
Jones Point, VA 138
HMS *Junon* 103

Ketchum, Richard 74
King, Rufus 42, 43, 152
Kinsale, VA 123–24

Lafayette, Marquis de 142
Lake Erie, battle of 97–98, 119
Lambert, William 121
Lancaster County, VA 121
Langguth, A.J. 1
Lawrence (sloop) 97
Lawson, Richard L. 116
Lee, Henry "Light Horse Harry" 52–53
Lee, Jesse 85
Lee, Richard E. 13–14, 17
Leftwich, Jabez 83
Leftwich, Joel: command of VA Brigade 83, 90–91; later career 145
Lemmon, Sarah McCulloh 1
HMS *Leopard* 9, 14, 20
Lewis, Garland 59–60
Lively, Robert 109
Lorrain, Alfred M. 95–96, 97, 98; at Fort Meigs 89, 92–93; joins volunteers 84–85; later career 145; march to Ohio 85–87
Lossing, Benson J. 1, 72, 143, 144
Lundy's Lane, battle of 124
Lynnhaven Bay 10, 13, 17, 38

Machodoc Creek, VA 123
Macon's Bill No. 2, 29
Madison, Dolley 129
Madison, George 88
Madison, James 6, *28*, 29, 100, 149; appoints peace delegation 120; at Bladensburg 125; briefly reopens trade with Britain 27; decides on war 33, 34–35; elected to first term 26; role in Henry Affair 31; second term 35, 42; wartime embargo 117–18
Mahan, Alfred Thayer 101, 143
HMS *Maidstone* 102
Marrin, Albert 2
Marshall, John 34, 53, 113
Martin, Daniel 10, 20
Mason, Armistead Thomson 139, 140
Massie, Thomas 112, 124
Mathews, Thomas 11, 12
Mauer, Maurer 86
McGehee, Thomas 60
McRae, Richard 84

HMS *Melampus* 10, 14
HMS *Meteor* 77, 127
Miller, John (VA militia officer) 61
Miller, John (19th U.S. Infantry) 93
Minor, George 125
Mix, Elijah 114–15
Mobile, AL 59
Monroe, James 6; appointed Secretary of State 30, 36; argues against peace 119; at Bladensburg 125; optimistic outlook on war 41–42; presidency 143; requests repeal of Defense Force Act 65; role in Henry Affair 32; Secretary of War 127; sends slave recovery agents 144
Monroe-Pinckney Treaty 23
Mordecai, Samuel 146
Mundy's Point, VA 123
Murphy, Pleasants 58–59

Napier, Charles: Craney Island 106–07; Hampton atrocities 111–12; later career 141; plans to raise slave army 71–72; on raiding 77–78; takes command of 102nd 71
HMS *Narcissus* 102–03
Native Americans: alliance with British 74, 80, *81*; at Fort Meigs 91–95; at Raisin River 87–89
New Orleans, LA, battle of 141, 143, 149
Newspapers 3, 44, 107, 152
Niagara (sloop) 97
Nicholas, Wilson Cary 29, 144
Niles' Register 70, 149
Nomini Church, VA 79, 123
Nomini Creek, VA 122–23
Non-Intercourse Act 3, 27
Norfolk, VA 3, 10, 101, 105–07, 137–39; impact of embargo 26; militia concentration 63; population 4; postwar 147–48
Norfolk and Portsmouth Herald 15, 45, 52, 82, 133–34
Norfolk Gazette and Publick Ledger 13, 19, 28, 44, 45, 51, 52, 54, 60, 124, 130
North Carolina 1, 103, 117, 137–38
North Point, battle of 135
Northern Neck 114, 116–17, 121
Northwestern Campaign 3, 80 84, 86–87, 89, 119

Orders in Council 23–24, 27

Panic of 1819 147–48
Parker, Richard E. 110, 123
Pennsylvania 1, 134–35
Perry, Oliver Hazard 97–98
Petersburg (barque) 16
Petersburg Volunteers: discharged 98–99; at Fort Meigs 89, 92–93; joins Perry's squadron 97; on the march 86–87; postwar compensation 144–45; raised 84–85; sortie 93; spearhead invasion 98
Peterson, Arthur G. 132, 147

Pierce, Franklin 144
Pinckney, Charles 26
HMS *Plantagenet* 114–15
Pleasants, Samuel 15, 44, 50
Pleasure House 38, 115–16
Point Pleasant, VA 84
Portsmouth, VA 10
Prevost, Sir George 142
Principles of '98 *see* Virginia and Kentucky Resolutions
Privateers 102
Procter, Henry 72–73, 88–89, 91–93, 95, 96–97, 98; court martial 141–42
Pungoteague Creek, VA 72, 122

Quasi-War 23
Quenzel, Carrol H. 46

Randolph, John 35, 40, 41
Randolph, Peyton 36
Ratford, Jenkins 10, 19–20
Rattray, James 114
Richmond, VA 3, 16, 112–14, 120, 124; population 4; postwar 146, 147–48
Richmond Enquirer 44, 56, 82, 110–11, 115, 121, 123–24, 130–31
Richmond Washington Volunteers 85
Ritchie, Thomas 44, 85, 111, 113, 121, 125, 130–31, 133, 144
Roane, Spencer 44
Rodgers, John 129
Rodney, Caesar A. 24–25
Roosevelt, Theodore 143
Ross, Robert 70, 135
Rounsavell, N. 47–48
Royal Marines 68, 72, 102, 106, 111, 115, 123; Colonial Marines 121–22, 144; Royal Marine Artillery 76; uniforms 76
Royal Navy 3, 25, 34, 101, 102–03, 106–07, 114, 122, 138, 143; Alexandria 127–29; Baltimore 135–36; conditions 9–10; desertion 79; impressment 9, 149–50; tactics 77–78; uniforms 77
Rush, Benjamin 82
Russell, Jonathan 120
Russia 25, 53, 118

Sapio, Victor 1
Scorpion (sloop) 114
Scott, David 87
Scott, Winfield 17, 54, 55
HMS *Seahorse* 127
Second Iraq War: comparison to War of 1812 151, 153, 154
September 11, 2001: comparison to *Chesapeake-Leopard* Affair 151
HMS *Shannon* 20
Sharp, William 57
Sheads, Scott S. 101, 140
Sheridan, John 138
Sigourney, James Butler 114

Simms, Charles 46, 127–29, 132
Simms, John Douglas 46
Slaves 4, 5, 6, 14, 123, 138; assist British 71–72, 116, 121; fear of revolt 58, 63; postwar 144
Smith, George William 36
Smith, John H. 97
Smith, Robert 29, 30, 31
Smith, Samuel 29, 30, 134–36
Smithfield, VA 112, 113
Snowden, Samuel 11, 46, 49, 52, 118, 132, 133
Stagg, J.C.A. 31
Staunton Political Censor 24
Staunton Republican Farmer 44, 51, 85–86
Stewart, Charles 105
Stonington, CT 131
Strachan, John 10, 20
Strong, Caleb 66
Surveyor (revenue cutter) 102–03
Swift, John 120–21
Swoope, Jacob 28–29

Tangier Island, VA 121–22, 134, 141
Tappahannock, VA 59, 79, 138
Tarbell, Joseph 103, 107, 117
Tatham, William 11–12, 17, 37–38, 115, 146
Taylor, Alan 148
Taylor, John 41–43, 51–52
Taylor, Robert Barraud **37**, 62, 111–12, 154; Norfolk command 103, 105, 107; later life 142
Taylor, Zachary 149
Tazewell, Littleton Waller 14
Tecumseh 73, 81, 83, 91, 93, 94, 95–96; death 98
Tenskwatawa 81
HMS *Terror* 77
Thames, battle of the 98, 119
Thomas, Joshua 134
Tippecanoe, battle of 81–82, 96
Tompkins, Christopher 62–63
Travis, Samuel 102–03
Treaty of Ghent 4, 140, 149–150
HMS *Triumph* 14
Tyler, John, Jr. 149
Tyler, John, Sr. 18, 35–36

United States Army 3, 54–55, 105; Bladensburg 125, 153; in the Northwest 96–97; in Virginia 65
United States House of Representatives 28, 39, 143
United States Marine Corps 103, 105, 125
United States Navy 3, 95, 97, 117; Bladensburg 125; Craney Island 105–07, 109; gunboats 101
United States Senate 4, 28, 34, 39
Urbanna, VA 138
Urwin, Gregory J.W. 55

Vassar, Peter 59
Virginia 4, 5 **6**; antiwar sentiment 44;

defense difficulties 63; military expenses 63; national influence 148–49; number of actions 140–41; postwar 144, 146–48; 12th Congress delegation 40
Virginia and Kentucky Resolutions 6, 148
Virginia Argus 10, 12, 15, 44–45, 50–51, 53, 55, 61, 65, 85, 110, 126–27, 132–33
Virginia Arms Manufactory 11, 57
Virginia Dynasty 3, 6, 148
Virginia Militia 3, 153; arms 57; Baltimore 135–37; Craney Island 105–07; Defense Force 64–66; desertion 61; discipline 59–60; 1814 raids 138; Hampton 109; Kinsale 123–24; Leftwich's Brigade 83, 84, 86, 89–91, 145; Machodoc Creek, Mundy's Point 123; mutiny 61–62; "militia myth" 141; Norfolk 137–39; officers 62–63; organization 56–57; Pungoteague Creek 122; response to *Chesapeake-Leopard* Affair 11, 16, 17, 18, 19; Richmond 112–13; total served and losses 140; trade with British 143; uniforms 56
Virginia Patriot 27, 44, 49, 124, 140

Wagner, Jacob 111
War Hawks 31, 40

Ware, William 10, 20
Warren, Sir John Borlase 68, 100, 103, 107, 111–12, 114, 118, 122, 154
Washington, George 6, 22, 80
Washington, D.C. 4, 126, 143
Washington National Intelligencer 15, 44, 70, 116, 129–30, 133
Wehtje, Myron F. 43
Wellington, Duke of 67, 75, 132
Wertenbaker, Thomas J. 26, 148
West Virginia 4
White House, VA 129
Williams, John S. 133
Williamsburg, VA 37, 58–59
Wilmington American Watchman & Delaware Republican 100
Wilson, Woodrow 149
Winchester, James 87–88
Winder, William H. 125, 126, 134, 137
Wirt, William 16, 58, 112–13, 144
Wood, Eleazar 89, 90–91, 92, 94
Worrenigh Church, VA 58
Wray, John 11

Yorktown, VA 59

www.ingramcontent.com/pod-product-compliance
Ingram Content Group UK Ltd.
Pitfield, Milton Keynes, MK11 3LW, UK
UKHW042015140426
5217IPUK00015B/1188